CUBA
THE AUDACIOUS REVOLUTION

Frank:

Enjoy the book!

George

GEORGE GEDDA

ISBN: 1-4564-8022-7

ISBN-13: 978-1-4564-8022-6

With love to Larry, Debbie and Sara

CONTENTS

ADDENDUM 1

ADDENDUM 2

ADDENDUM 3

PREFACE

At some point during my travels as a diplomatic correspondent, I concluded that perhaps no country was more interesting than Cuba. I first visited there in 1974 and returned thirty times. I saw a lot of other countries—eighty-seven, all told—while covering the State Department for The Associated Press. All countries have their peculiarities and charms and rough edges, but, to me, Cuba was in a class by itself, and I was delighted that it was the one I got to visit most and know best.

Cuba seemed to be following the same trajectory as other Latin American countries after its independence in 1902—a mixture of dictatorships and elected governments, as well as instability. There were no fewer than eight presidents between 1933 and 1936; this followed an imperialistic age of more than thirty years in which U.S. intervention in Cuba was permitted, under U.S. legislation enshrined in the so-called Platt amendment, anytime the United States thought it necessary to protect American business and financial interests. Obviously, many Cubans saw this as an indefensible incursion on national sovereignty.

Few countries undergo the kind of upheaval that Cuba experienced starting in 1959 when Fidel Castro, at age thirty-two, seized power from an unpopular military dictatorship after a two-year guerrilla war. But his promise of a return of freedom and democracy turned out to be a facade he used to buy time. He re-vealed his true intentions in 1961 when he disclosed that he had been a life-long Marxist-Leninist. To deter the Americans, just ninety miles away, he forged close ties with the Soviet Union. His ambitions were not limited to Cuba. He saw his revolution as a catalyst for leftist upheavals throughout the Third World. His anti-Americanism was unwavering during all of his forty-seven years in power. Castro said the plight of the Third World was attributable to the economic system "imposed" on it by the the United States.

Many saw Castro as an adventurer with an agenda far out of proportion to Cuba's modest size and resources. He could not possibly last, people said. And surviving may have been his most noteworthy achievement. It would not be enemies who finally felled him in 2006 but illness.

Raúl, of course, succeeded his brother at that time and formal-ly became the constitutional president in 2008, elected by party leaders. He differs from Fidel in form and substance. He lacks Fidel's charisma but is a more skillful administrator. He has a more collegial approach to governing than Fidel, who preferred to make decisions on his own. Fidel thought everybody should work for the government; Raúl believes the country is in crisis and must abandon the dogmas of the past. (Fidel and Raúl do not look like brothers. In size and facial features, they have nothing in common. In contrast, Ramón, a cattleman and oldest of the three brothers, almost could have been mistaken for Fidel's twin.

Fidel's health care and educational programs were universal and won wide international acclaim (along with many critics). But his revolution clearly fell short in other areas. He promised abundance and delivered shortages. The country produced little and had to rely on the charity of outsiders (Venezuela in recent years). In his early years in power, he railed against the *"sueldos de miseria"* (miserable salaries) that people earned under the military regime he replaced. Under Castro, rock-bottom salaries persisted, excluding the "social wage" of cost-free health care and education. For sustenance, countless Cubans counted on generosity of relatives and friends who had fled.

When Castro wanted something, no matter how bizarre, he got his wish. In a show of friendship toward Russia in the 1990s, he ordered the construction in Havana of a Russian Orthodox church. It was not clear from where the congregants would be drawn. Oddities were common during the long Castroite rule:

—A sizable, but declining, majority of Cubans from the president to the night watchman worked for the government and made the Cuban equivalent of one dollar a day or so, at least as of 2010. A sterling academic record at the university did not yield more income or a better life. Earnings, barring possible modest raises now and then, stayed basically the same. Castro said in 2005 that his own salary was thirty dollars a month. (Twenty years earlier he had said, "I don't get paid nor have I ever asked for a single cent for this work.") Either way, autocrats never have cash flow problems, Castro included.

—Cuban doctors were churned out in droves—eighty-eight thousand in the first forty-six years of the revolution, according to Castro. He once said there were more doctors in Cuba than there were in all of sub-Saharan Africa.

—Health care was universal and free. The clinics may be shabby and the lines may be long, but a Cuban with a health problem can count on seeing a doctor. Obtaining the prescription medicine the doctor may recommend is another matter.

—Frustrated by poor working conditions, an average of more than one Cuban doctor per day, encouraged by U.S. officials, abandoned their overseas posts between 2006 and 2010 and resettled in the United States.

—It may be difficult for an outsider to contemplate but the peso salary paid to most Cuban workers was worthless in many shops because they accepted only national hard currency—even for everyday necessities. The have, have-not divide these days consists of the minority of people who have access to hard currency and those who don't.

—In housing, the supply fell far short of demand. The selling and buying of houses was illegal (though changing). Often, several generations were forced to live under the same roof in extraordinarily cramped conditions. Privacy was an unfamiliar experience for many. It was common in Cuba for children to live and die in the house where they were born.

—Acute shortages of building materials prompted some entrepreneurial Cubans to rush to the scene of newly collapsed apartment buildings in Havana. There they sifted the rubble in search of unblemished tiles, sinks, wooden beams or other items they could sell or use themselves.

—Alberto Jones, a Cuban exile, writer, and frequent visitor to Cuba, spoke for many when he said: "Everyone knows that in order for every individual to solve their otherwise intractable housing crisis, every Cuban has had to bend the rules, find shortcuts, pay bribes, or purchase stolen goods..."

—Thousands of 1950s-era American cars are still in use in Cuba. The absence of auto supply stores anywhere on the island poses a problem. If the owner of one of these dinosaurs needs brake fluid, a mix of alcohol, brown sugar, and shampoo is sometimes used as a substitute. If a fender is needed, a creative option is to reshape and install a tin roof purloined from an unoccupied shack.

—Prison sentences in Cuba could be severe, even for a petty crime. A man was sentenced to twenty-two months merely for driving a pedicab without a license, the same period a youthful Fidel Castro served for leading a rebel attack that left fifteen soldiers dead in 1953.

—Since privately owned cars were scarce in Cuba, there was usually minimal competition for parking spaces. It was possible for a car owner to park free right by the front entrance of Havana's main baseball stadium minutes before game time.

—Asked whether he had ever seen a traffic jam in Havana, a veteran taxi driver said simply: "No."

—A Cuban journalist, desperate to emigrate, started e-mailing blogs to foreign publications, highlighting Cuba's social and economic problems. His objective was not to muckrake but to seek a right to asylum in the U.S., citing fear, albeit self-induced, of persecution.

—An elderly Havana woman asked a state agency to send an expert to reupholster her pre-revolutionary sofa and chairs. She was put on a waiting list. After five years, the agency was shut down. Eventually, a private contractor did the job illegally—at a cost of two months of her small pension. (Pensions often average between $6 and $10 a month.)

—Garish displays of wealth by well-connected Cubans were discouraged. When a close relative of Raúl Castro summoned state workers to build an extension to her Havana house in the middle of a depression, neighbors were enraged. She was ordered out of the country.

I covered the State Department for The Associated Press from 1968 until my retirement in 2007. I was sent by the AP on all but a few of my thirty-one Cuba trips, which began in 1974. Normally my on-the-job travels outside Washington were on trips overseas with secretaries of state. My job during Cuba trips usually was to cover speeches by Castro and his one-of-kind revolution. On many trips, I would follow Castro to the sites of his annual speeches on July 26, the anniversary of his debut as a guerrilla fighter in 1953. I was able to visit places like Santiago, Holguín, Sancti Espíritu, Cabaiguán, Trinidad, Bauta, Pinar del Rio, Guantánamo (the city and the nearby U.S. naval base), and, yes, the Bay of Pigs. But the bulk of my time over these visits was spent in Havana. My last visit for the AP was in February 1996, the same month that the Clinton administration temporarily banned all flights to Cuba following the shooting down of two Miami-based Cessnas that had approached Cuban air space. In 1999, the AP was allowed to open a bureau in Havana for the first time in thirty years, obviating the need for AP outsiders like myself to make reporting trips to the island. (I made several private visits to Cuba starting in 2001.)

My world view, to the extent that I had one, was shaped by my middle-class upbringing in Valley Stream, Long Island, New York, the four years I spent at Southern Methodist University (B.A. 1962), my stay in Venezuela with the Peace Corps, and, most importantly, the decades I spent covering the State Department in Washington, D.C.

I brought to the task of writing this book the normal mindset and prejudices of someone accustomed to basic freedoms, elected leaders, a steady job, a free press, well-stocked supermarkets, health insurance, heating and air conditioning, reliable transportation, and a plethora of entertainment outlets.

Each Caribbean country has a sizable population that is "poor." So when an American observer notices the across-the-board shortages in, say, Cuba, he has to make a judgment as to whether that is a geographic or cultural phenomenon, a product of the communist system, or of the American embargo that was imposed in 1962 and took from Cuba its best market. As with any assignment, a reporter has to provide context and rely as much as possible on facts, no easy task in a country like Cuba, where facts, like consumer goods, are in short supply.

For every Cuban who lives in substandard housing or is underemployed, there are probably more per capita in the Dominican Republic, a neighbor with a limited social safety net, where I spent six months between August 2007 and February 2008. This book attempts to draw comparisons between that country and Cuba, a difficult and inexact process but perhaps somewhat illuminating. It is safe to say that significant percentages in both countries would prefer to live elsewhere. Some conclusions are risky because Cuba has always been far wealthier than its neighbor to the east.

Fidel Castro, self-described champion of the poor, thought he had the answer for not only Cuba but for all Third World countries and spent almost fifty years trying to export his ideas—but with limited success. His best selling point was his health care system. It was far from perfect but it was quite possible that no Third World country provided more access to professional health care than Cuba. Former World Bank President James Wolfensohn once said that Cuba had done "a great job" on both health care and education. There were far more Cuban doctors per capita than American doctors, if Cuban statistics are to be believed. Castro earned goodwill from his export of doctors to needy countries. But the idea of Cuba as a role model for the Third World never caught on. Democracy never seemed stronger in Latin America than in the first decade of the new millennium. Even Castro acknowledged in a 2010 interview that the Cuban model did not have much appeal to the outside world.

People used to migrate to Cuba before the revolution. Afterwards, it became a country from which many people departed— for good, fed up with shortages and the lack of freedom. Norberto Fuentes, a pro-Castro intellectual who turned against the revolution, decried Castro's "absolute personal dictatorship" and willingness "to do anything necessary to stay in power." Fuentes left the country in 1994, asserting that "Cuba is dead, dead, dead.".

The history of Cuba might have been far different if Castro had been born and raised in Havana and not in the east, Cuba's most deprived region—"a sea of poverty," as he once said. Castro himself was born into a farm family in Birán. The family was well-to-do but had few aristocratic trappings. Their home, although large, was built on stilts. His father was a Spanish immigrant, his mother, a housekeeper. Ann Marie Bardach says in her book *Without Fidel* that lands bordering on those of his father were owned by the West Indies Sugar Corp., in which major shareholders were from the Bush family, forebears of the forty-first and forty-third presidents of the United States. According to Castro, that corporation, coupled with the adjacent holdings of the U.S.-based United Sugar Co. (previously the United Fruit Co.), covered four hundred and forty-three square miles of eastern Cuba, roughly six times the size of Washington, D.C. (Of the ten U.S. presidents whose terms coincided with Castro's tenure, the Bushes were probably the most loathed by the Cuban leader for their perceived aggressive attitude toward the island.)

As a youth, Castro was educated mostly by Catholics, then enrolled at the University of Havana in 1945. He soon became involved in politics. His sheer size, brains and speaking gifts enabled him to stand out. He was a twenty-five year old law school graduate with a wife and baby son when Fulgenio Batista seized power in a military coup in March 1952, ending Cuba's experiment in democracy. This was a turning point—one of several—in Castro's life. He decided almost instantly to take up arms against Batista.

His 1953 attack on a military barracks in the far east city of Santiago with some eighty companions occurred just sixteen months after Batista seized power. It did not go well. It did not spark the insurrection that he had hoped for. Castro was arrested. Many of his colleagues were killed. At his trial, Castro sought to justify his actions by describing Cuba's squalor, citing "the 500,000 farm laborers who live in miserable shacks, who work for four months of the year and starve the rest, sharing their misery with their children, who don't have an inch of land to till and whose existence would move any heart not made of stone."

He was found guilty of insurrection and sentenced to twenty-five years. He sulked at an off-shore island prison. But his audacity had made him a household word among Cubans. Thinking that hothead from the east had learned his lesson, Batista pardoned him after just 22 months' imprisonment. It was a grave miscalculation.

Far from being chastened by the 1953 fiasco, Castro wasted no time in regrouping for another attack, using Mexico as a base of operations. In December 1956, just nineteen months after his release from prison, he and eighty-one rebel colleagues sailed from Mexico and launched a guerrilla campaign against Batista from the mountains of eastern Cuba. It was supplemented by rebel groups operating in urban centers. Again, it seemed like an unfair fight, given the advantage of the military in manpower and armaments. But Castro was not one who was easily spooked by long odds; his three-hundred man rebel force was arrayed against thousands of regular Army soldiers. Remarkably, the will and the smarts of Castro and his guerrilla companions prevailed. As the country was ushering in a new year, 1959, Batista fled. Castro, a mere thirty-two, was in charge. Cuba would never be the same. He was about to turn the country upside down.

For Cuba, it seemed a golden moment when Castro entered Havana in early January 1959, welcomed by an adoring crowd. He had an aura that had many Cubans dreamily optimistic after years often-ruthless military rule and long years of warfare. He promised to reinstate democracy under terms of the constitution of 1940. He swore that he was an anti-communist. On both counts, he lied. He moved quickly to establish security and trade ties with the Soviet Union. Only when he felt secure enough, at the end if 1961, did he confess that he had been a Marxist-Leninist all this life.

In the early going, many supporters of the *ancién regime* and virtually the entire business elite were either chased out of Cuba or dispatched by a firing squad. There were reportedly more than five hundred such killings in the first three years; an undisclosed number of others were concealed.

Soldiers loyal to the deposed Batista regime were dealt with harshly. Over time, all independent newspapers and TV and radio stations were shut down. Huge swaths of rich agricultural land were nationalized, not to mention homes, factories and commercial establishments.

The Havana elite who managed to escape left their homes and business infrastructure behind—all of it for the cost-free use by the revolution, an immense inheritance. There never was any discussion of compensation. Based on claims filed with the State Department, Americans suffered combined property losses in Cuba of almost two billion in 1958 dollars. In 1961, Castro's forces easily put down an American-backed invasion force of Cuban exiles at the Bay of Pigs. It was a grave humiliation for the United States and its young president, John F. Kennedy.

Castro was to have a mutually beneficial relationship with Moscow for thirty years, one which had its share of drama. The installation of Soviet missiles on Cuban soil in 1962 brought the world closer to nuclear war than at any time before or since. A compromise between Moscow and Washington ended the standoff peacefully. Castro played no role.

One of Castro's his most trusted lieutenants in the early years was a young Argentine named Ernesto "Che" Guevara. Castro's view of neglect and suffering growing up in eastern Cuba paralleled what Guevara had found in his extensive travels through backwater towns of South and Central America in the early 1950s. A particularly radicalizing experience for Guevara was his presence in Guatemala when the CIA orchestrated the ouster of an elected leftist government in May 1954.

The paths of Castro and Guevara crossed in Mexico when Castro was preparing for his guerrilla campaign against Batista. They were to form a ten-year alliance that had international repercussions that no one could have predicted. Once the guerrilla campaign against Batista began in late 1956, Guevara, though sick with asthma, proved to be a fearless warrior, serving as second-in-command under Castro. And when Castro was in power, he tapped the Argentine as a top lieutenant. He was involved in a national literacy campaign in which one hundred thousand volunteers were deployed. He also was minister of industries, head of the agrarian reform program, president of the National Bank, and chief international salesman for the revolution. Such was Guevara's authority on money matters that he was dubbed Cuba's "economic czar." A medical doctor, he had no training for any of these tasks; he was barely thirty when he began assuming them. Castro obviously was more interested in loyalty than in professional credentials. (Many of the supposed allies he sent off as ambassadors simply defected.) He wanted real revolutionaries in his government, not merely people who had good professional resumes. In Che Guevara, he got total commitment. Che tackled his work with a fervor bordering on mania, at times reportedly working thirty-six hours without sleep. He once said, "...(I)f Christ himself stood in my way I, like Nietzsche, would not hesitate to squish him like a worm."

Guevara believed that Cuba's economic possibilities were limitless. He told a conference of Western Hemisphere leaders in Uruguay in 1961: "What does Cuba intend to have by the year 1980? A net income per capita of around three thousand dollars, more than the United States currently has. And if you do not believe us, fine, here we are ready for a competition, gentlemen."

Obviously, such talk was foolhardy but Guevara was not around long enough to see the full scope of the economic descent that was to befall Cuba. He mysteriously left Cuba in late 1964, hoping to promote revolutionary possibilities in the Congo. Did he leave Cuba voluntarily or was he pushed? Castro has never told the full story.

According to Washington-based historian Piero Gleijeses, Guevara's stay in the Congo, lasting only a few months, may have reflected disillusionment with African revolutionaries who, as he saw it, were more interested in high living than in pursuit of high ideals. He was killed in rural Bolivia by security forces while on a revolutionary mission there in 1967, never having returned to Cuba, so far as is known. At his death, he was thirty-nine.

For the United States, nothing was more dispiriting in its approach to Cuba than defeat at the Bay of Pigs. To that obscure outpost on Cuba's south coast, the United States in 1961 dispatched over one thousand four hundred U.S.-trained Cuban exiles to depose Castro. They were routed in seventy-two hours, a catastrophic American miscalculation that left Castro even more firmly entrenched. The Bay of Pigs played into Castro's hands like no other event could have. He had said that for a revolution to succeed, it had to be attacked. The United States obliged in two ways. It sponsored an attack on Cuba—and lost. America, proud victor (allied with others) over imperial Japan and Germany just sixteen years earlier was made to look foolish by a revolutionary upstart just a decade out of law school. Castro must have felt invincible at the time. And indeed, his grip on power was firm for decades but he never delivered the abundance that he so frequently had promised his people.

There is little doubt that the U.S. embargo hurt the Cuban economy but Castro surely knew that American reprisals were inevitable given his nurturing of guerrilla movements abroad and plotting alongside the Soviet Union during a peak Cold War period.

Political support for the embargo in the United States remained strong even after the Soviet Union disappeared, and with it the Cold War, in 1991. Castro was far less of a menace to American interests in the aftermath but the embargo nonetheless remained, largely because of the influence of Cuban-American anti-communists, who dominated South Florida politics.

On occasion in the post-Soviet period, Castro made it clear that his strategic vision had not changed even when he was without significant allies and was flat broke. When Castro met with Iran's supreme leader, Ayatollah Ali Khamenei, in May 2001 in Tehran, he said, according to AFP, "Iran and Cuba, together, can bring the United States to its knees. The U.S. regime is very weak, and we are witnessing its weaknesses from up close." His best hope during his later years was not that Cuba would ever become a glittering showpiece but that capitalism would some day implode once its self-corrective mechanisms no longer worked. During the 2008-11 recession period, it was not hard to imagine the retired Castro reveling in America's downhill slide.

In the long years of acrimony between the United States and Cuba, no period quite matched the early 1960s. In a 2008 interview with a Cuban correspondent, President Raúl Castro recalled that contentious time when he served as number two in the Cuban hierarchy and as Minister of the Armed Forces. Highlights of his remarks as translated by the author:

"Once defeated at the Bay of Pigs, the Kennedys, the U.S. administration and the system could not take that affront, that humiliation, that defeat by a tiny little country facing its military might... The (next) objective was a direct invasion, probably in 1962 itself, which was only prevented by the presence of Soviet nuclear rockets in Cuba... I am only noting the most visible aspects, the most talked about, the most significant of those years. They were five or six very hard years. The blockade (embargo) was already in place (by 1962), but the Soviet Union existed under the leadership of the Communist Party and (Communist Party Secretary General Nikita) Khrushchev, who had a very positive attitude. These played a very important role given that the revolution was able to survive and resist. We were endowed with a good quantity of weapons of every type, until attaining the strength that we have today from the military point of view... Then came *Operación Mangosta* (Operation Mongoose, a post-Bay of Pigs U.S. assassination program) directed by... Robert Kennedy, the U.S. attorney general, who also participated in the contacts made with the U.S. Mafia for the known and already investigated attempts on the life of Fidel, out of the many that they planned.

"They were five years of constant internal struggle; thousands of dead and injured, victims of state terrorism, directed, organized and led by the United States.

"At that time a CIA station was created in Florida, the largest after its central offices in Langley. Hundreds of CIA officials directing activities against Cuba... that center was only superseded by the one established years later in Saigon...

"As is known, (there were) 179 armed (Florida-based) counterrevolutionary bands of different sizes operating all over (Cuba); sometimes they joined up, delivered a blow, split up again; on two occasions they were in six of the country's provinces... That was for six years, I think it wasn't until 1965 or January 1966 when we annihilated the last band in that stage; after that more emerged in different periods, which were rapidly eliminated."

Fidel Castro, whose official title in those days was prime minister, was constantly on the lookout for new opportunities to expand socialism. He saw them in Africa, which in the 1960s was undergoing its transition from colonial rule to independence. He sent troops to Algeria in 1961 to help rebels there oust the French. He attempted to foment revolution in the Congo a few years later. By the mid-1970s, Cuban troops could be found in a dozen African countries and Cuba hosted training exercises for African troops as well. His most ambitious undertakings took place in Angola and Ethiopia in support of pro-Soviet causes. The commitment in those countries was breathtaking, considering Cuba's small size and its location thousands of miles away. (Castro also helped develop revolutionary groups elsewhere in Latin America, but the political costs were high; virtually all hemispheric countries broke diplomatic and trade relations with Cuba for an extended period. All but the United States have since resumed them.)

Castro said the new order in Cuba was the product of historical forces, not men. He saw Cuba as being in the vanguard of a global revolutionary movement that would overwhelm capitalism. *"Nothing Can Change the Course of History"* was the title of a two-hundred-and-twenty-page book published in 1985 based on interviews Castro had with two visiting Americans. Speaking of South America, he told them: "There cannot be the slightest doubt that an explosive situation exists and that if an urgent solution is not found... more than one revolution will take place." That did not happen. To the extent that there has been a trend in Latin America since 1985, it has been in the consolidation of freedom and democracy. (*The Economist* magazine said in 2010 that economic advances had lifted tens of million of Latin Americans from poverty. Talk of Castroite revolution on the continent has all but ceased. But leftist, anti-American politics lingered in some countries.)

Meanwhile, prosperity continued to elude Cubans. A country hell-bent on promoting international revolution, Cuba's own survival depended on generous support from the Soviet Union (and later from Hugo Chávez's Venezuela). In between, absent external support, Cuba suffered the worst economic crisis in its history. Adoption of capitalist remedies starting in 1993 spared the country from possible collapse—remedies that Castro halted after the economy picked up. But Castro nonetheless was in many countries an admired figure. He had a reputation as a fighter for the poor, a man able to stand up to the United States. Late in his tenure, he earned goodwill from his export of tens of thousands of health care workers to poor countries and training of medical personnel from abroad in Cuba. Cuban opposition to the American embargo, implemented in 1962, enjoyed steadily increasing support in the U.N. General Assembly. During most of the first eighteen years of annual voting, the United States was virtually alone worldwide in defending the embargo.

This book attempts to focus on aspects of Cuba about which little has been written, partly because too few foreign reporters have been allowed in the country for lengthy stays or made only a few brief visits. The work of the handful of American and other Western reporters based in Cuba is often excellent, considering the less than optimum conditions in which they labor. I benefited from the frequency of my visits to the country and my knowledge of Spanish, thanks to a stint as a Peace Corps volunteer in Venezuela in the early 1960s. I probably spent nine or ten months combined in Cuba between 1974 and 2008. Along the way, I talked with countless Cubans about their lives and learned from them the singularity of the Cuban experience. (I regret that I did not have more information for this book on life in small town and rural Cuba.)

Despite limits on freedom, seldom did any Cuban express fear in conversations with me about being seen speaking with a man who was easily identifiable from dress and physical characteristics as an American. (Some other American visitors found many Cubans to be fearful and uncommunicative.) I remember chatting with a Cuban couple in my hotel room years ago. They regretted the path Castro had taken and said they would have preferred a democratic outcome. *Was the room being bugged?* I wondered. Obviously, I was more worried about that than they were.

Gaining an understanding of what the Cuban revolution has wrought was not possible from mere visits to the island, however frequent mine were. The media is relentlessly uninformative. Besides, I spent most of my time during visits dealing with my assignment; having free time to explore was sometimes a luxury. In putting together the book, I took advantage of e-mail contacts on the island as well as a relatively new online English-language publication, *the Havana Times,* a useful window on everyday life on the island available only outside Cuba. I must also credit authors who, like me, were able to see Cuba up close: Ann Louise Bardach (*Without Fidel*), Lydia Chávez (editor, *Capitalism, God and a Good Cigar*), Robert Quirk *(Fidel Castro*), and Ignacio Ramonet (*Cien Horas Con Fidel*) *(A Hundred Hours with Fidel*). Also helpful was the staff at the Cuban Heritage Collection of the University of Miami Library. I did not have the benefit of a trip to Cuba for purposes of this book. I did not believe that the authorities there would have tolerated for very long an American wandering around the island asking questions of ordinary Cubans about life under the Castros. I would have very much enjoyed talking to Cuba's potato or tobacco farmers or to visit day care centers or homes for the aged. Conversations with ordinary Cubans were easier when I traveled with papers showing that I had authorization of the Foreign Ministry to be in the country. That was enough to assure police that I should be left alone. Mere tourists got less slack.

When I was traveling to Cuba once or twice a year, the authorities never objected when I visited the homes of dissidents, including those who were under constant surveillance. And the dissidents themselves never seemed to fear that meeting with an American would lead to reprisals. On one occasion, however, during a visit to Havana by Soviet President Mikhail Gorbachev in 1989, a dissident friend was arrested as he was making a several-mile trek to my hotel to deliver a press release to me. He was imprisoned and later was allowed to leave the country on the condition that he never return. Virtually all dissidents I knew were ex-prisoners. I found it strange that some of their homes were far more comfortable than the overcrowded, run-down dwellings of so many others. The explanation apparently was that they were born into the house and, according to common practice, were entitled, within reason, to stay there as long as they wished.

Having covered the stormy U.S.-Cuban relationship for thirty-eight years out of the State Department and on Capitol Hill, I felt I was up to speed on developments on that subject for purposes of this book. I knew all but one of the U.S. diplomats who headed the U.S. mission in Havana from 1977 on and all of their Cuban counterparts in Washington. All were generous with their time. I often exchanged impressions with CIA Cuba analysts in Washington over the years, especially after returning from visits to the island. I was grateful for those opportunities.

This book is part memoir, part anecdote, part history, and part analysis. I don't doubt that both the right and the left will find fault with parts of this book. That is the fate of almost anyone who touches this inflammatory topic.

Ray Suárez of *PBS* found that out when he was the lead reporter in a three-part series on health care in Cuba in December 2010. He spoke to a number of people linked to the Cuban medical profession, and also to other Cubans, both on-island and off, who criticized the health care system or the Cuban system itself.

Mary Anastasia O'Grady, of the *Wall Street Journal,* said the series clearly had a pro-Castro tilt. "The series was taped in Cuba with government 'cooperation' so there is no surprise that it went heavy on the party line," O'Grady wrote. "Still, there was something disturbing about how Mr. Suárez allowed himself to be used by the police state, dutifully reciting its dubious claims as if he were reporting great advances in medical science."

Suárez said he found it "horrifying" that O'Grady reached that conclusion, citing on the *PBS* web site critical quotes in the series from several interviewees who were unaffiliated with the regime. These people hardly qualified for roles in a "state propaganda film," Suárez said, mocking O'Grady's description of the series. Suárez noted that after the series was broadcast, the Cuban government informed *PBS* that any future requests for visas by the network would not be approved.

The most interesting aspects of the book (to me, at least) relate to the daily struggles of ordinary Cubans: the rundown, overcrowded housing and the overstretched transportation system. There was an "only in Cuba" quality to some of these experiences, and I hope readers will find them illuminating. Some early chapters focus on these issues. Later chapters deal, perhaps predictably, with the economy, particularly its decline in the early 1990s; the key role of block committees in providing security; the stormy relationship with the United States; the media; and the black majority population, among other subjects. Also included is Addendum 1, featuring quotes from Fidel Castro and an essay on Che Guevara. Addendum 2 includes essays by, or interviews with, ordinary Cubans about their particular (usually unhappy) experiences. Addendum 3 is a paean to AP photographer Charles Tasnadi, who accompanied me on many trips.

CHAPTER 1

AMERICAN SENATORS COME TO TOWN

It seemed like an ordinary Italian restaurant, the lights appropriately low, the waiters decently attired in dark suits. The customers were chatty and numerous and the mood cheerful. Our party of four, all American reporters, was seated with no waiting. We had just begun to check our menus when our waiter offered a recommendation. This, he said, pointing to one particular menu item from a long list, is *"la especialidad de la casa"* (the speciality of the house).

It was spaghetti topped with plain, unadorned tomato sauce.

Anyone who wanted pasta with a chunky marinara or a tasty pesto sauce was out of luck. It didn't take my colleagues and I long to realize why the waiter had singled out that particularly unexciting dish. It was the only item on the menu that was being served that evening (and who knows how many other evenings?).

The year was 1974, Fidel Castro was a still youthful forty-eight, and still in charge, having survived numerous U.S. attempts to get rid of him, including an invasion, a suffocating embargo, and myriad assassination plots. More than thirteen years had passed since the last U.S. government official had set foot on the island. So it was considered a newsy event when Senators Claiborne Pell and Jacob Javits traveled to Cuba to see whether a diplomatic opening was possible. I was among a group of twenty-nine American reporters and photographers who covered the visit, my first of many to Cuba.

We found the streets of Havana to be tense. It was possible that security measures were heightened out of concern that dissidents could see the visit by the senators as an excuse for a demonstration or at least whisperings of discontent to the visiting press. I heard nothing of the kind until two days into the trip when a man who appeared to be in his forties startled scores of people in the *Habana Libre* lobby and loudly denounced the regime. Security officers permitted him to finish but there was little doubt that he was dealt with harshly.

Cubans knew their limits. In a street conversation, when people wanted to refer to Castro without saying his name, they would reach for their chin, press their thumb and index finger together, and stroke downward, as though stroking a beard. If the military needed to be referenced, a hand would be raised across the chest to a shoulder, the index and middle fingers extended. This would signify military stripes.

Castro's principle security arm was the block-by-block committees, known as CDRs, set up to monitor suspect activity. Thanks largely to CDR sleuthing, thousands of dissidents were imprisoned.

In 1976, Castro acknowledged fifteen thousand such prisoners. That number has descended sharply over the years.

The visit by the two senators, by chance, coincided with the fourteenth anniversary of the street committees' founding. Castro commemorated the occasion with a speech, a blistering, hour-plus, anti-American diatribe before a Havana street crowd of thousands. Castro held the U.S. government "directly responsible" for the ousting of Chilean Socialist President Salvador Allende, a close Castro ally, a year earlier. As a result of U.S. complicity, there are "thousands of Chileans who have been tortured, murdered, jailed and banished" or who live in "awful conditions of repression, unemployment and poverty," he said. (The United States has denied having any direct role in the September 11, 1973 coup. It has been widely reported that the United States funded a conservative Santiago newspaper before the coup and also provided financial backing for a truckers' strike.) At least Pell and Javits were not on the podium with Castro that evening. I was seated about seventy-five yards away, next to a fellow American reporter, in the grandstand. Unbeknownst to me, the reporter spoke no Spanish. He asked me, somewhat sheepishly, at the end of Castro's speech, "What did he say?"

Among our "handlers" (officials who monitored foreign reporters) during the senators' visit were two young, English-speaking Cuban women. They both spotted a copy of the *Time* magazine that I had brought. Both expressed interest in looking at it. I gave it to one, and she drew a wrathful look from her colleague. Their behavior seemed to reflect a need to read something livelier and more informative than the drab fare available in the communist media. (Castro had declared himself a Marxist-Leninist about thirteen years earlier.) Throughout his rule, his people were largely oblivious to activities in the outside world beyond the scant information provided through official channels. As for my magazine, I never got it back.

During my stay, the radio in my room at the *Habana Libre* could be tuned to only two news and opinion stations, both all-day propaganda outlets. On one, the announcer periodically intoned, *"Cuba, el primer país libre de las Américas"* ("Cuba, the first free country of the Americas"). I heard the same message in subsequent visits; eventually, the blurb was withdrawn.

I was startled during that 1974 visit by the amount of radio coverage the stations were giving to the transition to independence from colonial rule in Africa. Castro obviously saw in this process opportunities for the establishment of one-party socialist states much like his. Cuban troops were scattered throughout Africa in the 1970s. Some were sent to the continent's most vile dictatorships, such as Equatorial Guinea. Through radio, the Cuban regime tried to sensitize public opinion to developments in Africa, though it was hard to imagine that more than a handful of people actually were paying attention. But if you wanted the latest on, say, the independence movement in

Portuguese Guinea in 1974, Cuba's *Radio Rebelde* or *Radio Reloj* were there for you.

The *Habana Libre* was formerly of the Hilton chain. Hilton opened it with a big splash in 1958, a year after Meyer Lansky, the American mobster, opened the by-the-sea *Hotel Riviera*. Both were spectacularly bad investments, made amidst a civil war. Just ten months after the *Habana Libre* opened, Castro took power— and soon laid claim to both hotels and, eventually, thousands of other properties belonging to Cubans and Americans. Within days after Batista's ouster, top officials took over the twenty-third floor of the *Libre* using it as an office. (Castro was constantly on the move and had no office of his own in the early period.) After sixteen years, at the time of the senators' visit, the former Hilton had a seedy look, a far cry from the opening-day glitter. (Nowadays, the *Riviera* also has a seen-better-days look, especially when compared with the plush, more youthful, *Sol Meliá* nearby.) In my room at the *Libre* during that 1974 visit, the desk lamp had a bulb almost too dim to cast shadows. Working at night there was an ordeal. (In subsequent visits, I remembered to bring my own sixty-watt bulb. "Don't leave home without it," was my mantra.)

Even the phone book was a curiosity during that first visit. It was strikingly thin, considering Havana's size. But what caught the visitor's eye even more was the presence of revolutionary phrases placed neatly at the bottom of each page. (Nineteen

months after the senators' visit, Castro delivered another unre-
strained anti-American speech marking the fifteenth anniversary
of the U.S. defeat at the Bay of Pigs. Afterward, as part of a campaign to tout the speech, telephone operators around the country
answered calls by saying, "We support Fidel's statement. Good
morning.")

Pell was a Democrat from Rhode Island, Javits, a Republican from New York. Both were steeped in the liberalism of the
American northeast and were members of the Senate Foreign
Relations Committee. Most foreign trips by senators attract little
attention but this one was different because of the destination.
Ironically, the last prominent American to visit Cuba before the
Pell-Javits trip was made by Senator-elect Pell himself in December 1960, between his election as a new senator and the break in
relations with Cuba.

The two senators arrived on a Friday afternoon aboard a U.S.
government plane. Pell, worried about possible hostile action by
anti-Castro exiles, insisted that the time and other departure details of the flight to Havana be kept secret. The press flew there
on a charter flight from Miami and was treated to a briefing shortly
after arrival by a Cuban economic affairs official. A reporter for a
well-known U.S. newspaper was in a somewhat inebriated state
during the briefing. He had a notebook in one hand and a glass
of wine in the other. With no obvious place to set the glass down

when the briefing began, he put it in the pocket of his shirt, of all places, and took notes. His aggressive questioning of the Cuban official annoyed and embarrassed the rest of us. I have no recollection of whether there was any wine spillage on the reporter's shirt when we departed.

Our Cuban hosts kept us busy. We went to a late night performance of high-stepping dancers at the *Tropicana* and also toured a psychiatric hospital outside Havana (it was described years later as a torture center by a dissident; in January 2010, two dozen patients died of cold and hunger there). Another stop was the Lenin School, where students, when they weren't laboring in the fields, were subjected to rigorous course work. The students were well-mannered, a behavior perhaps encouraged by monitors who were present for exchanges with reporters. Were the students there offspring of Communist Party functionaries? We didn't know but that certainly was a suspicion.

Given the stridency of Castro's anti-American remarks at his Saturday night speech, the event was a humiliation for the two senators, especially Javits. He was seeking re-election in New York that fall and, in the ensuing weeks, endured rebukes from critics back home for seeming to sidle up to one of the world's most anti-American leaders, a man who was at his Yankee-baiting best in Javits's presence. Five weeks after his foray to Havana,

Javits survived the re-election bid but by a smaller margin than his landslide win six years earlier.

In light of developments after the senators left the island, their visit turned out to be not as ill-conceived as it may have seemed at first. The evening after the speech, Pell and Javits dined with Castro, who told them that his fiery speech was not intended to embarrass them, and that the subject matter had been decided well before the date had been set for their visit. The senators said that Castro seemed open to an improvement in relations with Washington. "The ice has been broken," they said. Days after they had returned home, Castro released four political prisoners, making it clear that it was a gesture toward the senators and not toward the U.S. government.

Pell was known around Washington for his courtly manner and his propensity for gaffes. Accompanying him on the trip was a cousin, Christopher Iselin. Introducing him to Castro, a somewhat flustered Pell identified him as "Christopher Columbus." Castro smilingly wondered whether the man who stood before him was the actual discoverer of America. Pell then came up with the proper identity. At another point, Castro was waving goodbye to the senators, a cigar resting between his fingers. Pell grabbed the cigar and said, "Thank you." Reporting on the encounter years later, the *New York Times* said Castro was completely nonplussed.

Undisclosed at the time of the senators' visit were the preliminary contacts that the U.S. and Cuba had begun in secrecy. They had been authorized by President Ford, who had replaced the Cuba-hating President Nixon just seven weeks before the two senators' visit. Castro's own thoughts, as relayed by the two senators back to Washington, were useful to the administration as it contemplated actually opening substantive discussions. (One evening after his return from Havana, Javits briefed Secretary of State Henry Kissinger in a basement office in the Senate. I waited for two hours outside the office, hoping for a pithy comment from Kissinger on prospects for U.S.-Cuban talks. The stakeout, as I suspected, produced nothing. Kissinger breezed passed me without stopping, saying only, "Very interesting." Alas, long stakeouts that produce no news are the norm in Washington.)

Almost exactly one hundred days after the senators' trip, officials of the two governments met secretly in New York. In March, Kissinger, without directly referring to ongoing contacts with Cuba, said: "We see no virtue in perpetual antagonism between the United States and Cuba. We are prepared to move in a new direction if Cuba will." This was a startling disclosure. The United States had broken off diplomatic relations with Cuba in early 1961 during the waning days of the Eisenhower administration; there had been virtually no diplomatic contact since aside from the undisclosed contacts in early 1975. In the ensuing months, the two countries made conciliatory gestures toward one another. The process might have led to re-establishment of normal ties—were it not for developments in Africa.

Castro had taken a keen interest in the continent, hoping for socialist inroads in the post-colonial era. Attempts over the years to promote revolution in Latin America had yielded little and, besides, it ran the risk of provoking a hostile response from the United States. So Castro began looking east, across the Atlantic. He dispatched troops to a number of African countries in the early 1970s. The southwest African country of Angola caught Castro's attention in 1975 because of a power struggle that erupted following the end of Portuguese colonial rule. A pro-Moscow faction was arrayed against two non-communist groups. By the end of the year, troops from the apartheid regime in South Africa entered the fray. Castro's use of Cuban troops in Angola on behalf of the pro-Soviet faction angered Washington, which abruptly called off diplomatic discussions with Cuba.

The Pell-Javits visit, however intriguing the trappings, was relegated to history's footnotes. As for me, I was happy to go along for the ride—and happy there were more Cuba trips. The country was filled with surprises. One constant seemed to be Fidel Castro. He outlasted nine American presidents. Would there be an uprising when he surrendered power, as many of his enemies in Miami supposed? Or would it be a quiet exit? The answer would not come until 2006.

Fidel Castro, Senator Javits, and George Gedda

Cuban President Fidel Castro gestures with visiting Sen. Jacob Javits of New York standing to his left. Javits (bald-headed) and Sen. Claiborne Pell (not shown) conferred with Castro in September 1974 in Havana on ending a 13-year freeze in U.S.-Cuban relations. Author is standing behind Javits.

Thirteen of the twenty-nine reporters and photographers
pose at Havana airport after covering Cuba visit of Sens.
Jacob Javits and Claiborne Pell. Author is fourth from left in
white shirt. September 1974.

CHAPTER 2

THE SUCCESSION

Transition or succession? As Castro approached his eightieth birthday in 2006, still firmly entrenched, the more urgent the question became. He had long made it clear that brother Raúl was next in line.

Borrowing a baseball term, Castro said Raúl was his "*relevo*" (relief pitcher). The regime envisioned a seamless succession. The Castro family dynasty would be preserved. Castro and his younger brother (by just under five years) had collaborated in carrying out the revolution for almost fifty years. The Bush administration was lobbying for a transition to democracy, a preference made clear in a lengthy report in May 2004 that spelled out how the United States opposed a dynastic succession and, if asked, would assist a post-Fidel, democratically-oriented government in Cuba in the areas of health, education, food, transportation, and a surfeit of others.

A follow-up report issued on July 10, 2006, said, "There should be full agreement that the only acceptable result of Fidel Castro's incapacitation, death, or ouster is for a genuine democratic transition to take place in Cuba. This is an historic and stark choice between the continuation of dictatorship or the restoration of freedom and sovereignty to eleven million men, women, and children." The report said the United States would attempt to "undermine" any Fidel-to-Raúl succession.

It repeated the offers of two years earlier of assistance in a number of fields, including health and education, both touted by Castro and other officials as the crown jewels of the revolution's advances.

In a speech in far eastern *Granma* province sixteen days after the report was released, Fidel Castro, in effect, dismissed the American offers as nonsense.

"Granma has no need of any Yankee transition plan to teach people how to read and write, vaccinate or care for the health of its population," he shouted.

So long as Castro was hale and hearty, any discussion of who came next in Cuba was pure conjecture. Who knew on that steamy evening in *Granma* when that potentially explosive issue might come to the fore? And when it did, what would Cubans— and the Americans—do? How about the Miami-based, first-generation exile community, implacably opposed to Castro from the revolution's earliest days? And what, if anything, did the Bush administration have in mind? Was there any substance to its opposition to a succession from Fidel to Raúl? Or was it just rhetoric? The answers came sooner than anybody had expected.

On that very July day in 2006 when Castro spoke in *Granma*, he had made earlier appearances in Santiago and in Holguín, also in the east. Before that, he had just spent several exhausting days attending a Latin American summit meeting in Argentina and flown forty-three hundred miles back to Cuba. He had had little sleep. As it turned out, the *Granma* speech would be Castro's last public appearance for almost four years. On a short flight from *Granma* to a nearby airport in Holguín, he became desperately ill with an acute intestinal disorder. As no doctor was aboard the flight, the plane landed at the nearest airport for emergency treatment. He was near death—stricken hours after his mocking reference to Bush's hopes for a post-Castro transition to democracy. After the brief stop for treatment, Fidel was flown to Havana, where he underwent emergency surgery for diverticulitis of the colon the next evening. (According to a Wikileaks account of a note from Michael Parmly, the chief U.S. diplomat in Havana, most of the doctors attending Fidel recommended one type of procedure. There were two dissenters: a Dr. Selman, chief of the medical team, and Fidel himself. The operation performed was consistent with the latters' wishes, but the procedure failed and a new operation was ordered.)

A day after Fidel became ill, Raúl replaced him as Cuba's leader for what was supposed to be several weeks. This was something new for the Cuban people. It was the first time that the "*comandante en jefe*" had surrendered power. Would he really come back, as planned? Power had shifted from the charismatic Fidel to his deeply private and very loyal younger brother, No. 1 in the line of succession and the defense chief. He was known as a hard line enforcer during the revolution's early years and as a champion of pragmatism later on in dealing with economic decline. He espoused the opening of Cuba to foreign tourists and of limited private enterprise.

As power transferred from one brother to the other, large numbers of security forces were deployed nationwide, in accordance with a long-standing plan, perhaps the biggest such mobilization since the Bay of Pigs. They were on guard against possible hostile acts by Cubans, or even by the United States. Yet, so far as is known, there were no incidents. To the extent that Castro's opponents on the island were encouraged by his sudden illness, they no doubt were inhibited from voicing that sentiment by the imposing security deployment.

Perhaps there was worry among Cubans about the future. Would things get better without Fidel? Or not? Tom Gjelten, a Cuba expert at *National Public Radio*, has written that anxiety is a normal state for Cubans. "People live so precariously that the prospect of dramatic change frightens even those who want it," he said in an essay. He quoted a friend in Santiago: "We have so little but that only means we cannot afford to lose what little we have."

In 2007, as Castro appeared to have survived his health crisis, the Bush administration told reporters that the true test of Cuba's succession strategy would come only after his death. He remained gravely ill for a time and eventually began to receive close foreign leaders. President Hugo Chávez of Venezuela visited several times. Also in 2007, Wikileaks released a note from Parmly, the head of the U.S. diplomatic mission, saying that first, before anything substantial will happen, "Castro's presence has a chilling and retardant effect on Cuban society. The high expectations for change are still out there, but are mostly associated with the idea that the dictator has to die."

Occasional pictures of Castro, looking older and gaunter, appeared in the official media in the months after he fell ill. Consistent with a party-approved succession process, Fidel formally surrendered to Raúl, following a party conclave, his role as president of the Council of Ministers and the Council of State in February 2008. But he kept his name before the public by writing frequent columns, called *Reflexiones*, (Reflections), which were displayed conspicuously in regime newspapers. Some were read on TV news shows. On an official website, links to his columns received higher billing than links to Raúl's speeches. Ranking third in the digital hierarchy, at least for a time, were quotes from Hugo

Chávez. This alignment left the impression that Fidel in some ways was still number one, even though he no longer held his government and state posts. (It was thought that he had retained his role as first secretary of the Communist Party but, curiously, he disclosed in March 2011 that he had resigned that post without announcement five years earlier, presumably at the time that he fell ill.) Raúl said he always consulted with Fidel on important decisions. When Fidel was asked over the years about the possibility of retirement, he often said, "Revolutionaries don't retire." He also was consistent in his unwillingness to use his columns to discuss Cuba's economic problems. He knew that his enemies abroad would seize on any critical remarks as reinforcement of their view that the revolution's economic policies were a fifty-year flop.

Raúl was one of the few people Fidel trusted. They had worked together continuously from about 1955, when the two brothers were released from a Batista-era prison, until Fidel succumbed to his illness. Raúl registered his disagreement with Fidel on economic policies over the years but his loyalty to his brother and the revolution were never in question.

CHAPTER 3

TRANSPORTATION WOES

Car ownership is relatively rare in Cuba, so commuting usually but not always means walking or taking a bus, a bike, a horse-drawn carriage or a truck in the case of peasants heading for the field. The number of cars in Cuba available for a daily home-to-office commute is, unlike America, exceedingly small. To the extent that there are cars in Havana, aside from American leftovers from the 1950s, most are linked to tourism or other government-sponsored activities. The elder Castro once heaped scorn on what he saw as the truest expression of American consumer excess: the changing of perfectly decent cars for new ones every three or four years. That may be a valid point but the regime has yet to come up with a comfortable, efficient public transportation alternative. For many Cubans, commuting can be a tortuous exercise.

In Cuba, it was not uncommon to find workers who spend hours each day commuting. The arrival of twelve hundred Chinese buses in recent years was helpful. But they tended to look run-down before their time. No one was predicting a long life span for these buses, not with all the overcrowding, overuse and potholed roads. Some bus drivers did their best to serve their customers. Others, their vehicle half empty, inexplicably drove past stops irrespective of how many people were there waiting to be picked up.

I have seen traffic jams in dirt-poor countries from Haiti to Mali, but hardly ever in Cuba. (In fairness, Cuba has far more roadways than either of the others.) A veteran Havana taxi driver once told me that he had never seen a traffic backup in the city. Schools can be found in Havana every few blocks, sometimes hidden on an upper floor of a building constructed for another purpose. Almost all kids walk to school. School buses are a rarity. When it rains, students sometimes don't bother to show up rather than get soaked. Cubans often have to get by without raincoats. As a substitute, some use the equivalent of lawn bags, carving out spaces for their head and arms.

In 2005, Castro amplified his aversion to consumerism and the car culture in particular. "The consumer society is one of the most sinister inventions of developed capitalism," he told interviewer Ignacio Ramonet. "I try to imagine 1.3 billion Chinese with the same level of car ownership as the United States... Under a diabolic and chaotic order, consumer societies in five or six decades will have drained the proved and probable reserves of fossil fuels." (This is an unconvincing argument. Can anyone imagine society waiting around until the last oil well produces the world's last gallon of oil before it looks for a suitable alternative? That process is already well under way.)

The lack of private cars was underscored one late fall day in Havana. I was having a phone conversation with my friend Jorge. He was fortunate enough to have three cars because his wife worked for a foreign currency-paying European embassy. Even though his cars were rundown Soviet-made *Ladas*, having three gave Jorge almost aristocratic status in Cuba. I mentioned to Jorge that there was a baseball game that evening at Havana's "*Estadio Latinoamericano*." He promised an eight-fifteen pickup at my hotel. It occurred to me after we hung up that we would have only fifteen minutes to get to the game and see the start. In the U.S., fans have to leave for the park one or two hours beforehand because of traffic and problems parking. Jorge showed up on time; I braced myself for a late arrival at the stadium. Roughly seven minutes later, Jorge was parking *directly in front of the main entrance.* I was flabbergasted. I wondered whether he was going to drop me off while he found a permanent space. No, he said, this is where we park. We entered the stadium, paid a few pennies each for tickets, and were seated in two of the best seats in the house by an attendant after Jorge told him I was a *visitante importante.* And it was only eight-twenty-five p.m. So much for my concerns that we wouldn't arrive before the third inning. Glancing around the park while awaiting the first pitch, I noticed a sign on the right field fence: "*Luchar para Vencer*" (Fight to Conquer). I asked Jorge whether the sign was a reference to baseball or revolution. He looked at me with eyes that said, "Dumb question." The answer was obvious: "*Revolución.*" There must have been twenty thousand fans at the game. I assumed many of them had no choice but to hoof it to get home. In my case, I was back at the hotel in five minutes once the game was over, thanks to Jorge and the predictably sparse traffic.

On Cuba's streets, Soviet *Ladas* can be found along with Toyotas and Nissans. But many hand-me-down American cars from the 1950s and even the '40s are still around. No one knows how many there are but estimates range between sixty and one-hundred thousand. If it weren't for the rust, they might remind Americans of a Jimmy Stewart-era movie. As there are no businesses that spray paint cars, house paint applied with brushes is the unfashionable substitute. The cars are kept rolling by ingenious mechanics who make their own parts, up to a point. If a fender is needed, the solution could be a tin roof lifted from an unoccupied shack. For brake fluid, some use a mix of alcohol, brown sugar, and shampoo. If a car lacks a mirror, windows, or door handles, so be it. There is no place where replacement parts can easily be located. The nearest parts store is in the Bahamas or maybe the Dominican Republic. And if your tires need air, you have to get to your *Cupet* gas station before four-thirty p.m., the time air pump operators go off duty. To prevent theft, they take the air hoses home or lock them up at the station. Another quirk: there is no requirement for a car owner to have insurance, according to author/blogger Michael di Lauro, who wrote an article on cars in Cuba.

I remember a 1951 Plymouth pulling up alongside a taxi in which I was riding. I asked the driver the sale price. He said eighteen-thousand dollars—and wasn't kidding; prices in that range, I learned, were common for foreign buyers, even rusting hulks that have passed the half-million-mile mark and would have been left for dead in a normal country. A seller is more realistic if a Cuban inquires. The price would be closer to three thousand. The high price of limping lemons of a long-gone era reflects the acute state of transportation in Cuba.

Transportation problems worsened in the depression of the early 1990s when the demise of the Soviet Union and communism's disappearance from Eastern Europe left Cuba high and dry. Because of a lack of gasoline, oxen were mobilized to plow the fields. Half the bus routes in Havana were shut down. An estimated 75 to 85 percent of Cuba's international trade was eliminated. Many workers had to sit at home because they couldn't get to work. Long lines formed at bus stops because sometimes hours passed before a bus appeared. Those that did were often too full to take on more than a few additional passengers. Bus stop attendants, dressed head to toe in yellow, would stop passing government cars with empty seats. The drivers were obliged to pick up stranded commuters who were headed in their direction. Thousands of bicycles were imported from China, and the government touted the health benefits of pedaling to work. Many accidents occurred, often involving people in their fifties or older who hadn't been on a bicycle in decades.

Hitchhikers were a common sight on highways in those days of acute fuel shortages. They could be found jammed together in the cargo area of trucks, perhaps the only mode available to them. I can recall traveling on the highway east of Havana, with hardly a sign of other vehicles or human life for many miles except for hitchhikers.

A Cuban man told me that the gasoline ration for his 1966 Buick Century, a guzzler, was six liters a month—a gallon and a half. I saw him and his friends arrive in his car at a Havana beach one day. My guess is that this Sunday outing probably wiped out his entire gasoline ration for the month.

Petty theft was rampant in the early 1990s because of scarcity. People stole items that they could exchange for cash. Pilfering of silverware in hotel restaurants by staff (and perhaps customers) was so common that these items were often locked overnight at these locations. Only the wait staff had access. But when lack of bus service prevented some waiters from going to their jobs, the silverware remained locked up and some customers had to use their fingers at mealtime—or go hungry.

Communist Party and government stalwarts often have cars not because they buy them but because they receive them as bonuses that come with their jobs, compliments of the party. Sometimes the car comes with a driver. If the functionary loses his job for subpar performance, he loses his car as well. Cars also are available to others who are both frugal and fortunate enough to work at least part time abroad and receive expense money in euros before departure. One example was a couple who worked for *Cubana de Aviación*, the national carrier; aside from their car, they had an impressive array of household goods. In another case, a party loyalist transferred in mid-career to diplomatic work after many years' service to the Havana city government. He retired after a few postings overseas, having saved enough to buy a Toyota in Cuba, which he used to help his son start a taxi business. The fare in his cab, like many others, was payable only in hard currency. He and his family lived well; thanks to a satellite connection, they watched American programs on their flat-screen TV. (Such connections are illegal but not for the elite, so long as the satellite dish is hidden from view.) A taxi driver with a decent hard-currency paying clientele can live much better than a teacher or doctor.

Less fortunate was another Havana friend. For a time, his wife had a dollar-paying job for a foreign firm. On Saturdays, she was assigned to close the distant office where she worked until

2:00 a.m. Sunday. There was no public transportation at that hour. Taxis were too expensive. Walking home alone was too danger-ous. So her husband walked five miles to pick her up and the couple then walked all the way back—a sacrifice worth the price all because she got paid in dollars. (After an 11-year run, the gov-ernment ruled in 2004 that dollars could no longer legally be used for routine transactions but still could be exchanged at state cur-rency shops for euros or newly introduced CUC's, the national foreign exchange currency.)

In the interior of the island, horse-drawn carriages have been common in good times and bad, especially for commuting to work. The government calculated in 2009 that the number of horse-led trips actually increased over the previous year. At times, the horses are called on to work into the night. To avoid accidents, drivers light fires in small buckets that hang from the back of the carriage. The system is quaint and not out of place in leisurely rural Cuba. The price per passenger is also is right—just a few cents. Tourists are driven around in most villages on noisy scoot-ers, normally paying five dollars.

In farm areas, trucks are the normal mode for transporting workers. Truckers also deliver goods to markets but, with their vehicles and the roads often in poor condition and with supplies of gas unreliable, a trucker's life in Cuba is often trying, a situation certainly not limited to Cuba. The Economist Magazine reported in 2008 that much of the tomato crop the previous year was lost for lack of fuel for transport to the markets.

The rail system is in a sad state of neglect and disrepair. A *Toronto Star* reporter describes a short trip she took through an area east of Havana: "The Electric Train pulls up only a half hour late. Rust has turned its roof reddish brown. On top is a transformer that looks older than electricity. Four bent poles reach for the sagging cables that miraculously manage to deliver power to the engine. Slowly, we sway though miles of overgrown fields, some seats swaying considerably more than others. I feel like I'm inside the skeleton of a double-jointed contortionist." It is hard to envy the Cuban budget gurus who, with limited resources, have to make choices between competing entities whose claims for new equipment, however legitimate, can't all be funded.

In Havana, people who ride the bus to and from work spend about 4 percent of their income on these trips. A Cuban government study said that 30 to 40 percent of the fares paid don't reach the home office. This implies that theft by drivers or refusal by passengers to pay is widespread. Drivers commonly let pleading passengers off in the midst of heavy traffic—a dangerous practice to be sure—so to they can race to catch the next bus at a nearby stop before it takes off. Missing the bus could mean a long wait for the next one. Another option for commuters in Havana are the "*maquinas,*" cars that load up at a bus depot and head for a specific thoroughfare or other location. The drivers stand at curbside at the departure point and bellow the names of their destinations until their cars are filled, a system not unique to Cuba. The cost is low, much cheaper than a taxi for individual riders.

In October 2010, the newspaper *Trabajadores* (*Workers*) underscored the problems with bus service in Havana: "The obvious deterioration in urban transport is worrisome for commuters who need it each day. Crowded bus stops at all hours of the day, drivers who drive past bus stops, people running from place to place on the sidewalk as if they were athletes in training to see if they were lucky enough to find a bus. These scenes are repeated wherever you go."

Private, hard currency-only taxis in Havana charge the equivalent of about eleven dollars for short trips and twenty-two dollars for longer ones. This may not seem like much to a tourist but it is out of the question for dollar-a-day Cuban workers. Many pensioners are forced to get by on the equivalent of six dollars a month. But if you're a student at the University of Havana, a trip home to a distant eastern province can cost several weeks' pay. To afford it, the student has to earn hard currency in a side job. It would never occur to him to call home for money. He knows better. There is none, unless his family has a foreign benefactor.

This Cuban woman has the look of despair and the state of her truck tells why. She needs more than just a new tire. Is there a Good Samaritan out there?

Where will all these people fit? The car, an aging American clunker, takes paying commuters along a specific Havana route. It looks better than most cars almost seven decades old.

There are easier ways to earn a living than peddling passengers around tropical Havana. At least he can earn hard currency rather than low-value pesos.

CHAPTER 4

NO ROOM TO SPARE

José and Claudia, university students, dated for a long time and talked of marriage. But they lacked a place where they could comfortably live together. Often, a young married couple in Cuba move in with the parents of one or the other but, as is often the case, the homes of both José and Claudia were already overcrowded. So they decided to postpone their marriage—and hope for a housing miracle.

Sometimes a related dynamic comes into play. Take the case of a male university student from an overcrowded home. He starts dating a fellow student who lives in a home with extra space. His emotional attachment to his girlfriend may be somewhat thin but he may see marriage to her as his best, perhaps only, chance to escape the mob scene at his home.

Under law, buying and selling of homes has been prohibited but more flexible rules are being contemplated. The government view traditionally has been that the wealthy would simply buy up available property and resell at a profit. The downside of the existing system has been a gross lack of maintenance of housing stock. Grown children often have little choice but to stay in the home where they were born, perhaps for a lifetime. But as part of economic reform, more rental units were coming on the market, meaning more opportunities for people eager to relocate—a possibility only if they have a foreign benefactor to pay for a new arrangement.

Courtney Brooks, a young American who lived in Cuba for three months, said a fundamental difference between the United States and Cuba was the lack of choices young Cubans face compared with Americans.

Of the Cuban students she encountered, she said "...(T)heir lives are stagnant. I will never know what it is like to live with your parents throughout your adulthood. I will never know what it is to have no privacy. And I will always have options, even if I don't have a lot of money. It is amazing to me that Cubans can stay so resilient despite all of this."

The problem of overcrowding would be far worse were it not for the exodus of over a million and a half Cubans since 1959. Abortions, which are both legal and frequent, also have helped to reduce demand for housing, as does a law banning relocation to the capital without permission. In addition, use of a ration card is barred outside a citizen's own province.

There are no such barriers to in-country migration elsewhere in Latin America and the result is an abundance—more so than in Havana—of shantytowns that ring almost all capitals in the region.

In Havana, there is a widespread lack of maintenance because the responsible state agency is slow to respond to requests for help (bribes can speed the process). The small number of carpenters authorized as of 2010 to work at market rates normally require customers to provide their own wood, which is very scarce and expensive. New furniture is extremely costly. Anecdotal evidence and personal observation indicate that the furnishings in most Havana homes pre-date the revolution.

Sometimes, doctors and other professionals, saddled like everyone else with low salaries, inhabit rundown apartment buildings and are flanked by equally poor but less cultured neighbors. Says social critic Alberto Jones, "These people have transformed those residential areas into infernally noisy and dingy tenements where they show their absolute disrespect for their own neighbors."

Aside from hotels, there has been relatively little new construction in Havana since 1959, a point underscored in a color-coded scale model at a Havana exhibit hall that describes the city according to construction activity during three eras: colonial, post-independence (1902-1958), and the period since the revolution. The most active by far was the 1902-58 era. The display emphasized how energetic the Cuban construction industry was—on behalf of people with means—in Havana in that period, and the disheartening neglect since then. One multi-story

Centro Habana home built a century ago by an oligarch for his family is now home to forty-three tightly packed families, according to a *Wall Street Journal* story in 2009. It should be noted that the revolution probably had focused far more on development of housing in the interior than did predecessor governments, which appeared to be wholly indifferent to the needs of that area.

The most ambitious housing project of the revolution was a 1970s-era apartment complex known as *Alamar,* built near the sea about eight miles east of Havana. Regina Canó, a resident there, remembers the hope that the project galvanized at the outset, a time when, she said, children believed that "the future belonged to us and that in Cuba everything was provided for."

Writing in the *Havana Times*, an online publication available only outside the country, Canó said that thirty years later, "*Alamar* is a dirty city with garbage everywhere and few parks. The buildings suffer from years of neglect, their paint peeling off, with makeshift additions by residents trying to add rooms for their growing families."

She blamed a lack of planning, poor decisions, haste, and opportunism. "For many, living here is a last resort. An odd situation given that *Alamar* is a seaside town with beautiful natural surroundings that could be better used and enjoyed," she added.

In his 1994 book, *Last Dance in Havana*, Eugene Robinson of the Washington Post echoed Canó's view that *Alamar* was a dreaded choice for a house hunter. "The construction was shoddy, roofs were leaky, electricity intermittent," he wrote.

To make matters worse for the government, Alamar was an excellent place to listen to anti-Castro radio broadcasts from Miami because of the community's proximity to the sea.

In Havana, government-assisted home maintenance and construction is slow because building supplies are generally reserved for hotel and post-hurricane reconstruction. At least there are no property taxes for the great majority. The rest pay a fee of about two dollars per home.

Yoani Sánchez, a Havana blogger and government critic whose writings appear only abroad, says some Cubans resort to scavenging to acquire building materials. "On an island where acquiring cement, cinderblocks or steel is comparable to obtaining a bit of lunar dust, destroying in order to build has become a common practice," she wrote.

"There are specialists in removing bricks of clay intact from the walls in which they have been embedded for 80 years; experts in disengaging blue ceramic tiles from demolished mansions; and skillful 'deconstructors' who extract metal beams from heaps of rubble. They use what they have recovered to create their own living space, this in a country where no one can legally buy a house. The main 'quarries' where they obtain their material are houses that have collapsed or workplaces that the state's inactivity has left abandoned for many years. They fall upon these with an efficiency in their plunder that one would wish to see in the lethargic bricklayers working for a salary.

"Some of these skillful recyclers have died when a roof collapses or when a wall too riddled with holes at its base falls. But sometimes luck smiles on them, and they find a toilet without cracks or an electrical outlet that the owners of the demolished house could not—in their haste—take with them. A kilometer from the looting site, a small house of tin and zinc slowly begins to change. They have added the tile pavement from a building that collapsed at the corner of *Neptuno* and *Águila*, a piece of the exterior grating from an abandoned mansion on *Linea* Street and even a stained-glass window plucked from a convent in the old part of Havana. Within this home that is the fruit of looting, a family—equally ravaged by life—dreams of the next factory to be dismantled and carried away on their shoulders."

Alberto Jones, the social critic, says that any Cuban wishing to improve his housing situation cannot go by the book and expect to get anywhere. He has to "bend the rules, find shortcuts, pay bribes, or purchase stolen goods" to get what he wants.

Isadora Tattlin (a pen name) wrote in her book, *Cuba Diaries*, about a dinner party she and her husband were hosting for two Communist Party officials, who had their own driver. During dinner, someone slipped into the back yard and somehow cut off from the garden hose the piece of copper that connected to a sprinkler. The next day, an employee pinpointed the driver as the culprit. It should be noted that theft of copper was not unusual even in advanced countries because of high prices. But this particular theft has to rank of one of the more bizarre examples of such pilfering. Were the paltry proceeds really worth the risk?

Tattlin came down hard on Cuban authorities for not preserving more of "*Habana Vieja,* perhaps the most treasured part of Havana's storied past." It reminded her of bombed-out Berlin after World War II.

"It's hard to believe that 30-odd years of mere neglect could destroy so much," she wrote. "It looks more like an assault or, if not an assault, as if someone really hated the place, hated it in spite of its beauty or because of it, as if being beautiful were a taunt. Touring *Habana Vieja* is like stepping into a feud you don't know all the details of and being stunned at the strength of the hatred, at the force of the negative energy, and at the monumentality of the ego, or egos, behind the feud."

Years later, blogger Danae Suárez conceded that strolling the streets of Old Havana made her nervous. "I would always proceed cautiously and looking up," she wrote. "It wasn't because I liked to contemplate the sky or the colonial architecture, but for fear that at any moment some old balcony would come crashing down on me."

The 2006 movie, "The Lost City," describes the mystique of Havana early in the Castro revolution, as portrayed on screen by one of the actors: "Havana is very much like a rose. It has petals and it has thorns...so it depends on how you grab it. But in the end it always grabs you."

The government has tried to spruce up *Habana Vieja*, with its baroque, Neo-Classical and Neo-Gothic architecture. As of 2011, the renewal project had benefited a substantial area but there was still a long way to go. Government officials say the situation would actually have been worse without the revolution because Batista-era developers had plans to bulldoze large swaths of the old city into rubble and construct shopping complexes in their place.

One way out for a family wanting to relocate is to trade houses with another family. Often, house-trading is motivated by families interested in living closer to their employment. Havana's *Plaza del Prado* is the unofficial gathering point for prospective house-traders. There were hardly any options other than the street for finding alternate housing opportunities because newspapers generally lacked classified ad sections and the Internet was in its infancy in Cuba. Ads and access, however, were increasing. Some who wish to move advertise their interest on a bed sheet hung over the side of a balcony.

Some homeowners wish to trade because of overcrowding and people who can't get along. Eviction of a problem tenant is difficult because the legal system often favors the tenant. The law would rather preserve the status quo as opposed to forcing the eviction of someone who has no place to go. One solution would be a trade of one large, overcrowded house for two smaller houses or apartments. The two residences might yield more space and would separate families unable to get along. It also could spare a divorced couple from having to continue sharing the same space.

A couple must be careful about allowing, say, a visiting nephew from a distant province to stay at their Havana home even on what is supposedly a brief visit. If the nephew remains in the home beyond a certain period, the law considers him to be a legal resident there. He may be a disruptive presence but he cannot be evicted. Again, the law sides with tenants to avoid homelessness. But Cuba is not spared that problem. Some people sleep in the streets or in hallways, on benches, at bus stops, bus terminals, in empty buildings—or any place where there might be room to lie down. Case in point: a graduate of the University of Havana who had no place to go after receiving his diploma and slept in a funeral home rather than return to his impoverished hometown.

It is not hard to understand why so many houses in Havana have fallen into disrepair. The home technically belongs to the family with the title but, since no home can be sold in Cuba, the incentive for upkeep is diminished. Even if selling were legal, materials to make a home more presentable, such as paint or wall board, are either scarce or prohibitively expensive—or both.

Added to that is the often comatose government bureaucracy responsible for authorizing home improvement projects.

Homeowners are basically stuck with the furniture they have had, often since before the revolution. Replacing furniture is not an option for the great majority because so few people have any disposable income.

The state phone company is sometimes lethargic. A friend called the company when his phone stopped working. Months passed with no house call. A phone man did show up one day but only a painter was there. The painter, instead of telling the repairman to check the phone, told him to come back some other time. Upon learning that the repairman had shown up only to be turned away, my infuriated friend fired the painter on his return home.

Cubans often remain in their hometowns for life because government rules make it difficult to move elsewhere. One who left, at least for part of the year, was a star baseball player, Freddie Cepeda, who moved from *Sancti Espiritu* in Central Cuba, to Havana. Cepeda, born in 1980, has been a sensation in post-season international play. In Cuba's top league in 2010-11, the outfielder hit .397 in eighty-three games and hit twenty-eight home runs. His baseball skills have earned him a lifestyle that few Cubans can match. He reportedly earned a salary well into the hundreds of dollars a month, much higher than the average player and infinitely higher than average worker. Cepeda, as of 2010, spent the off-season living in a large middle-class Havana home with three big-screen televisions, all connected via a discreetly hidden roof dish to American television stations by satellite. Who his benefactors were is not clear. It's hard to imagine a Cuban living on the island who wants to see Cepeda leave for the U.S. and, so far as is known, he has shown no inclination to do so. During the season, he plays for the *Sancti Espiritu* team, living in a one-story stucco home and driving a Russian Lada, both provided by the government.

One avenue for Cubans to have a home of their own is to work on a *"micro- brigada,"* or small construction brigade. A friend in his twenties took such a job years ago with the understanding that he could claim one of the apartments he worked on for himself and his family. After years of hard work (long hours were part of the bargain), the friend was told that the apartment he was expecting was being assigned to a senior military officer who had served in the Angola war. Obviously, the friend was devastated. The many years of labor had gone for naught.

A Cuban mother who earned hard currency working for a foreign diplomatic mission was tormented because there was no room in her house for her youngest son, a twenty-one-year old who spent his day sweeping parks and his evenings living uncomfortably with roommates in a tiny apartment. His enterprising father found a woman, eighty-one, who had her own apartment with no children or other relatives to bequeath it to. The father offered her a deal: he would give her fifteen hundred dollars in exchange for granting his son the right to inherit the apartment. She quickly agreed. Months later, she died; the twenty-one-year-old's housing problem was solved. Obviously, the number of Cuban families with fifteen hundred dollars available to help a needy family member is microscopically small.

Cuba's housing situation worsened considerably as a result of three hurricanes in 2008. Government figures say six-hundred-forty-seven- thousand units were destroyed or damaged, almost 20 percent of the total. The figures also show that almost forty-five thousand replacement units were built in 2009. In a July 2006 speech in the eastern province of *Granma*, (the same day that he fell ill) Fidel Castro summarized the government's home reconstruction progress following a devastating hurricane there a year earlier: "The province has received two-hundred-fifteen-thousand-three-hundred thirty-one zinc tiles, one-hundred-two-thousand, one-hundred-seventy-five cement boards, one-thousand-four-hundred-sixty-one tons of steel and fourteen-thousand-six hundred-sixty-one tons of cement. It has also received twenty-five-thousand-two hundred-thirty-three mattresses and three-thousand-eight-hundred television sets to be delivered to the victims of the hurricane...

"I can assure you that this has been one of the greatest efforts ever been made by the country," he said, adding that several thousand homes still needed to be reconstructed or repaired. To the outside observer, these figures, if accurate, seem impressive and make the American response to Hurricane Katrina a year earlier seem all the more inadequate.

No country's housing stock is believed to have suffered more from storms than Cuba's in recent years. *Pinar del Río* province in Cuba's far west was struck by two hurricanes and a tropical storm over a three-week period in the summer of 2008. The worst was Hurricane Ike, which entered the island not far from its eastern tip and traversed it on a destructive six-hundred-mile westward path before finally entering the Gulf of Mexico.

Millions along the coast evacuated their homes and fled to higher ground. The sugar crop, covering some eight-hundred-forty-thousand acres, was destroyed, along with countless farm animals, according to Cuban government accounts. Food supplies in several areas of Havana disappeared from shelves.

In a column, a grieving Fidel said of the impact of Ike in the western farm region: "What will remain of the bananas, fruits and vegetables in the intensive farming areas? Where will there be any beans and other grains? Will there be a sugarcane or rice plantation? Where will there be a poultry, pork or dairy production center? The entire nation is now in what in military terms is defined as combat alert."

Comparisons between hurricane-prone countries and their respective ability to cope with hurricanes are difficult. But Cuba appears to do a better job than the United States and the island's Caribbean neighbors. In 2007, Dominican President Leonel Fernández visited Cuba to consult with Castro on ways the Dominican government could respond more effectively when hurricanes strike.

Unlike the U.S., evacuations in Cuba are mandatory. Looting is less of a problem in Cuba, partly because almost everybody is poor and there is less to steal. At the time of Katrina in 2005, valuable resources were spent by government agencies guarding homes and businesses against looting. And unlike the U.S., there are never arguments in Cuba over who is directing relief efforts and whether their mandates should be carried out.

Natural disasters, far from softening Cuban-American hostility, seem to have had the opposite effect. When the United States offered a five-million dollar assistance package after Ike struck, Cuba accepted it so long as it was part of a six-month moratorium on the U.S. embargo against Cuba, then in its forty-sixth year. The Bush administration rejected the proposal, prompting this response from Castro, as stated in a column: "It is obvious that the government of that powerful country cannot understand that the dignity of a people has no price... If it was one billion instead of five million, they would meet the same response. There is no way to pay for the harm to thousands of lives and the suffering, or the more than two hundred billion that the blockade and Yankee aggressions have cost."

Three years earlier, a few days after Hurricane Katrina struck, Castro notified the U.S. government privately that eleven-hundred doctors were ready to fly to New Orleans from Cuba on short notice to assist victims. Pictures of the team, all seated together and clad in rescue gear, were shown on television. Cuba waited for word from the Bush administration for several days but heard nothing. The idea was dropped.

CHAPTER 5

A SOCIO-ECONOMIC VIEW

Superficially, Enrique could be a life-is-good poster boy for the Cuban revolution.

When I met him, he was in the last year of his studies at the University of Havana, just a few months from graduation. While many American college students are ensnared in six-figure debt, Enrique's education has been cost-free, compliments of the revolution.

But the look on Enrique's face on a brilliant fall day conveyed more defeat than delight at his situation. Yes, his education was free, he said, but he had no spending money. The government gave him enough food ration booklets to last the first five months of the school year. But he had none for the second half. He was promised twenty pesos a month (about one dollar) for spending money, he said, but some months he received no payment. Besides, he was expected to use his allowance to buy notebooks, pens, and other items for class work. His family had no spare cash to send him.

After a few minutes of conversation on the campus of the two-hundred-and-eighty-year old institution, alma mater of Fidel Castro, he offered to show me around. Our stroll took us to several stately buildings and then to the broad *escalinata* (stairway), the university's signature architectural feature that boasts a view of the sea and descends into an off-campus area crowded with pedestrians. We visited a colorful shop where Haitian art was sold.

After the tour, Enrique told me of the difficulties he had in getting home to Santiago, four hundred and seventy-five miles to the east. The bus fare was expensive. He had to reserve fifteen days in advance and to establish a place in line (although without having to remain there throughout). He was annoyed when a traveler with hard currency showed up and was allowed to board the next bus. I gave Enrique five dollars (unsolicited) for the tour.

His travails as a student might be more tolerable if he could look forward to a better life after graduation—better than unforgivable dollar-a-day treadmill that the great majority of Cubans are stuck with. We met before talk of economic reform was in the air in Cuba. Perhaps he and other graduates may be able to take advantage of the new self-employment opportunities being offered. But on that day, before the concept of economic reform was on the table, he didn't seem particularly cheerful about his prospects.

Present-day Cuba is a far cry from what Castro envisioned when he took power. Having conquered the army of the Batista tyranny in just over two years, he felt that Cuba's possibilities were limitless. He brazenly predicted that Cuba would quickly eradicate unemployment and overtake the United States in per capita income. But within six years his optimism faded. He said economic development was infinitely more difficult than the guerrilla struggle he had waged. The best measure of discontent has been the continuing exodus of Cubans from the country. Those who got caught trying to flee faced three to seven years' imprisonment. It should be noted that people emigrate from all Caribbean countries, usually because of a lack of economic opportunity. More than half of all Puerto Ricans, for example, are transplants to the American mainland. All are American citizens and need only a plane ticket to leave or return. If it were that easy for Cubans, the exodus would be extraordinary. U.S. law has an annual ceiling of twenty thousand migrants from Cuba, with priority given to those seeking political asylum.

Where Castro got the idea that he could create in Cuba a land free of economic want is a mystery. Not until his brother, Raúl, succeeded him did the idea take root that reform—with capitalist trappings—was needed for the revolution to advance economically, and perhaps even be saved.

In September 2010, four years after Fidel stepped down because of illness, the Cuban government announced that, over time, one million or so redundant government workers would be fired. They had been assigned to jobs where they had little or nothing to do. They would be urged in many cases to become micro-entrepreneurs or to open small businesses with the right to hire employees. Cooperatives also were envisioned. The first phase of the job cutbacks were to affect sugar, farming, construction and the health and tourism industries. Warehouses were being built to supply new businesses. The plan represented a significant expansion of Fidel's experiment with for-profit activities during the depression of the 1990s. For ideological reasons, it was never allowed to flourish. The scope of the new plan represented the most ambitious economic reform in the revolution's history. As of July 2011, two hundred twenty-one thousand government licenses for small businesses had been issued. Questions inevitably arose about the fate of those who, for whatever reason, couldn't make a living under the new rules. Unlike the earlier, more limited experiment in the 1990s, Raúl pledged that there would be no stigma attached to being a *porcuentista*, or one who worked for himself. He saw economic reform as an urgent national priority. "Either we make corrections or the time will run out for continuing to skirt the cliff – we will fall," he said. But some wondered about the impact of inevitable bureaucratic resistance from those accustomed to, and preferred, traditional ways. In any case, It was a shocking, almost desperate, move by a regime which once proudly proclaimed it had achieved its goal of full employment.

In any other country, it would have been inconceivable for a national labor union to make an announcement on the firing of a significant percentage of the national work force without taking a stand in opposition. But in Cuba no eyebrows were raised when it fell to the union, officially known as the *Confederación de Trabajadores Cubanos* (Cuban Confederation of Workers) to make public the mass pink slip plan and the new opening to private initiatives. The CTC supposedly represents all workers but it actually is merely an arm of the government. It has no independence. Its writ does not include input on wage levels, dismissals, or related issues.

Raúl said the goal of the self-employment plan was to create "honorable work" for the people as opposed to fake state-created jobs. Transportation, plumbing, and construction, among other occupations, were being opened to private entrepreneurs. Others on the list drew derisive comments simply because they could not possibly have more than a microscopic impact on the overall economy. Among them were musical instrument tuning and repair, water delivery, animal rental, formal wear rental, knife and scissor sharpening, party entertainer (clowns, magicians), mule driver, arts and crafts specialist, and mechanical saw operator.

(There were no openings for professionals such as lawyers or engineers.) Danae Suárez, a Cuban blogger who writes for foreign readers, spoke for many when she said: "Does the state really believe that the income of a society (including this one packed with competent professionals) can rest on 'palm tree pruners,' 'bellboys,' or 'public restroom caretakers'?" she asked.

Lisandro Pérez, of Florida International University, agreed. He wrote in March 2011, "The list of permitted private sector activities is ridiculously small, too narrowly defined, referring mostly to artisanal activities which are unlikely to absorb in a significant way the dismissed workers from the public sector.

"Professionals in Cuba need to be allowed to exercise their professions independently. Entrepreneurs should be allowed to open companies without restrictions on the number of employees they can have. Only this way, there will be an increase in productivity."

That kind of reform is not being contemplated. But for a start, an attitudinal change among Cubans toward entrepreneurship is essential, as the newspaper *Granma* pointed out: "The aim is to distance ourselves from those policies that condemned self-employment to near extinction and stigmatized those who decided to join its ranks legally in the decade of the 1990s."

Left unanswered after two generations of Castroite rule was whether rigid socialism had extinguished the entrepreneurial spirit that Cubans were once known for. The reform movement announced in 2010 could settle that issue. It seems apparent that economic liberalization can succeed only if the state is an ally and not an impediment to the process. Some anecdotal evidence is not reassuring. One entrepreneur, Juan Carlos Montes, said in 2011 that he gave up an attempt to run a restaurant after five years because of overbearing inspectors and government inefficiency. "People can't get what they need to run a business," he said, quoted by the *New York Times*. "The carpenter has no wood. The electrician has no cable. The plumber has no pipes. Right now, there is no flour in the shops. So what are all the pizzerias doing? They have to buy stuff that is stolen from bakeries." Some other entrepreneurs voiced similar frustrations.

Benjamin Smith, an American researcher, said the economic opening authorized by Fidel in the 1990s was highly successful during the few short years it was tolerated. Among the activities permitted: rental of spare rooms to foreigners, use of extra space in private homes as a restaurant, street sales of food, drink and trinkets. According to Smith's research, entrepreneurs on average earned fourteen times more than they had in their previous state sector jobs. The experiment might have succeeded but the government forced many entrepreneurs out of business through high taxes and other disincentives. Fidel was uncomfortable with the inequalities that were being created and the ideological deviationism of the initiative.

Almost fifteen years later, with Fidel semi-incapacitated and in retirement, and the economy in dire straits, the regime announced at a Communist Party Congress in April 2011 additional reforms. In the planning stages was the legalization of the buying and selling of houses for the first time under the revolution. The implications were far-reaching. Havana's aging housing stock, for example, was in a sad state of decay. Under the new proposal, there would be powerful incentives for upgrades on homes that hadn't been treated to coat of paint or a kitchen makeover since the Korean War.

Officially, the housing deficit in Cuba is listed at more than five-hundred-thousand, a figure that seems low to some economists as do official estimates that only 50 percent of the nation's homes are in poor or subpar state.

If indeed the ban on the sale or purchase of homes is lifted, as has been suggested, it will be a major step forward, says Canadian Cuba expert Archibald Ritter. "To have a housing market, for example, will be of tremendous importance to Cuban citizens, because there hasn't been a market in fifty years," he says. "In Cuba, people are born in the same house they die in."

Also, while the new rules would forbid absentee ownership, Cuban-Americans would be allowed to finance home purchases on behalf of relatives on the island. Also on the reform drawing board were plans to permit the buying and selling of cars for the first time.

Except for high government officials, the great majority of Cuban workers have no idea what it is like to drive themselves to work or to the store. Presumably, any car transactions also would be financed by overseas Cubans on behalf of relatives on the island.

Anecdotal evidence suggested that the public supports reforms so long as transactions are not hobbled by nagging bureaucratic requirements, a common dread in Cuba. The government has promised streamlined procedures.

Suspicions were strong that Fidel, mistrustful of reform, was not happy with his brother's handiwork. He saw his revolution as a historic breakthrough for socialism, with implications for the entire international community. He once said that there was a direct connection between the Soviet reforms of the late 1980s and the ensuing dissolution of the communist system—and the country—a few years later. But he has not discussed in public his thoughts on Cuba's economic situation since before his disabling illness in 2006. He is still the same man who over the years ended hundreds of speeches with the words: *"Socialismo o muerte, venceremos."* ("Socialism or death, we shall conquer.") (Fidel announced the revolution's commitment to socialism in 1961 on the eve of the Bay of Pigs invasion. In no time, a catchy tune could be heard on Cuban air waves: *"Somos socialistas, p'alante, p'alante. Al que no le guste, que tome un purgante."* ("We are socialists, forward, forward. Whoever doesn't like it, take a laxative.")

Raúl said he, too, remained a committed socialist despite his openings to for-profit activities. In April 2010, he told the Communist Party Congress after his pro forma election, "I assume my post to defend, preserve and continue perfecting socialism, and never permit the return of capitalism." His actions, however, suggest that he rejects dogma and seeks practical solutions.

Alcibiades Hidalgo, a former chief of staff to Raúl who defected to the United States in 2002, said Raúl had opposed for years the policies of Fidel because they "ignored the economic realities of the country." The division between the two brothers persisted after Fidel stepped down, said Hidalgo, a former ambassador to the United Nations. The fact that Fidel was still alive deep into Raúl's presidency was "perhaps the greatest obstacle" to change, he added.

Alberto N. Jones is a Cuban who emigrated to the United States but who has been allowed to make return visits despite his public criticism of the system. Jones made a seventeen-hundred-mile tour of the country in the summer of 2010 in which he talked to a broad cross-section of Cubans.

"What I found was everyone clamoring in unison for a change in the country's socio-economic situation, while a few called also for political change," he wrote. He added that Cubans "confront the greatest threat to our integrity and sovereignty that our country has had to face in its 500-plus years of existence." Jones, who was born on a segregated sugar plantation, said that while Cuba needs a new system, he does not favor a resurrection of the pre-revolutionary capitalist system.

The food rationing system, which has been a sore point with many Cubans since it was created in the early 1960's, may also be reformed out of existence, according to Cuban officials who spoke during the Communist Party Congress. Rationing was designed to ensure all Cubans access to food and other neces-sities at nominal prices. This sounded reasonable so long as the system provided enough food for each citizen for an entire month. But two weeks, is more typical—and then the consumer is on his own. He must turn to hard-currency stores, the black market—or get by on his wits. (Cubans rely heavily on coffee to get their day off to a good start. So there were complaints in 2011 when the government, trying to cut import costs, began selling in markets coffee blended with ground peas.)

Jacinto Ángulo Pardo, a government economist, made the case for preserving rationing. The alternative, he wrote, "is the establishment of the blind laws of the market, which would leave without protection thousands of families with low income, the dis-abled, single mothers."

Following is a list of ration book products and the monthly, per-person authorized quantities as of 2010: two hundred and thirty grams (eight ounces) of *picadillo*, a spicy dish whose basic ingredient normally is ground beef but soybean is used as a substitute in Cuba; one pound of chicken; one pound of fish (eleven ounces without the head); seven pounds of rice; ten ounces of beans; eight ounces of cooking oil; one bar of bath soap; one package of soap for clothes every two months; ten eggs; one tube of toothpaste every other month; four ounces of coffee; a quart of dish soap every four months or more; three packs of strong cigarettes and one mild pack for seniors; four pounds of sugar; and salt (quantity depends on availability).

In 2011, soap and toothpaste were removed from the ration card list, meaning they were no longer available at subsidized rates. Indeed, many of the above items were available items through the ration book only intermittently. Given the average Cuban's purchasing power, the prices of these items in hard-currency stores were exorbitant. The majority of Cubans have virtually no discretionary income. Even simple treats carried a high price tag for wage-poor Cubans: just under an hour's pay for a piece of candy, more than a day's pay for a can of Cuban beer.

Cuba's Agriculture Ministry insists that there are bright spots in the farm sector. It cited in particular the establishment in Havana in the 1990s of private gardens, state-owned research gardens and family patches. Combined, they are said to employ around twenty-five thousand people.

The family gardens, a ministry communique said, range in size from a few square meters to large plots of land, which are cultivated by individuals or community groups. Aside from food supplies, these farms also produce medicinal plants.

Sometimes food problems have a tragicomic quality. Danae Suárez, a blogger, was hoping to treat visitors from Italy by making spaghetti a la *carbonera*. But the boxes of spaghetti she bought were filled with little beetles. She wound up serving her guests fried egg with rice.

Medicine chest and other health-related items are often lacking or are of poor quality. For many Cubans, their happiest days occur when friends or relatives arrive from Florida or other foreign locations bearing a suitcase filled with aspirins, Tylenol, Dayquil, NyQuil, Alka-Seltzer, soap, Band-Aids, heating pads, ice packs, sleeping pills, eye drops, hair pins, anti-itch cream—the list goes on. In some ways, Cuba can lay claim to being a medical power. In other ways, it can't.

There is one small cluster of Cubans who make big money legally. They are Cuba's artists, the best of whom sell their works legally through intermediaries to buyers in the United States. The paintings are considered part of "informational" exchanges, which are exempt from embargo restrictions. Some Cuban artists make more from a single painting than most of their compatriots do in a lifetime. Over time, the most talented boast hard currency earnings in the six figures (in dollars), according to one American dealer.

Some of the most sought-after jobs in Cuba involve those that permit contact with travelers from wealthy countries. One such job is airport customs inspector. In a 2010 article in the *Havana Times*, Julio de la Yncera, a Cuban who resettled in the United States, described his airport experience with an overeager customs agent on a return visit to the island:

"The customs employees apparently select some passengers to check the contents of their baggage, and I had the misfortune of being one of the people they selected. I remember that after examining the contents of my suitcase, when the customs official attending me saw that I had fifteen rolls of film, she asked me why I had so many. I responded saying that I was going to a friend's wedding and that he wanted me to take pictures.

"The official then asked me if she could have a roll and I told her she could. She was afraid that her supervisor would see it and indicated to me how to stand so it wouldn't be seen when she put the roll of film in her pocket. Then she saw batteries and began explaining that her son had a toy that didn't have batteries. This time I immediately told her no, because I needed them for the camera's flash. I was also carrying a computer book that my friend wanted. She thumbed through it to see if it had anything negative against Cuba. She wanted me to give it to her but I again told her no, explaining that I had bought the book for my friend and that it was a personal gift for him.

"Ten years after having left Cuba, these first few minutes gave me sour impression. First there was the intimidation by a guard who had nothing to do in the full view of all of us, unarmed civilians, and then there was the corruption—right there in the airport itself. Much later I was able to appreciate the discrimination that existed between those who possessed dollars and those who had only domestic currency. Those with dollars could make purchases in stores full of goods, while those who didn't could only buy using their ration books. Those stores that sold goods in domestic currency had very few products available, and these were of very poor quality."

Fidel's view was that the average person doesn't need more than simple meals, a few shirts, a couple of pairs of pants, shoes, a roof, and a bed. Living well meant serving your community and your country well. Small meals are good; they don't slow you down, Castro believed. If one shunned materialism and was imbued with a revolutionary spirit, he could lead a productive, purposeful life. Compare that to the barren, consumer-driven life in America, or so the official Cuban thinking went.

It would be wrong to assume that no Cuban has consumer goods. A large number of senior Communist functionaries boast a car, a computer, a wide-screen TV with a satellite connection, a DVD player, the latest kitchen appliances, and the like. But deluxe accouterments should be out of the view of ordinary Cubans. Ostentatious displays of prosperity are forbidden. (I never saw a luxury car in Cuba.) Those who possess valuables know that they can be taken away at any time because of disloyalty or corruption. Another perk for some loyalists is daily home delivery of meals so that they need not stand in line at the market like most people. When illness strikes, they need not go to an ordinary hospital. They have a well-appointed one for themselves. Perks for the favored ones is not unique to Cuba. They were a feature of all countries of the old Soviet bloc.

Reinaldo Escobar, a dissident and social critic, discusses his view of the supposed correlation between bureaucratic rank and the type of perks available: "In some drawer, sealed by State security, they now keep the obscene specifications of these sinecures," he surmised. "I dream of a day in which they publicly come to light and then we will be able to know who had the bag with oil, chicken and detergent, and who was the one with Serrano ham and imported whiskey, which level or military grade corresponded to a supply of vitamins and which to a quota of Viagra."

Many Cubans are attracted to the delights of gadgetry. When DVD players began appearing in Havana stores in 2008, people crowded around display cases. They were also transfixed by the wonders of the Internet, but computers, like DVD players, were not a viable option for average Cuban because of cost. Rental of computers at Internet cafés or hotel business offices is possible but, again, the cost per hour is high. Home Internet use lagged behind most countries. On the plus side, speedier Internet access was on the horizon with the completion in February 2011 of a Venezuelan-financed fiber-optic cable along the Caribbean seabed from Venezuela to Cuba.

There are web sites in Cuba for buyers and sellers of a wide range of products and services. *Revoltico,* or "commotion" in English, offers information on arranged marriages for people who want to resettle outside the country. It also serves as a forum for people interested in buying used furniture and other items. In November 2010, a woman in need of more living space advertised, as part of a trade, her one-bedroom, one-bath apartment on *Revoltico.* To generate interest (at the expense of political correctness), she pointed out that the home was of "complete capitalist construction." Her unstated message was that construction under the revolution invariably was shoddier than that under the predecessor system.

American-made refrigerators bought before the revolution were treasured by many families, not least because they were so reliable. But Fidel decreed not long before he stepped down that these energy-guzzling antiques had to be replaced by more efficient Chinese models. Homeowners did not have a choice. To pay for the new model, the government charged a pricey (for the average Cuban) sixty pesos month, equal to three dollars, perhaps three days' pay per worker. Many people complained about the price and said the replacements were not as reliable as the U.S. models. The government also decided to revolutionize the way Cubans cooked at home, ordering a shift to pressure cookers, rice cookers, electric cookers, electric stoves, and thermos-like devices for heating water electrically. Electrical appliances were in; gas, kerosene, and firewood were out.

The kitchen makeover plan did not work out well, at least according to popular commentary. The new appliances wore out or broke down, said Fernando Ravsberg, a Havana blogger, writing in the (foreign subscribers only) *Havana Times*. The first to stop working were the thermoses, followed by the electric stoves, he wrote. The Chinese refrigerators, Ravsburg said, acquired the nickname "big crybabies" because they were constantly dripping. Spare parts for these appliances were in short supply. The *Granma* newspaper reported that one repair shop in Havana had one hundred and sixty-four customers waiting for replacement parts for one appliance or another. One local woman was quoted as saying: "I'll return all those pots and I'll even pay if you just give me back my gas cooking tank."

One reader (anonymous) responded to Ravsberg's article by repeating a view held by other Cubans that "socialist" Chinese firms "shouldn't be producing—and then dumping—such inferior products on anyone, let alone fellow socialist countries." In a similar vein, another anonymous respondent wrote that Ravberg's article showed that poor countries cannot progress because they "can only afford bad quality products from Chinese production which are not meant for the rich countries. It's incredible how many failures those products have. A whole bunch of Orange printers (didn't work) due to a too-small motor inside. What sense does this make?" (Many Chinese exports to the United States have not worked out well either, but defects seem to disappear over time as manufacturers work out kinks.)

Another contributor to the *Havana Times*, Rosa Martínez, wrote that she was outraged when informed that the utility company was planning a price increase on the heels of one imposed not long before.

"If I have to pay more than 200 pesos ($10) for electricity, I think my lifestyle will slide back to the Middle Ages: no more TV, no more refrigerator and zero DVD. We'll light the house with candles or firewood and cook with firewood or coal. But pay 300 pesos (fifteen dollars)—NEVER!" she wrote.

The number of political prisoners in Cuba has dropped dramatically since the early days of the revolution. But rights groups contend that repression persists. In a 2010 report, the Washington-based Human Rights Watch said: "Cuba remains the only country in Latin America that represses virtually all forms of political dissent... (T)he government continued to enforce political conformity using criminal prosecutions, beatings, harassment, denial of employment, and travel restrictions.

"Since inheriting control of the government from his brother Fidel Castro in 2006, Raúl Castro has kept Cuba's repressive legal and institutional structures firmly in place. While Cuban law includes broad statements affirming fundamental rights, it also grants officials extraordinary authority to penalize individuals who try to exercise them.

"Following the death of a political prisoner on a hunger strike in February 2010 and the subsequent hunger strike of a prominent dissident, Cuba's government has released more than 40 political prisoners, forcing most into exile. Many more journalists, human rights defenders, and dissidents remain behind bars, while the government increasingly relies on short-term, arbitrary detentions to punish its critics."

To some analysts, Cuba's harsh treatment of dissent should be viewed in the light of decades of American efforts to undermine the communist regime through a policy of economic denial, support for dissenters on the island and tolerance of armed anti-Castro groups in South Florida. (I once asked a Miami-based FBI agent why there was no crackdown on the Florida groups, which clearly were operating in violation of U.S. law. He said the Florida office of the FBI was reluctant to go after these groups because many members were neighbors and friends of FBI personnel. To me, the argument was not convincing. A more likely explanation was that decision-makers in Washington had concluded that the political costs of dismantling these armed groups, given the mood in South Florida, simply would be too high. To be in Miami and be a known supporter of lifting the embargo could be a fearsome experience in an earlier era. I remember sitting in a Miami coffee shop with one such friend in the late 1980's. Every few seconds, he would look over his shoulder to see if anyone with hostile intent was coming his way.)

Fidel, meanwhile, saw the United States itself as a major human rights violator. In a May 2009 column, he chastised the human rights commission of the Organization of American States, an official body from which Cuba had been excluded for decades (and doesn't want to rejoin in any case).

Castro objected to a commission report reprimanding Cuba for rights abuses. "Has it ever condemned the government of the United States?" he asked. "No, never. Not even the genocide committed by (President George W.) Bush (in Iraq), which took the lives of millions. How can they (the commission) commit that injustice? Not even the tortures at Guantánamo. As far as we know, not a word."

Yes, but there were plenty of words in the American and foreign media about presumed rights abuses of suspected terrorists held at the Guantanamo detention facility. A February 2006 report by Amnesty International said: "Many of these (Guantanamo) detainees allege they have been subjected to torture or other cruel, inhuman and degrading treatment... Guantánamo Bay has become a symbol of injustice and abuse in the U.S. administration's 'war on terror'. It must be closed down."

Competitive elections to the largely powerless people's assemblies have been held in Cuba since the 1970s. Candidates are picked according to party loyalty. They are forbidden from making speeches or issuing political statements. Voters base their election-day choices on biographical information on the candidates. The media trumpets these elections as important developments in the nation's political life. Fidel has maintained that the Cuban system is superior to the American system because turnout is much higher. Only a handful of aging Cubans have ever voted in an election which offered a choice between candidates. Cuba is the only country in the hemisphere that forbids bona fide choice among candidates for election to public office.

Like many politicians, Fidel had a penchant for trafficking in partial truths. For years, the railed out at the United States for a 1966 law that permitted undocumented Cubans fleeing on boats to be granted migrant status so long as they were able to land their vessels in Florida. Any who were picked up en route by the U.S. Coast Guard were returned to Cuba. Castro said that the law had induced many Cubans to risk their lives by attempting the crossing. Countless would-be migrants did die. He blamed the U.S. law for the loss of life, never mentioning the hopeless situation in Cuba that these unfortunate Cubans were trying to leave behind.

Clearly, the idea of a career in one of the many dead-end jobs in government offices has been unappetizing to many Cubans. One young Havana woman was determined to avoid that fate. She had heard about an opening at a European embassy that was to be filled the following year, and Cubans were allowed to compete. The salary would be paid in highly prized euros but there was one daunting prerequisite: fluency in the language of the host diplomatic mission. The woman had some knowledge of the language and worked tirelessly to master it. She succeeded and, In the end, she got the job. Her salary was modest by international standards but in Cuba it probably put her in the top two percent of Cubans employed legally. She and her family lived comfortably in an apartment in *Nuevo Vedado*, one of Havana's better neighborhoods.

To Fidel, the supposed penury of Cubans was all relative. He never wanted to measure Cuba's standing by per capita income.

He was interested in developing "human capital" and providing social services. He frequently called attention to the hunger, disease, and lack of proper schooling that afflict hundreds of millions in scores of countries elsewhere. He said the capitalist system "imposed" on these countries by the United States was to blame. From time to time, billboards appeared around the island declaring that *"40,000 niños se murieron ayer en el mundo. Ninguno fue Cubano"* ("Forty thousand children died in the world yesterday. None was Cuban.") Castro argued that Cuban children get for free the same quality health care available at the renowned Mayo Clinic in the U.S. (a doubtful claim). He constantly reminded his countrymen of Cuba's extraordinary levels of school enrollment. He noted that in some Latin American countries, desperate youths directed the fire from flame throwers into their mouths at busy intersections to get money from drivers, a wretched practice that he said was unheard of in Cuba. Meanwhile, he said, Cuba had no beggars or abandoned children, in contrast to almost all other countries. (If any are found in Havana, they are quickly picked up by street patrols.)

Alcoholism appears to be less of a problem in Cuba than in other Third World countries, the result, officials say, of artificially high liquor prices. Castro tried to offer alternative forms of entertainment, including outdoor movie presentations and concerts in squares with locals invited to dance along. He said that every municipality in the country had a movie house, a library, and a museum. (I once heard him say, "We build museums; the Americans built bordellos.")

Violent crime appeared to be on the upswing in Cuba, according to anecdotal evidence. (There is almost nothing in the national media on the overall issue.) In Guantánamo province, one of Cuba's poorest, violence against women was a particular problem. Roxanne Rodríguez, a local psychologist, said in a rare on the record quote by a Cuban professional that the blame rests with "poor economic conditions... The basic needs of the individuals and family are not satisfied; inadequate housing conditions that force divorced couples to share the same housing with other relatives; the lack of communication between couples; (and) drug abuse..."

Says Rosa Martínez, a blogger: "We Guantanamo residents are exasperated with the speed with which we've seen increases in aggravated robberies, racketeering, assaults, purse snatchings, murders, brawls and much more. We're especially worried about the summer vacation because our children are going out into the streets daily in search of amusement."

There was more support for the revolution during the earlier decades. I heard many references among Cubans to the "good Soviet times" of the 1970s and 1980s. Indeed, an analysis in *The Economist* magazine said that earning power of Cubans was

50 percent higher in those days compared with 2010. Fidel rue-fully acknowledged his country's hard times in the summer of that year. American reporter Jeffrey Goldberg of *The Atlantic* maga-zine had asked Castro whether Cuba was still an example for the Third World. "The Cuban model doesn't even work for us any-more," he replied. Castro tried to backpedal from the comment when it received widespread attention internationally. He said his intention was just the opposite of Goldberg's interpretation. But given Cuba's dire economic straits, Goldberg's account was widely accepted. In a clarification made later in a speech, Castro said it is the capitalist system that is a proven failure.

"My idea, as everybody knows, is that the capitalist system does not work anymore either for the United States or the world, which jumps from one crisis into the next, and these are ever more serious, global and frequent and there is no way the world could escape from them," he said. "How could such a system work for a socialist country like Cuba?"

But it was clear that his revolution was not inspiring copycat systems, as he had hoped and had fought hard for. The rebel groups he had supported in a number of Latin American countries decades earlier had long since disappeared. Communist regimes in Eastern Europe imploded starting in the late 1980s. He had said years earlier that the inability of communist regimes to pros-per was a mere temporary setback. He insisted that the evolution of socialism, like Christianity, was uneven, that he was confident of socialism's ability to endure, and only needed time to fine tune. (He offered these assessments before the disappearance of communism from Europe and after the embrace of the capitalist model by China.) At least Castro could take satisfaction in the rise of leftist governments sympathetic to Cuba in Venezuela, Bolivia, Ecuador, and Nicaragua starting late in his tenure. But, unlike Cuba, all had some democratic trappings.

None was as important to Cuba as Venezuela, which played the role as Cuba's benefactor, replacing the defunct Soviet Union. Venezuela provided Cuba with multi-billion dollar annual subsidies to the island, mostly in oil subsidies. Cuba reciprocated by sending tens of thousands of teachers, doctors, and sports trainers to Venezuela. Cuba also helped run Venezuela's ports, telecommunications, and police training, and it issued identity documents. In addition, Cubans provided security advice to key Venezuelan ministries and to the presidential palace as well. (A State Department cable released by Wikileaks in 2010 said Cuban intelligence officers "have direct access to Chávez and frequently provide him with intelligence reporting by Venezuelan officers."

Cuba's education system has drawn praise as well as criticism. Cuba expert and Harvard professor Jorge Domínguez, writing in the New York Times in 2003, said: "Cuban schoolchildren are among the word's best performers, with Cuban fourth graders outscoring all Latin American students in mathematics tests." Cuba has kept kids in school through eighth grade to a degree achieved by few other Third World countries. If a child lived in a remote area miles from the nearest school, Fidel has said, a teacher would be assigned to educate him one-on-one under Cuba's mobile teacher program.

A 1998 report by the UN Economic and Social Council said testing showed that Cuban children in the third and fourth grades were academically well ahead of students from twelve other Latin American countries. Students from the Dominican Republic and Venezuela had the lowest grades. Cuba had come a long way since the pre-revolutionary period when a U.N. estimates showed a 24 percent illiteracy rate.

Shortly after taking power, Castro dispatched young people to the countryside to teach the peasantry, and literacy rates rose dramatically. For a time, city children were sent to rural schools where classwork was combined with agricultural work. Indoctrination was easier in these surroundings. Also, children were spared exposure to the negative influences of city streets.

Throughout the revolution, education at all levels has been free in Cuba. It may be the only Third World country where poor children who need glasses get them—and without cost. In a 2003 speech, Castro said that Cuba "has the highest school retention rate—over 99 percent between kindergarten and ninth grade—of all the nations of the hemisphere. Its elementary school students rank first worldwide in the knowledge of their mother language and mathematics. The country ranks first worldwide with the highest number of teachers per capita and the lowest number of students per classroom."

(The *Granma* newspaper once carried a regular feature in which ordinary Cubans wrote about the positive impact of the revolution. The columns were titled, "*Si no fuera por la revolución*" ("If it weren't for the revolution"). Some contributors recounted how the revolution gave opportunities to their own families, which previously had known only poverty and illiteracy for generations. I can remember the account of one woman from the impoverished east who migrated to Havana after the revolution and became a bio-technician.)

The rap against the Cuban educational system is its strict Marxist orientation in the educational and cultural spheres. In addition to grades, all Cuban students are measured by their ideological reliability. Also, unlike almost every other country, there is no correlation between academic achievement and economic well-being after graduation. Raúl conceded in 2010 that one million Cubans hold down fake jobs. No doubt many were high academic achievers. Engineers and clerks in Cuba make roughly the same $1 a day salary. Some Cuban women armed with a college degree opt to clean the houses of foreigners rather than work for a state agency because the pay is better. Countless

Cuban teachers fled the profession in the early 1990s because higher paying jobs in tourism were becoming available in large numbers. Other degree-holders choose to sell trinkets to foreigners as opposed to working in their profession.

Fidel would prefer a culturally advanced country than one in which a good academic record can translate into a good salary. He once predicted that Cuba's education system will turn Cuba "by far, into the country with the highest degree of knowledge and culture in the world." That would appear to be an unattainable goal for a country which inhibits free inquiry, free debate, and free speech, where only a small minority have Internet access or have traveled abroad, where learned journals of opinion are non-existent, and where there is a notable absence of the kind of quality universities commonly found in the United States and Europe.

Damarys Ocaña, a Cuban-born writer who lives in the U.S., notes that Cuban schools start dossiers on students during elementary school. Their grades will be recorded as well as their political and religious activities. The *"expediente acumulativo escolar,"* as the dossier is called, will follow the student to his job, where bosses will keep similar tabs, she wrote. Defenders of the system, of course, point out that it is only natural for Cuba to its instruct its youth about the revolution's principles, not to mention the need for revolutionary awareness, given the hostility of the United States toward the island for almost all of the Castroite rule.

But there are signs that irreverence and deviationism are replacing revolutionary zeal in Cuba.

There is no letup in the number of Cubans who are eager to start anew elsewhere. Scores of Cubans write blogs for foreign consumption that highlight social and economic problems on the island. One Havana blogger, Yenisel Rodríguez, wrote that the *Granma* newspaper deliveryman for his neighborhood made his rounds telling whoever would listen: "I'm the one who distributes the most lies in Cuba." And on a main thoroughfare in Havana, Rodríguez said he saw a conga line of youths who were chanting: "To leave Cuba, mama, is what I want, to leave Cuba, mama." Such behavior would not have been tolerated in an earlier period.

The Cuban system does gives opportunities to children. Claudia Cadelo took classes as a youngster in piano, art, English, swimming, and gymnastics. She also became a university graduate. Afterward, disillusionment with the system set in. To pay for her university education, she began two years of mandatory social service. Her six-dollar-a-month salary was barely enough to buy food, even subsidized ration book items. Because of her low pay, she left her job and refused to seek alternative employment. Her displeased father wanted her to spend her time usefully.

Claudia agreed that work was good but only if there was fair compensation. She worked at odd jobs but each year brought an increasingly stagnant existence. Claudia failed in her effort to migrate to the United States. Eventually, though, she married

and was able to join the ranks of social critics who became bloggers for publications distributed abroad. Some people learned to
accept what the Cuban system had to offer and to defend it; others, such as Claudia, did not.

One friend, a widow who had migrated before the revolution
to the United States, was offended by American racism of the
early 1960s. She decided that she belonged in revolutionary
Cuba. She told me her story when I met her in the late 1970s.
None of her fervor had diminished. Our friendship persisted in my
subsequent visits. She loved her job as a manager in a medical
research center. She and her mother never missed a speech by
Fidel in the plaza. She spoke reverently about a cousin who was
a volunteer sugar cane cutter on weekends. Her grown daughter
so loved being a student in the Soviet Union that she didn't want
to return to Cuba.

Once Teresa (not her real name) went to an outdoor beachside café with me and two others. I threw fifty pesos on the table
when we sat down, and suddenly there was a hush. The waiter
hesitantly informed us that only dollars were accepted. (I was
aware that dollars had just been legalized but I was unaware that
pesos could not be used in certain places.) I pocketed the pesos
and substituted them with dollars. My friend was humiliated and
disappeared for fifteen minutes. On her return, she vented about
rules that forbade a thirsty Cuban woman from enjoying a drink

payable in the national currency. Only the "enemy currency" was accepted. I felt her pain. A much bigger disappointment for her occurred a few years later when the regime reneged on a promise to give her a car as a reward for her revolutionary devotion.

Obviously, many Cubans simply never acclimated themselves to the revolution, finding it too stifling. One was Carlos Manuel, who had tried to escape to the U.S. three times by boat, each unsuccessful. He was intent on a fourth try. "What I want is to work, and I want to be able to use what I earn with my job to have a normal life without having to steal or pretend," he said in an interview translated from *Entrevista* (*Interview*) magazine. "The truth is that I do not think so much about material things that can be found there (the U.S.), but about everything I can do there. For example, I dream about being able to navigate the Internet, because I believe in all these years I haven't been connected for even one hour reading all the information that interests me." (For more, see Addendum 2.)

All societies suffer from corruption and, in Cuba, that blight is often incited by shortages. Not surprisingly, some clerks who sell rationed food according to monthly quotas take unfair advantage. They sometimes withhold, in exchange for cash, prized items such as cooking oil, sugar, or rice for preferred customers, according to a *Latin American Herald Tribune* article in

September 2010. (Cooking oil has always been a fundamental requirement in Cuban kitchens, owing to the preference of Cubans for fried food.)

Customers at the *agro*, or food market, sometimes keep a close eye on clerks who weigh their purchases. While standing in line to pay for groceries, they share intelligence on which clerks have been known to put their thumb on the scale. At bakeries, the kitchen staff sometimes cuts the recommended amount of oil and flour for each loaf of bread. The result is smaller loaves. The end-of-day surplus can be used to make bread for hard-currency customers.

Bus drivers often pocket the fares of riders and riders often get on the bus without paying. As a result, bus fare revenues for the state are about a third lower than they should be, according to an official study. Jobs in homes where diplomats live or in restaurant kitchens are eagerly sought because food theft is relatively easy. A doctor told me that his wife earned seven times more than he did by cleaning the homes of foreigners. He said he had tried to flee to the U.S. by boat but was caught.

Cuban officials, of course, try to crack down on food thieves, some of whom can't rely on food markets for family meals because supplies are often erratic. A friend who had just graduated from law school said he turned down an offer to be a judge, explaining that he did not want to sentence people to prison who had stolen food only because their children were hungry.

It is not unusual in Cuba, not to mention other countries, for homeowners to mistrust housekeepers. The head of one Havana household informed his housekeeper that he periodically weighed rice, beans, and other cupboard items. If the scale showed that one or more food storage jars were unaccountably light in weight, he would know who was responsible. The encounter of the housekeeper with the homeowner left her humiliated. (In a similar vein, the American ambassador in one South American country routinely asked an assistant to draw lines on wine and whisky bottles that corresponded to the levels left after a reception at the residence.) Pharmacists have been known to set aside scarce prescription medicines for hard currency customers, often leaving less well-off patrons unable to fill their prescriptions. The most damaging corruption is that which occurs at the government level—the insidious large-scale siphoning of resources, leading to the further impoverishment of an already poor country, not an uncommon practice in dozens of countries.

The chronic shortages in Cuba can produce demoralizing consequences. Most families were reluctant to invite guests to their homes because they have nothing to serve or because the home had not been painted or decorated with new furniture for a half-century through no fault of their own.

The occasions when I covered Castro outside of Havana were usually linked to July 26 anniversary celebrations in observance of his emergence as a guerrilla fighter in 1953. In some of these venues, I watched as thousands of people in peasant garb walked through hot, dusty streets toward the speech site. They did not look and act like an oppressed people. Later, I would take my up-front seat in the press area but rarely watched Castro as he strode onto the podium. I preferred to turn and look at the faces of the spectators. The cheers and broad smiles of those nearest me came as no surprise because, unlike the thousands of other spectators, they had seats and therefore belonged to the local political elite. From my impressions, however, Castro was seen by many people as more than just a strongman. He was a man who somehow against all odds was able to withstand American determination to oust him and who tried very hard to make Cuba a better country but who had fallen short in many ways.

Attendance at these July 26 events, of course, was virtually mandatory, a point made clear beforehand through door-to-door reminders by party loyalists. Buses hauled people from outlying areas to the site, usually an empty field. The buses often arrived well ahead of time, leaving people to bake in the sun for hours while waiting for their leader. Anecdotal evidence suggests that some Cubans show up at speech sites to avoid punishment for non-attendance but slip away once they are seen by a supervisor from their workplace.

These summer festivities in one province or another were special occasions. The venue was based on a national competition.

The "winner" was the one deemed to have made the most social advancement in recent months. Brigades of workers would spruce up the town by filling potholes, applying fresh paint, and planting greenery. People were given time off from work. Extra food and drink was brought in. (I remember coming upon a crowd of hundreds in a square one morning in an eastern province during an anniversary celebration. They had gathered near a large truck. An onlooker told me that tins of Spam, newly arrived from Europe, were being passed out.)

Year after year, the ritual was the same. Radio reporters broadcasting nationwide would describe the unbounded *júbilo* (joy) that the people felt about the imminent arrival of their leader. Some even counted the hours before the grand entrance: "*En solo seis horas llega nuestro comandante en jefe.*" ("In just six hours, our commander-in-chief arrives.") Then, just before 6 p.m. Castro would arrive in his car caravan. In his speech, Castro invariably went over the progress made in the recent past in local school, library, road, and other construction. He always paid homage to the local Communist Party chieftains for their tireless service. The latter part of his speeches was usually reserved for international issues.

(I once watched a Castro speech from a TV monitor in a building not far from the speech site. Knowing that Castro would initially dwell on local issues, I slipped away to a nearby bar in the building and asked for a beer. The bartender replied that beer sales during the *comandante's* speech were forbidden.) Castro kept up the tradition of giving speeches on July 26 for decades. His disabling illness occurred in 2006 in the evening after his last such speech.

Castro was famous for long-winded speeches but none that I covered, so far as I can recall, lasted much more than two hours. (A sampling of some of his speeches in 2005 showed they averaged about three hours and forty minutes). There was good reason for him to keep his July 26 speeches shorter: the weather was invariably hot.

Housewives complained that drawn-out speeches by Castro, whatever the occasion, often played havoc with soap opera programming. That is much less of a problem under the more restrained Raúl. Early in the revolution, Fidel gave a speech that went on interminably. One independent paper still publishing then concluded that the length of the speech was more important than the content. The next day's banner headline: "*Castro Habla por Ocho Horas*" (*Castro Speaks for Eight Hours*).

July 26 was the most important holiday of the year but lately it has lost some of its cache. A long speech by Fidel was part of the annual trappings but Raúl has been far less visible, declining even to give a speech during the festivities in 2010 and 2011. He is not the orator that Fidel was and is probably more

comfortable with a lower profile. For decades, the summer festivities outstripped everything else on the revolution's annual calen-
dar. In effect, it replaced Christmas, which was viewed as inconsistent with the secular spirit of the revolution. Besides, Christmas
often coincided with the sugar harvest and therefore was a dis-
traction. To make sure that everyone understood the disfavor of
religiosity under Castro, the National Assembly routinely chose
Christmas Day as one of the handful during the year when the
assembly convened a meeting.

Shortly after the revolution, an estimated three thousand Spanish priests were chased from Cuba because Castro saw them as
a counter-revolutionary menace. In his book on Castro, Robert
Quirk said the only evidence of the Christmas spirit in Havana in
1960 was a representation of a "revolutionary" Nativity painted on
the marquee of a local TV station. "The Three Kings" were Fidel
Castro, Ernesto Guevara, and Juan Almeida, a co-insurrectionist
allied with Castro for years. Cuba officially became an atheist
nation in 1962. But Christmas has been making a comeback
since the 1990s, one of several indications of the revolution's
lighter touch compared with the much more ideological approach
of the early days.

Castro softened his attitude toward religion in the 1980s when
he indicated an affinity for the so-called "liberation theology,"
whose followers consisted mostly of leftist Christians. In 1991,
observant Cuban Christians were allowed to join the Communist

Party. Also, resources were made available for refurbishing Cuba's many rundown churches. The liberalization culminated with the visit in 1998 of Pope John Paul II to Cuba. Afterward, people could celebrate Christmas openly and attend Sunday mass without fear.

In previous Decembers, I remember evening strolls through residential streets of Havana and looking through windows for a Christmas ornament or a sprig of green, some reminder, however tiny, of Christmas spirit. Only rarely did I find any until the early 1990s. I wondered whether Castro ever had any second thoughts about the theft each December of one of the most important parts of Cuba's cultural heritage for all those years.

Analyses of what Castro's economic policies have wrought are difficult partly because of the paucity of official information. The secrecy surrounding the state of the economy has been derided by sources as diverse as *Granma*, the Communist Party organ, and Óscar Espinosa Chepe, the dissident economist from Havana. He noted in December 2009 that a supposedly comprehensive government report on the state of the economy lacked figures on industrial and farm production, income from tourism, oil, and gas, and information about commercial and payment balances and external debt. Important indicators such as nickel and sugar production also were lacking, he noted.

"There is also no information about the demographic situation, detailed levels of monetary circulation, among other data that is basic to determine the state of the economy and where it is heading," said Espinosa Chepe, who has served time as a political prisoner.

To the extent that economic data is released, independent experts often doubt its credibility. For example, in 2005 the government reported a healthy 5 percent expansion of the economy. But the University of Pittsburgh's Cuba-born Carmelo Mesa Lago wondered how that was possible in the face of "significant losses due to two hurricanes, the worst drought in a century, a poor sugar harvest, an electricity crisis that shut down several industries and high oil prices," among other factors. (But Cuba's tourism revenues in 2005 reached two-billion, four-hundred-million dollars, an increase of two hundred-eighty-five-million dollars over 2004, and one of the best years of the decade, according to the Cuban government.)

Another example of perceived data unreliability concerns unemployment. As Mesa Lago points out, many Cubans don't tell the authorities that they are unemployed because they worry they may be hauled off to work as farm laborers. But nothing skews unemployment figures more than the practice—now being phased out—of sending workers off to factories or government offices where there is nothing for them to do. A government plan is being implemented to eliminate up to a million supposedly fake jobs, starting in 2011 as part of shift toward self-employment and small business development. At this writing, the government, in the face of complaints, was reducing tax rates for entrepreneurs to stimulate investment.

One area where there was room for improvement was the export sector. According to a CIA analysis, Cuba had an estimated three-billion, three-hundred million dollars in exports in 2010. Products sold included sugar, tobacco, coffee, nickel, citrus, fish and medical products. Imports totaled $10.24 billion and included food, petroleum, chemicals, equipment and machinery. China topped the list of buyers of Cuban products and Venezuela was the leading seller to Cuba. Among Latin American countries, according to the International Monetary Fund, none had a smaller rate of export growth than Cuba between 1958 and 2000. A major contributing factor, however, was the U.S. embargo, imposed in the early 1960s.

As for the new openings for private sector activities, Katrin Hansing, a Cuba expert at the City University of New York, told an interviewer in Havana in 2010 that Cubans were caught between hope and fear about the new policy. Hansing, who spoke to a *PBS* reporter from Washington, said Cuba "has basically given its citizens a cradle-to-grave security blanket, right? Whether it's been good or bad is a different story. With all of these new announcements of potential unemployment, and that you have to kind of fend for yourself, that is scary to people, because, psychologically, this is something completely new." She had a point. It is hard to predict how career government workers would react if they are suddenly asked to summon the will and the smarts needed to make a living on their own. Espinosa Chepe says mere reforms within the existing Castroite formula are not enough. "To avoid social explosions, a change of system is necessary," he says.

During the long period of Soviet subsidies, Cuba basically gave low priority to tourism, which Fidel had felt was an undignified way to earn income. The Soviet subsidies, in effect, had served as a substitute for income from fancy hotels that, before the revolution, catered to well-to-do, sun-loving foreigners, mostly Americans, many with a penchant for carousing and gambling.

In 1989, tourism revenues were listed at a paltry two hundred and seventy million dollars, roughly double the figure from 1980, but still far below the levels of the late Batista years. Once the Soviet subsidies dried up, Cuba pivoted quickly to an emphasis on tourism, joining just about every other country and territory in the Caribbean. A hotel construction boom, led by Spanish firms, followed, and by 2010, tourism revenues were listed at two-billion-two-hundred-million dollars, a drop off compared with the pre-global recession period. (Until 2008, tourist hotels were off-limits to Cubans, partly because of concern that prostitutes would otherwise be filing in and out, blighting the hotel and the environs.)

The announced revenues generated by tourism were deceptive because they reportedly didn't take into account the high cost of keeping the hotel patrons happy with fresh seafood, newly picked fruits, and other delights. Other sources of foreign exchange for Cuba included remittances from expatriate families, nickel exports, earnings from Cuban medical services abroad, and, of course, cigars.

Sugar was once an export mainstay of Cuba. Soviet purchases of Cuban sugar, starting in the 1960's, offset the loss of the U.S. market but then Cuba lost much of the Russian market as well in the 1990s. Also, sugar was increasingly a high risk investment because of wild price fluctuations on the world market. In 1974, the average price was fifty-seven cents per pound; in 1977, it was eight cents. During the early part of the 21st Century, Cuban sugar production dropped to levels not seen in a hundred years. But, by 2011, sugar production appeared to be recovering after a disastrous 2010.

Random samplings of Cubans suggest that the dual-currency system (low-value pesos and higher value CUCs, the national hard currency) is extraordinarily unpopular. "There is one measure that the entire world is waiting for, that is the elimination of the dual currency... and it's a measure that our government and our economists must analyze sooner or later," Rubén Pupo, a peso-earning security guard, told an American reporter in 2009. Cuba may be the only country in the world where workers essentially are unable to buy many necessities in the currency in which they are paid. At the Communist Party Congress in April 2011, officials said the government eventually plans to eliminate the dual currency.

"In Cuba, money (the peso) is worthless," said Lizette Fernández, speaking to the *Miami Herald* in 2010 after leaving her homeland. "You get soap two times a year, and when you run out, you have to go to the dollar store, where it costs 75 (U.S.) cents ´ (about six hours' pay). There is virtually nothing you need that you can buy with Cuban pesos." The cost and frequent unavailability of cooking oil has been a sore point for Cubans for years. In April 2011, the cost was more than two dollars per bottle—more than two days pay. Says Espinosa Chepe: "It is known that the salaries in general are not enough to subsist on."

The food shortages of the 1990s posed a particular problem for Nitza Villapol, host of a TV cooking show in Havana. She told an American reporter that for weeks she built her shows around differing potato concoctions because market shelves had little else. Examples were potato with onions, and potato with an ounce of cooking oil and salt. In a more prosperous time, Villapol would tout such dishes as *rognons sautes au champagne, filet of boeuf a la perigordine,* and *poulet a la basquaise.*

An American diplomat one evening years ago patronized a Havana restaurant popular with foreigners. The menu, at least, offered him hope of a selection. A lobster dish seemed tempting. "Is there any of this?" the friend asked the waiter, pointing at the menu. "Yes, there is, but we don't have it," the waiter said, stone-faced. The friend pointed to a second dish. The response and the facial expression were the same. On the third try, the waiter burst into laughter, recognizing that his game had run its course. The friend laughed with him. He had to settle for a very plain pizza.

There is broad disagreement over the quality of life in Cuba before the revolution. Some of the earliest migrants to the United States after the revolution were from Havana's upper crust, peo-ple who fondly recall the city as an ultra-modern metropolis where life was good. Stories abound about the pre-revolutionary splen-dor of Havana. "*Havana, quien no la ve, no la ama*" ("Havana, one who hasn't seen it doesn't love it"), people said in the old days. Some cannot accept the crumbling metropolis that it has become. Many insisted that public education was good before the revolution. By some measures, Cuba had the fourth highest literacy rate in Latin America, after Argentina Chile and Uruguay in the 1950s.

But in his book *Cuba*, historian Hugh Thomas said his research showed that only 44 percent of Cuban children between six and fourteen attended school in 1953, six years before the revolution. He said another survey a few years later showed a fifty-fifty split between children of that age group who were enrolled and those who weren't. He added that 45 percent of children from peasant families had never been to school and that of the 90 percent of those who had, few had gone beyond the third grade. His research also indicated that only one in ten Cuban children between thirteen and eighteen were in school. Early on, the revolution dispatched many young people to the countryside in what was seen as a highly successful effort to bring up the literacy rate.

A month before he died in 1963, President Kennedy decried the misrule of the Batista years: "I believe there is no country in the world, including the African regions, including all the countries under colonial domination, where economic colonization, humiliation and exploitation were worse than in Cuba, in part owing to my country's policies during the Batista regime."

Arthur Schlesinger, a historian and top aide to Kennedy, had said earlier: "The corruption of the (Batista) government, the brutality of the police, the regime's indifference to the needs of the people for education, medical care, housing, for social justice and economic justice...(are) an open invitation to revolution."

In his early Castro-era book, *Listen, Yankee*, the leftist U.S. scholar C. Wright Mills assailed what he saw as the prior American domination of the island.

"The 'Old Cuba' rested of course on foreign-owned capital, which in Cuba meant Yankee-owned capital, and it wasn't only the sugar fields and the (sugar) mills and the oil refineries and the electric company and the rubber-tire plants and the telephone system. It was also the preferential tariffs given to U.S. capitalists— and only to U.S. capitalists who sold so many things to Cuba that Cubans had to have," declared Mills.

Other experts said almost two-thirds of the farmland, including much of the sugar-growing areas, was under American ownership.

Historian Paul Lewis says in his book, *Authoritarian Regimes in Latin America*, that the main aspiration of the Cuban people during the Batista era was the restoration of the democratic system that the dictator had taken from them in 1952. He staged his coup just months before Cubans were scheduled to hold their third presidential election since the constitution of 1940 constitution took effect.

Lewis says that in 1958 about half the Cuban population was middle class or higher and that their living standards "were among the highest in Latin America (and indeed the world) according to measures such as per capita income; literacy rates; infant mortality rates; the number of physicians and dentists per capita; the per capita consumption of meat, vegetables and cereals; the number of automobiles, telephones and radios per capita; the availability of electric power; and the level of industrial production."

Wages in Cuba nowadays are almost uniformly poor. In the Batista era, there was one sector that did very well: organized labor. Lewis points out that this group prospered at the start of Batista's rule and enjoyed a 14 percent increase during it, his second stint as president. This sector benefitted greatly as a result of contractual bans on worker dismissals and on mechanization. Workers in other sectors did not fare nearly as well.   it was not a surprise when Cuba's Communists and the Cuban Labor Federation ignored Castro's call for a general strike during Batista's final months in power.

Lewis notes that the rural population and unskilled urban labor lived in poverty and insecurity in the Batista era. "At least one-third of the labor force was unemployed or worked at poorly-paid or part-time jobs," he says. "The 25 percent of the population classified as rural labor seldom went beyond the third grade at school and had an illiteracy rate of almost 42 percent. Their housing lacked electricity, running water or indoor toilets. They were undernourished, suffered from intestinal parasites, and had almost no access to health care."

Havana's pre-revolutionary status as a glittering cultural and commercial centre was neutralized somewhat by the city's "sin" industries: gambling and prostitution. Americans had significant investments in these enterprises. At the gaming tables, Americans were a ubiquitous presence, easily identifiable with loud shirts on their backs and margaritas in their hands. Batista had close ties to Meyer Lansky, the well-known American mobster and gambling entrepreneur in Cuba until the Castro revolution.

According to a *New York Times* obituary of Lansky in 1983, Castroite troops, shortly after the revolution, "smashed hundreds of slot machines, dice and roulette tables and other gaming devices in Havana's tourist hotels and ended a multi-million dollar industry and Mr. Lansky's substantial interests in it." Even though Lansky built the *Hotel Riviera*, his preferred hangout was *El Nacional*. It still stands, lavishly remodeled after the revolution, boasting a lobby with mahogany-tiled walls and Elizabethan chandeliers. Nowadays, it caters to foreigners; unlike an earlier era, gambling is forbidden.

So how does Cuba compare with its nearby Spanish-speaking neighbor, the Dominican Republic, a democracy? Cuba has always been more prosperous than the Dominican, which shares the island of Hispaniola with Haiti. CIA estimates showed that in 2009, Cuba's per capita income was ninety-seven hundred dollars, compared with eighty-three hundred for the Dominican Republic, a country whose wealth is largely concentrated in Santo Domingo. In the social realm, Cuba is vastly superior with much higher rates of literacy and lower rates of infant mortality and unemployment.

Dominicans enjoy free speech, a free press, and freedom of association. Free presidential elections have been held every four years since 1966. None has been held in Cuba since 1948.

It is in the health care field that Cuba lays claim to being far ahead of the rest of the Third World. All Cubans have health insurance under Cuba's free health care system. According to U.S. statistics, only 18 percent of Dominicans do. The range of widely available medical treatments in Cuba is far greater than its neighbor's. Foreigners flock to Cuba for treatment, less so to the Dominican Republic.

Dominicans are free to travel abroad. Cubans generally were not, a source of abundant criticism among some Cubans. But in 2011 officials were discussing an easing of regulations, which until this point included a requirement for government permission to leave and an invitation from a foreign sponsor.

Young Dominican baseball players are free to sell their talents to U.S. Major League teams, and about five hundred have reached that level over the decades. Cuban players are prohibited from signing contracts with big league teams—unless they desert, as many have.

Salaries are higher in the Dominican Republic than in Cuba but the social safety net is far thinner. A Cuban who loses his job normally continues to receive some benefits, including subsidized food. Unemployed Dominicans are, for the most part, on their own. Huge numbers of Dominicans and Cubans rely on U.S.-based relatives to help them out economically.

The pockets of poverty I've seen in Cuba seem less daunting and less extensive than those in the Dominican Republic. A substantial percentage of Dominican homes lack electricity.

The Cuban media ignores the poverty and other shortcomings in the country, preferring to accent the positive, such as the opening of a new clinic. The shabbiness of many existing clinics is not discussed. The timidity of the Cuban media contrasts sharply with the far bolder and more informative Dominican press, which highlights such issues and poverty and corruption. "Poverty Continues to Afflict a High Percentage of Dominicans," the Santo Domingo daily *Listín Diario* said in a banner, page-one headline on October 16, 2007, the eve of the "International Day of the Eradication of Poverty." The accompanying story described the hellish existence of a neighborhood alongside Santo Domingo's Ozama River. Many other Dominicans suffer similar deprivation.

A 2006 World Bank report highlighted the factors that push so many Dominicans toward crime and violence: "poverty, youth unemployment, urban migration, drug trafficking, a weak education system, ineffective policing, the widespread availability of weapons, drug and alcohol use and the presence of organized gangs." Some older-generation Dominicans speak with nostalgia about the harsh 1930-61 Trujillo dictatorship, when streets were safer. There is no independent data on the extent to which Cuba suffers from urban crime and violence but, having spent long periods in both countries, I would say the Dominican Republic is worse off.

Cuba may be the world's most heavily subsidized country. The support it has received from, first, the Soviet Union and, later,

Venezuela, ran well into the tens of billions through 2011—all in the name of socialist solidarity. It also received several hundred million dollars in credits from China. By comparison, the subsidies funneled to the Dominican Republic from the United States and international lending institutions were much smaller. Remittances to the Dominican Republic from the U.S. were estimated by the Inter-American Development Bank to be three-billion, one-hundred- million dollars in 2008—with a 5 percent decline during the 2008-10 recession years. There are no official figures on remittances by Cuban expatriates back to Cuba but informed estimates put it at between eight-hundred million and one-billion dollars.

Use of the Dominican Republic as a way station for U.S.-bound drugs is believed to be much higher than Cuba. Among the reasons is better policing in Cuba.

Cuba came out less corrupt than the Dominican Republic on a survey of perception of corruption around the world by Transparency International, a German-based corruption watchdog group. (A joint study by the World Bank and Inter-American Development Bank found that a Dominican bank scandal early in 2003 caused six-hundred-seventy-three-thousand Dominicans to fall into extreme poverty.)

The survey said that, among Latin American countries, only Chile, Uruguay, and Costa Rica were seen to have less corruption than Cuba. In terms of political rights, the Dominican Republic was listed in a survey by the New York-based Freedom House as one of eighty-seven "free" countries and Cuba as one of forty-seven "not free."

Unlike Cuba, there are no income limits in the Dominican Republic. Jobs that pay three to four hundred dollars a month are common but such salaries don't go very far. And it is not easy for a dark-skinned Dominican from the interior to overcome his poor roots—and chronically weak education system—and have a chance at the "good life" in upscale areas of Santo Domingo. Cuba says it provides free universal education. The Dominican Republic has never given high priority to the concept of a decent education for all. (The same applies to health care.) Virtually all Dominican parents with means, mostly white, send their children to private schools. Each afternoon during the school year, late model cars, often SUV's, line up by the dozen in front of private schools in wealthier neighborhoods of Santo Domingo for child pick-up. There are no public schools in these neighborhoods because there is no demand for them.

A *Miami Herald* article on race in the Dominican Republic said Dominicans describe themselves as one of a dozen or so racial categories but rarely negro. In the same article, Dominican historian Celsa Albert said, "The Cuban black was told he was black. The Dominican black was told he was Indian. I am not Indian. That color does not exist. People used to tell me, 'You are not

black.' If I am not black, then I guess there are no blacks anywhere because I have curly hair and dark skin."

Like the Dominican Republic, Cuba also has a racial divide.
Fidel Castro said he believed that the guarantee of universal education in Cuba would minimize social divisions based on race
but he later acknowledged that inequalities persisted long after
his revolution began. An Afro-Cuban group asserted in 2011 that
race is a "taboo" subject in Cuba even though blacks constitute a
majority of the population.   (See "Afro-Cubans", Chapter 12, for
more)

In terms of Internet access, it is far greater in the Dominican
Republic than in Cuba, where few can afford computers and
where the government sees the web as a potentially subversive
instrument. Fidel, however, became an avid tweeter, amassing a
reported one hundred thousand followers since opening account
in 2010. His musings, much like his columns, usually focused
on international issues such as the potential for nuclear war and
the supposed evil machinations of NATO. On topics such as the
widespread desire for a better paycheck and more food on the
table, he had nothing to say.

The passions of these Cuban kids are evident as they cheer on their favorite hoops team.

A bunch of guys hanging out without much to do. This could be a scene from any Caribbean country. In this case, it's Cuba.

Idle men against a backdrop of a building sorely in need of an upgrade. The one next door has already had one and looks just fine.

CHAPTER 6

THE CUBAN MEDIA

During a chat with a Cuban acquaintance some years ago, a Washington Post reporter bemoaned the dull fare served up by the country's best-known newspaper and Communist Party organ, *Granma*. The Cuban replied that *Trabajadores*, a party daily for workers, might be a refreshing change. The Post reporter recalled that her hopes were dashed the next day when she saw the headline in *Trabjadores* over the lead story: "Tooth Paste Quotas Fulfilled."

Few in Cuba, even fervent Communists, defend the mundane output that passes for news in Cuba's media. The people in charge realize that exposing frailties in the communist system can wreck their careers. Their duty is to promote the system, not undermine it. (The Argentine journalist Jacobo Tímerman once described *Granma* as "a degradation of the act of reading.") Another biting comment about Cuban journalism in general was offered by Circles Robinson, the Havana-based founder of the *Havana Times*, an English-language online publication about Cuba available only outside the island. He told an interviewer in

2011: "There has been a distinct lack of critical everyday reporting and analysis of Cuba's political, economic and social spheres
throughout the country's 50-odd year revolutionary history."

In an attempt to find a silver lining to the output of the Cuban
media, National Assembly President Ricardo Alarcón once said
that Cuban journalists, unlike those from some other countries,
don't get killed in the line of duty. (There is no acknowledgement
in Alarcón's comment about the valuable service western journalists perform in reporting, for example, from areas of international
conflict, such as South Asia.)

It is hard to imagine any Cuban journalist winning an international reporting prize. One can only surmise what the career of
Bob Woodward, the renowned reporter for the Washington Post,
would have been like if he were Cuba-born: a regional director
in the Department of Revolutionary Orientation, perhaps? (The
DOR, as it is known, sets the guidelines for all media outlets,
among other duties.) Cuban journalists have to work within very
narrow parameters. They must be ideologically reliable, based on
files dating from grade school. Once hired by a media outlet, they
are on a short leash. Their bosses are not journalists but party
loyalists. The Paris-based media rights body Reporters Without
Borders has said Cuba's press freedom situation is "disastrous."
It adds that with less than 2 percent of the country's population
online, Cuba is "one of the most backward Internet countries."

Its 2010 Press Freedom Index ranked Cuba one-hundred-sixty-sixth out of one hundred and seventy-eight countries surveyed. Cuban authorities, of course, don't see a free exchange of ideas as a priority, whether through the media or other means. They believe that an embattled country such as Cuba must avoid giving any space to critical ideas or stories that would give aid and comfort to a determined and powerful enemy. Still, *Granma* and other party organs are not as uniformly faithful to party dictates as they once were. Ordinary citizens are being allowed to vent their frustrations in a special section in *Granma's* Friday editions, a relatively recent innovation.

The U.S. might have a different view of press freedom if it were under threat from a powerful neighbor, as Cuba has been for years. Cuba believes it must have its guard up at all times and sees little merit in "even-handed" media coverage. Less excusable is the lack of balanced reporting on the daunting problems Cuba faces internally. Difficulties in health, education, and other sectors are discussed in the Cuban media but newspaper readers and TV news consumers are assured that solutions are on the way. Rarely does a new health clinic open without a glowing media report. Corruption or other examples of wrongdoing are not reported without high-level party approval. Not surprisingly, anti-Americanism is a recurring theme. One of my earliest memories of my time as a reporter in Washington concerned the following approximation of a Cuban news agency rewrite of a 1971 AP story from Washington: The World Bank announced that it was no longer providing assistance to the leftist government of Chilean President Salvador Allende, citing the country's poor credit rating, the AP confessed today. (Note that verb: *confessed)*

Cuban officials say the American media focuses too much on trifling issues, such as scandalous behavior by the rich and famous. In contrast, the Cuban media trumpets news of social importance, such as the country's health care advances. (Cuba ranked twenty-eighth worldwide in incidence of infant mortality in 2009, better than any other Third World country and better even than the United States, which ranked thirty-third. Oddly, statistics on maternal mortality are not routinely disclosed.)

Murder cases are seldom reported. When a man killed his ex-wife and child in Guantánamo province, people talked of little else for days but the media remained silent. The purpose of the media is to defend the revolution; reports of violence could raise doubts about whether the country is on the right track. Beyond that, enemies of the revolution abroad could seize on accounts of brutal behavior to their advantage.

In contrast to the American media, Cuba guards the privacy of public figures. No media outlet was allowed to discuss Fidel's health problems in 2006 unless he himself issued a statement. No serious profile of Raúl Castro had ever appeared in the Cuban press before he became president. In interviews he has given over the decades, he has almost never talked about himself. He delivered only four speeches during his first eighteen months as Cuba's leader. This seemed to reflect his awareness that when he stands before an audience, he is not the master speechmaker that his brother was. Illness kept Fidel away from the podium but his newspaper columns kept him in the public consciousness. His "Reflexiones" output exceeded three hundred in less than four years after his retirement. Many of his literary labors were read verbatim on television news shows.

There was more evidence of his continuing clout. On August 13, 2009, at midnight on Castro's eighty-third birthday, eighteen months after formally surrendering his state and government posts, normal television programming was interrupted and replaced by a three-minute tribute to Fidel that featured flattery, photos, and videos of his life dating back more than fifty years. The accolade showed he was still a national force even though he had long since disappeared from public view. During all of his years in power, there were few public peeks at the private Fidel. The media, knowledgeable Cubans say, refrained from showing a picture of Fidel's girlfriend, the mother of five of his children. Once asked by American author Ann Marie Bardach how many children he had, Castro responded, "*Un tribu*" ("A tribe"). Bardach reported that Fidel had eleven children with seven women between 1949 and 1970. He was married at least once, perhaps twice. Such tidbits are not discussed in the Cuban media.

To catch up on the news, many Cubans tune in an evening show on *Telesur*, a Venezuelan-backed leftist news alternative that can be seen in many Latin American countries. Cuban blogger Alfredo Fernández says a narrator of an evening news show, Walter Martínez, is a master manipulator.

"...(A)n entire generation of older Cubans have in the journalism of Walter Martínez the exact dose of (dis)information they need to hear without caring that there exist more versions of the news than what this gentleman is presenting to them. While on occasion he doesn't misinform them completely, he does in fact limit reality to that precise portion that the government wants... one that they'll think is the sole account possible," he wrote in February 2011.

During the upheavals in the Middle East in early 2011, Fidel wrote a column about his unhappiness with international press reporting of these events. For enlightenment, he said, he tuned in *Telesur*. He reveled not only in the network's coverage of the unrest but in the ouster of Egypt's Hosni Mubarak. In his newspaper column, Fidel highlighted the thirty years of American support and friendship for Mubarak. He did not point out that the protestors who turned out en masse day after day were demanding freedom and democracy. Egypt's ties with America were not an issue. Graham Sowa, an American living in Cuba, said in an essay in the *Havana Times* that the ample coverage of the upheaval in Egypt contrasted with the absence of coverage of the nearly concurrent mass demonstrations in Bahrain, Algeria and Yemen. (The leader of Tunisia had already been forced out.) The coverage of the uprising in Libya, including columns by Fidel, was incomplete but supportive of Moammar Gadhafi because of his relatively advanced social policies. Sowa's point about the infrequency or selectivity of coverage of international news in Cuba is well taken. He wrote that "the absolute dearth of dynamic commentary on our contemporary world" is one of the "biggest struggles" he has as an American living in Cuba. Sowa, a medical school student, said he only learned about the unrest in the Middle East through the Internet well after the turmoil had started.

In an interview in 2005, Castro said Cuba has good reason to limit media criticism of the country's shortcomings. "Our news organs are not in the hands of enemies of the revolution, nor in the hands of agents of the United States. They are in the hands of revolutionaries. Our press is revolutionary, our journalists on the radio, on television, are revolutionaries... There has been the view here for some time that criticism, the denunciation of things poorly made, that's the enemy's game, it helps the enemy and the counterrevolution. (Still), we have discovered that in the fight against negative trends, the work of the press is very important.

We have encouraged the critical spirit. (It is) a fundamental factor in perfecting the system.

"If freedom of the press means that the counterrevolution and enemies of Cuba have the right to freely write against socialism and against the revolution, smear, lie and create conditioned reflexes, I would say we are against that 'liberty,'" Castro said. "As long as Cuba is blockaded by the empire (the U.S.)... a country threatened by the president of the United States himself (Bush), we can't give that right to the allies of our enemies whose objective is to fight against the reason for the existence of socialism."

Ron Ridenour, a Cuban blogger, wrote in a *Havana Times* commentary in March 2011 that the Cuban people would benefit from an unhindered media. "Strict government control of the media and other channels of information and debate cripple the ability of the common man and woman from acquiring adequate information and ideas necessary for them to become empowered," he wrote.

Castro has frequently ridiculed the notion that the capitalist press is "free" and therefore superior. He noted that no widely read U.S. publication would ever hire a reporter who extols the virtues of one-party socialism. But to the extent that this issue is deemed worthy of debate, a cursory comparison of the daily output of the American and Cuban media should end it. One informs, the other doesn't. A Cuban diplomat once expressed amazement to me at the quantity of information that the Washington Post was able to glean from unidentified government sources on sensitive issues. The Post, he said, was a better information source than any intelligence agency.

Once the United States and Cuba get beyond their ongoing impasse, perhaps conditions will exist for the emergence over time of a freer press in Cuba, something akin to the 1950s, when there were more than a dozen independent daily newspapers. There were censors in those days but their sole function reportedly was to intercept at the Havana airport each day's delivery of the *New York Times* and to clip out any Cuba-related stories (normally anti-Batista) prior to the papers' distribution to city newsstands. Since the revolution, sightings of the Times in Havana have been as rare as meteors.

The Cuban media has to rank as perhaps the least informative in Latin America. The bureaucracy's tight-fisted attitude toward release of routine information even drew the wrath of *Granma,* the Communist Party's official organ. In July 2011, the newspaper called it "incredible and even exasperating" that permission was needed from a vice minister to interview a school child or to take a picture of a classroom scene at the start of a semester. The article noted that Raúl had decried "excessive secrecy" and demanded that "all information be put on the table."

In lieu of a balanced account of the events of the day, anniversaries of trifling occurrences are sometimes fondly recalled by the Cuban media. On international issues involving Cuba itself, the regime was sometimes curiously silent—as when thousands of Cuban troops were deployed to Ethiopia starting in 1977.

Important international developments are routinely ignored by Cuba's media if they suggest a trend unfavorable to the country. A U.S. diplomat told me in 2006 that Havana's media had looked the other way for the preceding two years as the anti- Russian "Orange Revolution" unfolded in Ukraine. Cuba's leaders apparently did not want the word to get out that a Russian neighbor historically dominated by Moscow had elected a government eager to establish ties with the European Union and other creations of Western democracies. (A successor Ukraine government, also elected, has been far more sympathetic to Moscow.)

Occasionally, the triumphalist tone of the public discourse in Cuba can take an inexplicable shift. An example was an April 2010 opinion piece by Esteban Morales, a TV news analyst, on spreading corruption in Cuba. The article appeared on the web site of the official Union of Writers and Artists of Cuba, known by its Spanish initials UNEAC. "In reality," Morales said, "corruption is more dangerous than the so-called internal dissent, which still finds itself isolated: it still lacks an alternative program, it doesn't have real leaders and doesn't have a mass following. But corruption is the true counter-revolution, what can do the most damage, because it comes from inside the government and state apparatus, which are those who manage the resources of the country." Only a tiny percentage of Cubans actually saw the piece because it appeared on an obscure web site in a country where Internet access is minuscule. Was this an example of a new openness, a break with orthodoxy, a Caribbean "glasnost"? No. Not long after publication of the article, Morales was expelled from the Communist Party and his days as a TV news analyst were over. (The party reinstated him in 2011.)

Much like rice, coffee, eggs, and chicken, information is rationed in Cuba. A Cuban wishing to be informed is used to having no recourse. But now modern technology is producing cracks in the system. Yoani Sánchez, Cuba's most noted dissident blogger, credits mobile phones, digital cameras, and removable memories.

Sánchez says text messages she receives enable her to keep track, for example, of protests in leftist-led Venezuela and other information deemed too sensitive to be published in Cuba's official media. A torrent of messages during one busy week in Venezuela in early 2010 had left her cell phone "on the verge of collapse," she wrote. "I forward copies of these brief headlines to everyone in my address book, in a network that mimics viral transmission: I spread it to many and they in turn inoculate a hundred more with the information."

Not surprisingly, Sánchez has suffered harassment from Cuban authorities—she was once roughed up by state agents—but had yet to be silenced as of 2011. (In an earlier era she almost certainly would have faced a long prison term.) She has won press freedom awards from institutions in Europe and the United States but the regime has denied her permission to be present at ceremonies honoring her.

According to one count, more than one hundred bloggers operate in Cuba without authorization, some avowedly anti-government. Of the latter, Sánchez is clearly the best known. Dan Wilkinson, an American expert on Cuba at Human Rights Watch, a private group, wrote in 2010 that Sánchez's "Generation Y" blog gets more than 1 million visitors a month and is translated into fifteen languages.

The U.S. embargo against Cuba is obviously an inviting target for the Cuban media. According to one Cuban estimate, the embargo did three hundred and sixty-two billion dollars in damage the Cuban economy over a half century (other official estimates, including Fidel's, are much smaller). Each November since the early 1990s, the Cuban press has cheerfully—and extensively—reported on the U.N. General Assembly's overwhelming condemnation of the embargo in votes on Cuban-sponsored resolutions. The broad backing for Cuba is a tribute to the hard work of Cuban diplomats around the world. (Rare is the country that doesn't have a Cuban diplomatic mission.) It also reflects the international disdain for the continued American commitment to the embargo a full generation after the end of the Cold War.

Readers of the Cuban press following the January 2010 earthquake in Haiti were told that U.S. forces sent there for relief work had established a beachhead in Port-au-Prince. The reports ominously cited the presence of American troops in the vicinity of the presidential palace. The implication was that President Obama saw a devastated Haiti as ripe for an imperialistic grab, a mischievous interpretation, to put it mildly, of American motives. An alternative explanation was that Cuba was worried that the troop presence in Haiti was an American cover for an attack on Cuba, the mountainous eastern portion of which is just a short hop from Haiti.

(History taught Fidel that Americans can't be trusted. He interceded with Venezuelan President Hugo Chávez in 1999 not to allow American forces to assist Venezuela in clearing roads blocked by mudslides. Fidel told Chávez he thought the deployment might be a ruse designed to mask a military intervention. Chávez agreed and ordered Washington to cancel the mission. At the half-way mark of the trip, the ships reversed course and returned to their home port. This was an early sign for Washington that Chávez would not be easy to deal with. Fidel's concerns about a supposed stealth American invasion of Venezuela were never substantiated.)

While Americans took pride in the private and public assistance provided to earthquake victims in Haiti, the Cuban press focused on the large number of suffering Haitians never reached by official U.S. aid convoys and private relief groups. It depicted in heroic terms the help provided by Cuban doctors to injured or ailing Haitians at makeshift hospitals the Cubans set up. (I have no doubt that the sacrifices of many Cubans carrying out this work were substantial.)

Cuba reportedly had three-hundred and forty-four medical personnel in Haiti at the time of the earthquake. That number increased by almost nine-hundred personnel who assisted in earthquake relief as well as the ensuing cholera epidemic, according to official accounts.

Meanwhile, other donor countries and allied private aid groups dealt with the daunting and expensive tasks of removing thousands of tons of rubble and reconstructing hospitals and other infrastructure facilities. All agreed that progress was slow because of the magnitude of the problems and the often lethargic bureaucracies of donor countries and the Haitian government.

Cuba's coverage of hurricanes and other natural disasters at home tends to accentuate the positive. Typically, microphones from state media outlets are thrust in front of victims, who invariably express faith in government recovery efforts. The numbers of dead and injured are sometimes not reported. Also sometimes missing are reports on the fate of people who lost their homes.

Many reportedly end up packed together for prolonged periods in shelters under difficult conditions. Fidel said that Hurricane Dennis (2005) destroyed the homes of two-hundred-forty-five-thousand one-hundred-five people. Understandably, home reconstruction in Cuba often is no match for the immense need after a hurricane passes through.

Cuban officials see an hour-long evening news show called *Mesa Redonda* (*Round Table*) as a useful educational tool. Regime loyalists dissect a particular topic and, in the process, tout the government line. Before he fell ill, Fidel helped to shape the program, according to the aforementioned Alcibiades Hidalgo, a former Cuban ambassador to the United Nations, who defected in 2002. Hidalgo said Castro often decided on subject matter and on participating panelists, sometimes not making up his mind until 3:00 a.m. of the day of the show.

Raúl Rivero, a journalist who turned against the regime and eventually left the country, said *Mesa* and other TV discussion programs are "daily opinion carnivals of character assassination and verbal throat slashing." *Mesa*'s target is often the United States. American leftists are sometimes given a forum on the show. In 2008, Cindy Sheehan, who grieved the death of her son in Iraq by taunting President Bush near his Texas ranch, claimed on *Mesa* that only wealthy Americans have access to the American health care system. Her contention drew an approving smile from the moderator. (As of 2008, 85 percent of Americans had health insurance, according to the Census Bureau.)

At a pizza joint in Havana, a TV was tuned via satellite one evening in 2008 to an American baseball game. I was keeping an eye on the game while chatting with three companions. At one point, I glanced toward the TV and discovered that somebody had turned it off. I complained. A waitress dutifully turned it back on. About ten minutes later, the TV screen was dark again. "Why is this happening?" The waitress responded that each time a commercial came on, the staff assumed the game was over and that an American news show could come on at any minute. Someone would be in trouble, she said, if the authorities found out that the restaurant was being used as a forum for disseminating enemy propaganda. The explanation seemed understandable; I certainly did not want to see penalties meted out because I was a baseball buff. I dropped my request that the TV be turned on.

Two years earlier Castro had seemed relaxed about Cubans being exposed to the output of serious American newspapers or TV news stations. "Nobody here is worried about what they might say against the revolution," he said. It may have been the kindest thing he ever said about the American media.

Cuba lags well behind most countries in Internet use. Possession of computers with Internet access, as of 2010, was largely limited to government officials with a need for them. Many schools have computers with access only to Cuban web sites. Given the low salaries in Cuba, it is hard to imagine the day when home Internet use becomes routine and without limitations. Without it, fact-checking is difficult. With it, Cubans would have in their hands a tool with significant potential for expanding their knowledge horizons—and anti-regime mischief, as officials in China have learned. Dissidents there no longer have to rely on hand-delivered fliers to pass word, for example, of a protest rally. Dissemination can be instantaneous through the Internet. In Cuba, on the other hand, the lack of Internet access keeps Cubans largely clueless about the world around them. A Cuban friend once told me he had heard that, according to a poll, Fidel Castro ranked sixth among the world's most admired leaders. In Cuba, where digging for information is difficult, corroboration was possible for me only after my return to the U.S. An Internet search yielded no confirmation of the report. Serious research with Internet help is possible at Cuban advanced academic institutions but not without prior authorization. For most Cubans, unlimited Internet access never becomes more than just another wish list item.

Isadora Tattlin, the pen name of an American who lived in Cuba with her European husband in the mid-1990s, wrote in her book, *Cuba Diaries*, that a Cuban member of the National Assembly left her aghast when he repeated an obviously baseless rumor that 40 percent of American adults had had sex with animals. Again, it was the type of rumor could have been dispelled quickly with an Internet check. But in unconnected Cuba, such rumors can thrive.

It is not easy for the revolution to wage a propaganda war against the United States. Cubans are reminded every day of their own poverty, and many have an idyllic view of how Americans live, despite the negative portrayals—sometimes quite accurate—of the U.S. in the Cuban media. It is hard for the regime to counter the depictions of the good life as shown in American movies and in the narratives of Cubans who have resettled in America that they convey on return visits to the island.

Discrediting the U.S. is a high priority for the regime. The violent tendencies of America was the subject of a Cuban TV documentary. I can remember sitting in a crowded airport in the eastern city of Santiago in 1983, when I was startled by what sounded like a stampede. It was actually people rushing to watch something on a TV monitor in a remote corner. Scenes were being shown of the 1974 American movie, *Death Wish,* about a man who goes on a vigilante-style rampage against violent criminals in New York City. The theme fit nicely with Cuban portrayals of life in America. How much Cubans are swayed by such images is impossible to say.

The Cuban press ignores the abuses that occur in Cuban prisons but eagerly recounts conditions in U.S. prisons, drawing on American press reports. "One out of every four prisoners in the world is in a U.S. penitentiary," the Communist Party daily *Granma* said in a February 2010 article. "The composition of these prisoners is profoundly racist: one out of every 15 black adults is incarcerated; one out of every 9 is aged 20-34 years; and one out of every 36 is Hispanic. Two-thirds of those serving life sentences are African-American or Latino, and in the case of New York State, only 16.3% of prisoners are white." There is no discussion of whether inmates in U.S. prisons deserve to be there or of the numerous rights given to defendants in America, in contrast to the more arbitrary procedures in Cuba. In the *Granma* article, there was the curious suggestion that the prison population should somehow reflect the racial composition of the nation at large. Also missing was any reference to the racial makeup of prisoners in Cuba or prisoner treatment. (Yusimi Rodríguez, an Afro-Cuban and former reporter for a Cuban national newspaper, wrote in 2009 that "the greatest number of people in our jails are black.")

American consumer excess is another favorite theme of the Cuban media—the endless spending on useless gadgets, redundant clothing, and the like. It was not unusual for an American man to have sixty shirts in his closet, Castro once said in a speech in my presence, his arms thrust outward and a how-can-this-be expression on his face. American consumerism probably headed his long list of anti-American themes.

Castro's ideal is a citizen who thinks the most important value is service to revolution. A low salary is of no consequence to him because he can count on the revolution to meet his needs, such as food, health care, a place to rest, and a couple of changes of clothes. (As legend has it, Che Guevara had but a single pair of pants as he made his way from Argentina to Mexico looking for revolutionary opportunities, finding one when, by happenstance, he encountered Fidel in Mexico in 1955.

The American embargo is another favorite—and obvious—target of Cuba's media machinery. It claims that the measure, since its inception in the early 1960s, has caused unending hardships on the island. Castro called the embargo "criminal." (Secretary of State Hillary Clinton said in 2010 that Cuban officials had left U.S. officials with the impression that Cuba actually preferred that the United States leave the embargo in place lest the country "lose the excuse" for its poor economic performance.)

The Cuban press can be counted on to call attention to any critical comments from abroad, no matter how obscure, about the embargo. An example was an account of an anti-embargo resolution approved by a pro-Cuban entity in the town of Bayona in the Basque region of France in March 2010. Earlier came an endorsement, also duly noted in the media, of an anti-embargo stand taken by an association of pro-infant groups in Kazakhstan.

CHAPTER 7

TOUGH TIMES

Fidel Castro always was an avid consumer of news. He had his Foreign Ministry scour the international press each day for stories about Cuba. (One ministry reader told me he was awakened one night and heard a familiar voice on the phone line. "You missed one," it said. It was Castro.) He probably had seen my byline a few times, and acquaintances in Cuba said he had mentioned me in at least one speech. On one occasion in 1992, he was alarmed by a story I had written.

During the Mariel boat lift of 1980, a U.S. election year, one hundred and twenty-five thousand Cubans fled the island to Florida in boats. Countless Floridians were deeply resentful about the arrival of so many poor, uninvited foreigners and believed that President Carter was wrong in allowing it to happen. American officials informed Cuba afterward that a second rafter exodus would be considered "an act of war."

Twelve years after Mariel, I wrote a story for AP about American anxiety over an uptick in the number of migrants who were leaving the increasingly impoverished island for South Florida.

Did this indicate that was Castro was tolerating a piecemeal departure of discontented countrymen? In a phone conversation with me, a State Department official described the phenomenon as a "slow-motion Mariel." On seeing my story, a worried Castro wondered whether President George H. W. Bush was planning something drastic, perhaps even military action, to pre-empt a repeat of 1980. The Cuban leader called the number-two official at the Cuban mission in Washington demanding that he find out the name of my source. The diplomat called me the next morning and, over dinner that evening at an uptown Chinese restaurant, he asked me to identify the official. I refused. If I couldn't give the name, he suggested perhaps I could disclose the rank of the official. That was important because if it was somebody at the assistant secretary level or above, Cuban concern would be heightened. I said nothing. I didn't want to be known as someone who reports to the Cubans on un-attributable discussions with U.S. officials. The diplomat was obviously upset about having to report back to Havana that he couldn't get an answer to the *comandante's* question. In the end, nothing came of the "slow-motion Mariel." (Two decades later, I can report that the unnamed official was Vicki Huddleston, at the time the coordinator for Cuban affairs at the State Department, who a year later was named head of the U.S. diplomatic mission in Havana.)

It was not clear whether Castro took steps to brake rafter traffic that year. But in 1994, two years later, he gave the green light to an exodus at a time of steep economic decline coupled with unrest. Soon, more than thirty thousand Cubans set sail for South Florida, often in rickety vessels. Some tried their luck on inner tubes, a wooden door or even Styrofoam rafts. Floridians were appalled at the specter of another Mariel. Gov. Lawton Chiles pleaded with President Clinton to stop the exodus. Whether Clinton ever considered a military response is doubtful. He ended up ordering the Coast Guard to intercept the would-be migrants and send them to the U.S. base at Guantánamo. They were told that admission to the U.S. would never be granted. But in early 1995, Washington had a change of heart, deciding that all would be allowed to migrate, albeit in stages. Washington was concerned that confinement at the base so enraged the detainees that they were believed to pose a threat to their U.S. military guards.

For Clinton, the political price was muted partly because delivery of the migrants on military aircraft to U.S. soil was piecemeal and was completed a full year before the 1996 presidential elections, when he would seek—and win—a second term.

Witnessing the exodus in 1994 of so many Cubans escaping in boats, as I did aboard a U.S. military plane, was difficult for the mind to digest—a shimmering sea dotted with hundreds of vessels, many unseaworthy, each carrying desperate people yearning for a better life.

It was a country where milk, for example, was practically impossible to find because the East German government had disappeared, rendering null and void its commitment to be Cuba's main source of powdered milk. Milk production inside Cuba had dropped dramatically, reportedly because of a sharp descent in availability of quality animal feed. Just nine years earlier, a monument in the town of *Nueva Gerona,* on La Isla de Juventud (The Isle of Youth), had been erected in honor of a cow whose prodigious milk production seemed to foreshadow a nutritional breakthrough for the nation's children. Castro once visited the bovine and gently stroked her hide before the cameras. But the vision of a nation of happy milk-drinking children soon evaporated.

In his book, *Between Revolution and Reform*, historian Luis A. Pérez spelled out the magnitude of Cuba's economic collapse in the early 1990s, officially known as "The Special Period": "Life in Cuba settled into a grim and unremitting cycle of scarcity, in which shortage begat shortage and where some of the most basic daily needs and wants could be satisfied only by Herculean efforts. Inventories of available clothing, soap and detergent, and spare parts dwindled and often disappeared altogether. Rationing quotas frequently failed to supply enough food for more than two weeks of each month, driving vast numbers of people into the black market to supplement official monthly allotments."

Pérez wrote that the "disappearance of more than 300 medicines from local pharmacies, together with food shortages, threatened the health and nutrition of all sectors of the population, but especially the very young and the very old, the ill and the infirm."

Cuban imports of medicines and related products dropped 38 percent between 1991 and 1992 for lack of foreign exchange. Frequent blackouts added to the misery.

A Canadian Medical Association Journal report said that between 1990 and 1995, "Cubans essentially experienced a famine: adults had an average daily protein intake of 15–20 grams and lost an average of 5%–25% of their body weight... The famine in Cuba during the Special Period was caused by political and economic factors similar to the ones that caused a famine in North Korea in the mid-1990s. Both countries were run by authoritarian regimes that denied ordinary people the food to which they were entitled when the public food distribution collapsed; priority was given to the elite classes and the military.

"In North Korea, 3%–5% of the population died; in Cuba the death rate among the elderly increased by 20% from 1992 to 1993. Thirty thousand Cubans fled the country, and thousands of these emigrants drowned or were killed by sharks in the Gulf of Mexico. Cuba finally accepted US donations of food, medicines and cash in 1993, and a system of private farmers' markets was set up in 1994 to provide easy access to locally grown food."

Looking back, Rosa Martínez, a Cuban independent blogger, said many people still haven't been able to forget the hardest days "when it got so much worse that we thought we couldn't survive. People washed themselves with chlorine or water mixed with ashes. There were I don't know how many other inventions, and these destroyed my bed linen in less than a year," she wrote. Her saddest memory was seeing her father walk several miles each day loaded with firewood to sell. Thanks to those sales, she said the family was able to survive.

At the university, there were *jineteras* (prostitutes) who studied by day and 'hustled' by night. "It was a question of life or death," Martínez wrote. "Either you prostituted or you left the university."

One day came an unexpected blessing. "My group had an exchange with foreign students," Martínez said, "They gave us gifts that they called 'souvenirs.' (One) gave me $100. I couldn't believe that a student, the same as me, gave me more money than my dad could earn in more than six months."

The health care system was a study in contrasts. Cuba's hospitals were capable of delicate and complicated surgeries. But finding aspirins at pharmacies during this period could be a daunting challenge. A reporter friend visited five pharmacies and asked for aspirins at each. None was available at four of them. At the fifth she was handed four aspirins wrapped in tissue paper.

Many Cubans suffered the effects of a near 80 percent decline—from thirteen-million tons to one-million-eight-hundred-thousand tons—in Russian oil exports to Cuba between 1989 and 1993. After the fall of the Soviet Union in 1991, between 75 and 85 percent of Cuba's international trade was eliminated.

Poor quality and quantity of food had unexpected consequences during this period when, without warning, tens of thousands of Cubans suddenly became partially blind. (I was there for
unrelated reasons and was surprised when Cuban officials permitted me to meet with affected patients at a Havana hospital.)
Thanks to an efficient distribution system, in which neighborhood
block committees played a critical role, tablets of vitamin B-12
were made available around the country, and the problem eased
quickly. The Cuban media held the U.S. embargo responsible. *La
Tribuna de La Habana,* for example, called the United States the
"principal ally of the epidemic and its consequences."

Food availability was a continuing problem during this period.
The price of a chicken at the market was listed as two pesos
but finding one was virtually impossible. A shopper could go to
the black market and find—but not necessarily afford—one for
one hundred and twenty pesos, roughly a week's pay. A Cuban
friend who was a college professor received government permission to accept an invitation to speak at a Washington think tank.
He arrived in Miami thin as a rail, his stomach empty. Within two
weeks he had gained twenty-five pounds.

Food supplies were a problem before the actual collapse of
the Soviet Union—and the consequent drying up of Moscow's
aid program. In March 1991, a Cuban Air Force pilot, Orestes
Lorenzo, flew his MiG jet fighter to Miami from Cuba and asked
for asylum. He described a mess hall dish ironically called "*bistek*

de toronja" (grapefruit steak). It consisted of a grapefruit rind (the edible slices having already been consumed), some garlic, and bread crumbs. That was it, according to Lorenzo.

In an extraordinary display of daring, he later borrowed a private plane in Miami to pick up his wife and two children at an agreed meeting point on a highway outside of Havana, where he landed the aircraft. Lorenzo then flew his family safely to Florida.

His experience was one small measure of the economic difficulties that the military was having as part of the crisis of the country as a whole. To make the military more independent and less of a drain on the economy, it started growing its own food and dramatically reducing its numbers, chiefly through reduction in the length of mandatory service of recruits. It also became an arm of the tourism industry. The best known of its entities was *Gaviota*, which built hotels, transported tourists around the country by air, and took them on maritime excursions. The military experimented with business improvement practices in the hopes that, if successful, they could be adopted by historically inefficient non-military state enterprises. The new, business-oriented, military was a far cry from the one whose prime mission was fighting wars in the African bush. There was a side benefit for the regime: a money-making military would be less likely to revolt.

The early 1990s was a time when the country faced terrible choices. Food stocks were depleted and so were hard currency

reserves. The regime, at one point, decided that the latter problem was graver than the former and reportedly opted, without
announcement, to sell food abroad for cash—a wrenching trade-
off, to say the least.

Traveling around Havana one morning with a friend in his car,
I spotted a large open-air fruit and vegetable market about fifty
yards square. I saw no produce, nor customers, nor employees.
Scales swayed listlessly above the empty bins. I finally saw two
employees in the back. I asked whether the market was open.
"Of course we're open," they replied. Why was there no produce?
They explained that they were waiting for the delivery truck to
arrive. Their tone suggested it was more a hope than an expecta-
tion. Empty markets were common during that bleak period.

I almost always stayed at the *Habana Libre,* located in a bus-
tling area near a large park that housed a *Coppelia* ice cream
stand. Before dawn one morning during those dark depression
days, I took a walk toward the park and discovered thousands of
people in a seemingly endless line for ice cream. As I was to discover, the line was populated by people with empty or near-empty
cupboards—people for whom *Coppelia* offered the only hope for
something—anything—for breakfast. These were not peasants in
ragged clothes; their attire was not much different from what one
would find on a typical American street. I even stumbled upon a
friend from the Cuban Foreign Ministry. When I greeted him, he

evinced no particular discomfort about being seen in line with so many others for an ice cream breakfast before heading off to his diplomatic duties. Among other issues, we chatted about the low pay that farmers earn and how Fidel had tried to blame bureaucrats for the situation.

I returned the next day for a second look. The lines seemed just as long. I encountered an elderly woman who was a bundle of energy and good cheer even in those hard times. It seemed that nothing in her life was more important than the free turkey she was promised, presumably in recognition of her loyalty to the revolution, on International Women's Day in six weeks. Deep into our discussion, she acknowledged that it was not a whole turkey, just half of one. I was taken how bubbly her personality was, notwithstanding the hours-long wait in line for an ice cream breakfast. (The revolution taught Cubans to be patient—not a bad thing.) I wondered whether the woman needed anything but I was reluctant to ask, worried that she might be offended. I finally asked her. Hesitantly, she acknowledged that she needed a pair of sneakers.

I agreed to meet her at her home later that morning to deliver new sneakers. They cost only about six dollars at the dollars-only hotel store but she obviously had no one to help her with this type of purchase. I went to her home, as promised, with the sneakers. I had made her day and her joy had made mine.

In roughly the same timeframe, I called a Cuban government economist for a story I was doing on economic trends on the island. The official told me that his agency had produced several public reports on the subject. He agreeably offered to drop by my hotel room so I could look at them. After initial pleasantries, he said his agency sells the reports for five dollars apiece. Suddenly his offer to visit me made sense: he wanted some of my dollars. I thumbed through three of the reports and agreed to buy two. I gave him ten dollars—roughly the equivalent of two weeks' salary for him—and he left, probably with an extra bounce in his step. I never read the reports.

Cuban officials on occasion note that the United States was able to inflict pain on the island over the years but that Cuba was helpless to retaliate. Castro would be forced time and again to cope with continuing American moves to tighten the embargo. In 1992, legislation sponsored by Sen. Robert Torricelli, a New Jersey Democrat, barred subsidiaries of U.S. companies operating overseas from investing or trading with Cuba. The Torricelli legislation banned ships engaged in trade with Cuba from using U.S. port facilities for six months after the last visit to the island. As a result, some shipping companies skipped Cuba altogether rather than pass up a more lucrative stop at a U.S. port. In addition, the measure ordered the U.S. president to withhold economic assistance and debt relief from Cuba's aid donors. The same penalty applied to countries that signed free trade agreements with Cuba. Restrictions on travel by Americans to Cuba were tightened. Expressing confidence in the efficacy of his creation, Torricelli said that Castro, however resilient he had been until then, would be toppled "within weeks." That, of course, didn't happen. Clearly, Torricelli and his allies were trying to drag other countries into their campaign to choke the Cuban regime.

Many countries objected, rallying behind a Cuban proposal to have the U.N. General Assembly condemn the embargo. The vote, taken just weeks after the Torricelli bill was signed, was fifty-nine to three in Cuba's favor, with seventy-one abstentions. Cubans heartily welcomed the show of international support. Some in Cuba urged that the date of the vote become a national holiday. In subsequent years, Washington's international isolation in the U.N. on its Cuba policy became more acute as more abstentions became votes for Cuba in the annual, Cuban-sponsored balloting. By 2009, the margin was one hundred and eighty-five to three in support of the Cuban position.

Sales of U.S. medical equipment to Cuba have been legal since 1992 but have never reached their potential because of economic and political decisions on both sides. In 2008, the United States approved one hundred and forty-two million dollars in sales and donations of medical equipment to Cuba but only 1 percent actually was delivered. Cuba ordered equipment from the U.S. and then cancelled at least part of the purchase when a friendly country offered to donate it to the island cost-free.

Some U.S. medical supply companies are reluctant to try to do business with Cuba because there are no assurances that the Congress won't reinstate prohibitions on such trade. There are other deterrents. Licenses for sales must be approved by the Commerce and Treasury Departments. Approved sales then are subject to review by the State and Defense departments. A company making a sale must prove to the U.S. government that its product reached its intended destination, that it is not re-exported, and that it is not used for torture or other human rights abuses.

As Cuba's economic crisis deepened in the early 1990s, Castro responded by ordering an unprecedented series of reforms that were obviously painful deviations from his usual socialist orthodoxy.

A campaign to promote foreign tourism through construction of first-class hotels was initiated. The initial decision thirty years earlier to downgrade tourism was extraordinarily reckless. Fidel sacrificed a sure foreign exchange earner and, for ideological reasons, pinned his hopes on industrialization for national income. The perceived benefits of industrialization proved to be illusory. The impact of the reversion to tourism thirty years later has been dramatic. A number of lofty, luxury, five-star hotels have gone up around the island. The new additions to the Havana skyline brought sparkle to a city sorely in need of it and proved to be a reliable foreign exchange earner. For a truly relaxing time, a visitor can choose from among several hotels located in isolated but picturesque areas. In a normal year, more than two million foreigners, mostly Canadians and Europeans, visit the island. (Two million seven hundred thousand were expected in 2011.) Combined, tourists typically spend more than two billion dollars. Castro was initially loath to make tourism a centerpiece of Cuba's economy but, in the bleak days of the early 1990s, he felt he had no choice. It has the advantage of employing thousands, in addition to filling government coffers.

In another significant reform, the American dollar, once a hated symbol of American domination, and off limits to Cubans for decades, was allowed to circulate freely starting in 1993, leading to a sudden, sharp increase in remittances. Lorena Barberia, in an MIT working paper, says remittances jumped from forty-three million dollars in 1992 to four hundred and seventy million in 1994. The dollar was pulled from circulation in 2004 but still can be exchanged for euros or CUC's, the national foreign exchange currency.

There were other examples of a more flexible approach. Farmers during the early 1990s were permitted to sell part of their output at market prices. Also, electricians, plumbers, and other artisans were licensed to have private clients. European investors were authorized to enter into joint ventures with Cuba but all hiring of workers was done by Cuban entities. The European partner in a venture paid the Cuban government, say, two thousand dollars a month for a worker. The government would, in turn, pay the worker the peso equivalent of about twenty dollars a month—and pocket the difference. As a side benefit, the worker would receive each month a "basket" of items such as soap, shampoo, and perhaps canned goods. The system enabled the government to make foreign exchange, and reward ideologically reliable workers with above-average jobs while excluding those who were less committed to revolutionary norms.

One major irritant in the joint venture initiative in recent years was Cuba's refusal to allow the European co-investors to withdraw from Cuban banks the millions of dollars they had deposited in them. The reason was Cuba's chronic shortage of hard currency.

There were other innovations during those difficult years of the 1990s. Initially, a family with enough space could open a home restaurant so long as it had no more than twelve chairs. (Now the limit is fifty.) Proprietors had to prove with receipts that the food served was not bought from the black market. Homeowners could also rent spare bedrooms to foreign visitors. The names and other ID information of the visitor had to be reported to the state. If the landlord had two guests at the same time, they had to be related, presumably to lessen chances of in-house plotting by conspirators. A friend rented separate rooms in his home to two

Arabs who were in Cuba on business. When government inspectors found out they were unrelated, the friend was fined fifteen hundred dollars, a sum equal to about six years' pay for the average Cuban. If the friend gets caught twice more, he may be sent to prison.

Many landlords and self-employed Cubans, stifled by rules, simply gave up; their numbers declined by 43 percent between 1997 and 2003, according to Mesa Lago, the Cuban-born economist, citing research by an independent Cuban journalist. Socialist purity was making a comeback—at least for the time being.

The influx of tourists coupled with a sharply declining economy led to the reappearance of prostitutes on Havana's streets. They often could be seen patrolling tourism areas and were largely undisturbed by the authorities. Castro once said that Cuban prostitutes were a cut above their counterparts from other countries because they were better-educated (nine years was the norm) and therefore had alternate employment options, which young women elsewhere normally did not. On taking charge of Cuba in 1959, Castro vowed to eradicate prostitution and said in 1971 that goal had been achieved. "In our country all of those sad and horrible things of an exploitative society no longer exist," he said. Indeed, Cuba projected a somewhat puritanical image to the world during the earlier decades of the revolution.

The rebirth of prostitution in the early 1990s was a reminder of one of the most disreputable features of the Batista era. The phenomenon was the subject of a 2004 article in the journal *Transnational Law and Contemporary Problems*. It said that, over the objection of the Cuban Women's Federation, the government sponsored advertising campaigns featuring unaccompanied Afro-Cuban women frolicking on beaches. The March 1991 edition of *Playboy* magazine showed topless black beauties reveling by the surf at *Varadero*, Cuba's best-known beach. The journal report said that these visuals carried a subliminal message to some that a tourist can get sex in Cuba as part of a vacation package. Cuban tourism enterprises reportedly allowed the photo shoot in exchange for inclusion of pictures of the country's tourist facilities.

Castro clearly saw the limited opening in the 1990s to capitalist activities as temporary. For most of his adult life he had tried to repress the work-for-profit mentality. Once the Cuban economy had begun to recover, by 1996, he halted the reform measures or at least made it more difficult for these enterprises to survive. High taxes were the chief complaint.

As in virtually any country, Cuba has an underground economy. If a Cuban has a television with a VCR, he can tape movies and rent them. If an employee of a state company has a job with Internet access, he can sell the password to a friend. He can also sell it to a second friend so long as there is agreement as to the times when each would have access. Cuba's has a limited number of legal cybercafés, the first of which opened in 2000 in the domed, pre-revolution *Capitolio,* modeled after the U.S. Capitol building in Washington. According to *Capitalism, God and a Good Cigar,* a book edited by Lydia Chávez, only hard currency (five dollars an hour) is accepted at the enterprise and only foreigners or Cubans married to foreigners are allowed computer time. The government earns hard currency from the operation but employee theft diminishes its take. A customer can log on for two hours, pay for both, but only one hour is rung up. The difference goes to the proprietor or the employees.

The government took steps prevent the burgeoning tourism industry from becoming an island of privilege for the tens of thousands of Cubans it employs. As described by Mesa Lago, a government directive barred employees from "receiving gifts, donations, lodging, invitations to meals and parties, fellowships or trips abroad, and use of cars—without prior government permission. All gifts must be reported in writing to the immediate supervisor; electronic and video equipment will be kept by MINTUR (the tourism ministry).

"Tourist employees shall restrict their relations with foreigners to those strictly necessary; conversations and negotiations with foreign partners must be conducted in the presence of one witness (a euphemism for a security agent); employees must be discreet with information they have and not disseminate anything that could be sensitive; they must abstain from expressing ideas harmful to the government; be loyal to state politics; report in seventy two hours any contact from a foreigner not related to work issues or contrary to revolutionary morale—and exert permanent vigilance on any potential action that could damage state interests."

In small towns, tourists often have more contact with ordinary Cubans than in Havana. Tourists always have to be wary of street people hawking merchandise, as is the case in many countries. Take the elderly American gent who used to be the able to buy imported *Cohiba* cigars before the revolution and relishes a chance to savor one on a visit to Cuba. He comes upon a street vendor selling his favorite "*puro*". It may be the real thing but also may just be tobacco leaves rescued from the assembly floor and tidied up to look like the genuine article.

A Cuban can make a decent living in an interior town with beaches nearby. For a fee, hustlers help the foreign visitors find lodging, transportation, and restaurants.

In Lydia Chávez's book, there is a succinct description of the difference between Cubans who are able to take advantage of a tourist presence in small towns and those who aren't: "The division between the dollar-rich and dollar-poor is visible on any street. Bright white Adidas sneakers stand out against worn-out loafers. Well-off kids in their drab school uniforms crowd into dollar markets in the tourist part of town to buy sodas or little packages of cookies or candies. Flashy watches and gold chains are conspicuous next to naked wrists and calloused hands." Tourists thus contribute to prosperity but also to class divisions.

Faced with extreme shortages of food and other basic needs, many Cubans, often teachers, traded their profession for work in tourism, reportedly earning two to three times more. With schools suddenly short of teachers, universities began allocating far more resources to teacher training. Even some routine secretarial jobs or work as a hotel maid in tourist areas paid more than teaching. The flight from teaching was such that schools had to recruit young people, some still in their late teens or early 20s, to fill vacancies, using "fast-track" training to prepare them. Many parents complained of a sharp learning decline after veteran teachers departed.

A university dean, unhappy with his low pay, resigned and took a job as night manager of a Havana hotel. Countless other Cubans tried to make ends meet by selling homemade trinkets for dollars at street stands. A random sampling of these vendors indicated that many were engineers who simply could not get by with their meager peso wage. Vendors who relied on sales of wood carvings often had difficulty finding wood. They sometimes scavenged collapsed houses in search of wood from bannisters or stairs.

The headlong rush into tourism produced the kind of dichoto-
mies that Castro so wanted to avoid—pampered tourists at plush
hotels while a short distance away Cubans wait in line at charm-
challenged pizza parlors. In his book on Castro, Robert Quirk
quotes a woman with a small child saying, with tears in her eyes
as she waited her turn to buy food, "Why are they starving us?"
A friend who was a university professor told me the only meal he
could count on most days during the Special Period was a small
serving of rice and beans at the school cafeteria in the afternoon.
The friend told others that his hunger was so great that he seriously contemplated suicide.

Castro rarely talked about Cuba's food situation but Ann Louise Bardach went out on a limb during a 1994 interview with him
by using a joke popular in Cuba to broach that delicate subject.

"What are the triumphs of the revolution?" was the question.
The requisite answer being: education, health care, and sports.
"And what are the failures of the revolution?" Then the punch
line: "Breakfast, lunch, and dinner." To Bardach's surprise, Castro
laughed and said, "When you have too much breakfast, lunch,
and dinner, it's bad for your health." Bardach then observed that
the "master spinner had instantly turned hunger into a virtue."

The promise of more food for Cuban markets emerged in
2000 when embargo critics in the U.S. won a rare victory. Farm
state U.S. legislators, eager for new markets for their constitu-
ents, led the charge for allowing food sales to Cuba for the first

time in almost four decades. The measure was approved so long as Cuba paid cash for these imports. Instead of welcoming this important deviation from the embargo, Castro curiously ordered up a rally of hundreds of thousands in Havana to protest the pay-when-you-buy restriction. The condition seemed reasonable, considering Cuba's poor international credit rating. My guess is that the protestors had no idea why they were there. How bad is Cuba's credit? One useful indicator was reported in the spring of 2010 by the Paris Club, a group of nineteen developed countries. It showed that Cuba had a foreign debt of more than thirty billion dollars, the second highest in the world. (Other estimates put the debt at twenty billion.) Indonesia ranked first, China third, and India fourth. This meant that Cuba's debt as a percentage of population or of gross national product, was much higher than those of the other three countries. It also confirmed Cuba's long-standing status as a bad credit risk.

The easing of the embargo on food enabled the United States over time to become the leading food exporter to Cuba worldwide. Products included corn, wheat, chicken, soybeans, and powdered milk. Sales peaked in 2008 at seven-hundred-ten-million dollars and dropped by about a third 2009 largely because of a foreign exchange shortage in Cuba. Frozen chicken was the largest single sales item at one-hundred-thirty-nine million dollars. Overall, the United States was Cuba's fifth largest trading partner in 2007.

Besides legal sales, many American products find their way into Cuban markets surreptitiously. A *Miami Herald* account in August of 2009 said that at one downtown shopping center, Wilson baseball caps, Westinghouse light fixtures, Proctor-Silex juicers, and GE microwave ovens could be found. On the street outside, Sean John jeans and Ray-Ban sunglasses were for sale, the *Herald* said, adding that some government ministries operate with Dell computers. Fidel Castro was spotted once sporting New Balance sneakers. The *Herald* found the same item for sale in a shopping center at *Varadero* Beach, two hours east of Havana.

Few U.S. products available in Cuba come directly from the United States. Most are resale items from places like the Panamanian duty-free zone in *Colón.* By the time these goods reach Cuba, their prices are high, given the cuts each merchant takes along the way. The percentage of Cubans who can afford any of these goods is very small because of their trifling salaries. The *Herald* said that American companies are often oblivious to embargo violations involving their products because usually there is no way to trace them once they are sold in an American store. Still, OFAC, the U.S. government agency that enforces the embargo, at times levies fines against companies whose products end up in Cuba. Meanwhile, the prospect of more American products and dollars flowing into Cuba increased with the announcement in March 2011 that five additional American cities—San Juan, Dallas, Chicago, Pittsburgh, and Baltimore—were being added to the list of American cities authorized as departure points for direct flights to Cuba. Those previously authorized were Miami, New York, and Los Angeles. But Cuba remained off limits as a vacation destination for Americans. (Castro once said during the administration of President George W. Bush that the number of Americans who traveled to Cuba illegally was so high that additional prisons would have to be built if all were prosecuted.)

Many American officials quietly despised the embargo, partly because it hurt the Cuban people more than the leadership while also serving as a propaganda weapon for Castro. George Shultz, who served as secretary of state from 1982-89, admitted years after he left office that he thought the policy was "insane." In 2004, Lawrence Wilkerson, chief of staff to Secretary of State Colin Powell, called the embargo "the dumbest policy on the face of the earth." (He said later he thought the comment was off-the-record.) A sizable number of Republicans joined Democrats in opposition to aspects of the embargo. It was also a favorite target of free trade groups. The Cuban media routinely has called the embargo "an act of genocide." Bruno Rodríguez Parilla, a top Cuban diplomat, once said, according to *Granma*, that the embargo "covers so many elements that it affects every corner of the economy of our country; it is impossible to carry out a meticulous calculation" of its total impact. Defenders of the embargo say that lifting it would only make life easier for the regime and delay the day of its collapse.

Some Cubans blamed the revolution for the hardships. I had vivid memories of an encounter with a woman one summer day near the *Malecón,* Havana's seaside causeway. She said that more than a decade earlier, in the 1980s, she was one of Castro's true believers, so devoted that she was allowed to travel to East Germany for three years to teach humanities courses to college students. She returned to Cuba and taught at the University of Havana. When the economy wilted, so did her faith in the system. The turning point came when she was unable to find bar soap or a bottle of shampoo. She quit her university job and took another as a golf course cashier, earning tips in foreign currency from Canadian patrons. She lost the prestige she had as a scholar but at least she was able to keep clean.

For his 1991 book, *Castro's Final Hours,* author Andres Oppenheimer asked Cubans for their thoughts on the soap shortage. "You can fool your stomach with several infusions of coffee a day but there is little you can do to make up for soap, (Cubans) would tell you," he wrote. And not only women complained: "If there is ever going to be an uprising here, it will be over soap shortages," Oppenheimer quoted José, a young engineer, as saying.

There is no quick route to prosperity in Cuba. Castro decided early on to do away with the lottery, until then a popular fixture in Cuban society. There was, however, a rare rags to riches moment that I witnessed in front of the *Habana Libre* hotel one day in the late 1980's. A CBS TV crew was getting ready to leave Cuba after a stay of several days. There was a lot of heavy lifting of equipment for the attendants. On departure, the CBS team made it worth their while, handing over an eight-hundred dollar tip, a fabulous sum by Cuban standards, the equivalent of about three and a half years' pay for a worker. It was the norm, however, for the attendants to share their tips with the hotel staff. (Nowadays, there is heavy pressure at the traditional American TV networks to keep costs down. The days of eight-hundred dollar tips are over.)

Cuba is full of hard luck stories. Answering my hotel room phone one day, I heard the voice of a woman who pretended to know me. She asked me to mail a letter to an uncle living in the U.S. on my return home. (I presume that the hotel staff had given her the room numbers of Americans registered there.) Her request seemed innocent, so I suggested that she ask the front desk to put the letter in my mail slot. As I was ready to hang up, she pleaded that we meet so that she could hand deliver the letter to me. I agreed.

When we met, Carla (not her real name) talked about the misery of having to make do without life's basics, particularly soap and shampoo. We chatted for half and hour; I volunteered to buy her those items at a store in the hotel that catered to guests with foreign currency. I did not invite her to accompany me into the store because I wasn't sure whether hotel security would let her in, sensing that she might be a Cuban intent on shoplifting. I bought her a small bag of items. She was grateful. We agreed to stay in touch. In the ensuing months I received two letters from her at my home outside Washington. I called her on my return to Havana about a year later and we agreed to meet for breakfast at my hotel the following morning. To my surprise, her sister, Beatriz, showed up instead. The sibling explained that Carla was unexpectedly asked to start her job shift earlier than usual that morning. Beatriz and I ordered breakfast in the coffee shop. I noticed that she was not eating her meal. I asked why. She explained that she wanted to take it home so she could share it with Carla and two others who lived at the house. How generous, I thought. Food shortages tend to be an abstraction for the well-fed. In the case of this Cuban household during the depression of the early 1990s, it was a painful daily reality. It was a not question of lack of money or lethargy (all but one in the home had jobs). Availability of food at the markets was alarmingly inconsistent at best.

As Beatriz and I were leaving the hotel, she asked me if I could spare twenty dollars. I think she was embarrassed to make the request but did so anyway because of the dire needs at home. What did she have to lose? Indeed, I think Carla dispatched Beatriz to the breakfast because Carla knew that she couldn't bring herself to ask me for the money. I was pleased to oblige Beatriz's request. Her face reflected her joy. We said goodbye.

CHAPTER 8

GUNS RULE

Weapons of virtually all types and sizes helped define Fidel Castro's life.

"His speeches were studded with references to blood and to the prospects for violence and death," wrote Robert Quirk, a Castro biographer. As Castro saw it, the author said, "No man was complete without weapons. They assured protection from enemies. They symbolized the power to impose one's will, the assertion of virility. Attack before you are attacked. Weaponless you are emasculated, helpless, effeminate. With a pistol the world is yours."

If a man was not prepared to use a weapon, Castro believed, he should not carry it. "In school, he kept a pistol in his room," Quirk continued. "At the university, he joined a university gang in its bloody confrontations with rival groups. As a guerrilla leader in the *Sierra Maestra,* he kept within arm's reach his favorite—and famous—rifle with a telescopic sight. A pistol hanging from his military belt became a part of his habitual attire. When he conferred with subordinates, he drew his weapon from his holster and placed it on the table before him, as though to remind them of the source of his authority. When, as head of government, he began one of his marathon speeches, he made a show of putting a pistol on the lectern."

When Castro arrived at the University of Havana in 1945, he found a vibrant gun culture. As he began to attract attention there because of his outspokenness on political issues, he acquired enemies—some armed. Fearing for his life, he left the university.

When he returned, he was packing a weapon, says Brian Latell, a long-time Latin America expert, now retired, for the U.S. government. It was a turning point for Castro, as the Cuban leader recalled in a 1995 speech: "One could say that it was the beginning of my own personal armed struggle. I was faced with the whole Mafia gang that dominated the university," he said.

Latell, author of *After Fidel*, alluded to Castro's remarks in a newsletter of the Cuba Transition Project in September 2010.

"If there was one thing I learned through those years when I had to look death in the face, unarmed on many occasions, it is that the enemy respects those who do not fear him, those who challenge him. The action I took… won their respect," Castro wrote, according to Latell.

Castro attempted to assassinate a politically ambitious secondary student named Leonel Gómez, Latell wrote, citing "the undisputed testimony of two eyewitnesses." He added that Castro was provoked by Gómez's membership in a rival gang.

Latell said there is no record of the assassination attempt in any spoken or written record that he is aware of.

Quirk pointed out that University of Havana students at the time formed revolutionary groups ostensibly devoted to social reforms but instead "they employed terrorist methods against their enemies both on and off campus," he wrote. "By the time Castro had arrived to begin his law studies, violence and corruption were endemic in the capital." Quirk said there were sixty-four political assassinations during the term of President Ramón Grau San Martín (1944-48).

He also said the respective heads of the two leading groups, the MSR and the UIR, were given senior positions in the national police and had access to government funds and to "large stores of weapons. The action groups made machismo a way of life."

A few days after the triumph of the revolution, in January 1959, Castro talked about the transforming effect of the possession of a single weapon. "The revolutionary of my childhood walked with a .45-calibre pistol at his waist and wanted to live on the respect it commanded," he said.

Weapons always were an integral part of Castro's adulthood. At age twenty-six, he led a failed armed attack in Santiago on a military barracks of the Batista dictatorship. He was imprisoned. He also captained the successful 1956-58 guerrilla struggle against Batista's army. It was an astonishing triumph, one that was to have global implications for decades. Cuba says the war claimed twenty thousand lives, a number that seems wildly exaggerated to some Cuba-watchers.

When it became obvious that Castro, once in power, was no mere reformer but a revolutionary, he polarized the country. The year 1961 was known for the Bay of Pigs but also as "The Year of the Firing Squad," a reference to the deterrent used by Castroite enforcers that produced five-hundred eighty-seven deaths by one count. Agrarian Reform Chief Antonio Núñez Jiménez said in a speech, according to *Time* magazine, "We will erect the most formidable execution wall in the history of humanity." His opponents promised a hanging for each rebel shot to death.

In 1962, armed struggle took on a whole new meaning with the introduction of Soviet offensive missiles in Cuba. The prospect of nuclear war had millions around the world sitting on edge for almost two weeks as the U.S. and USSR tried to reach a settlement. In the end, the Soviets withdrew their weapons in return for U.S. concessions, including a promise never to invade Cuba. But the guerrilla war waged by Florida-based groups persisted for another three years before forces loyal to Castro finally prevailed.

(Castro once said years ago that Cubans are the only people threatened twice by nuclear weapons. Aside from the crisis in 1962, he said, there was the possibility in 1988 of a South African nuclear attack against Cuban forces fighting alongside the leftist MPLA forces in Angola against South African troops. The weapons were never used. A negotiated settlement to the conflict was reached late that year. In 1989, South Africa disposed of its nuclear arsenal.)

When the Bay of Pigs invasion failed, the United States tried more unobtrusive ways of getting rid of the Cuban leader, including CIA-sponsored assassination attempts in the early 1960s. A U.S. Senate study in 1975 uncovered eight such plots. Castro said the actual figure was much higher. In his 2001 book, *Body of Secrets*, former National Security Agency official James Bamford wrote about a 1962 U.S. plan known as Operation Northwoods. Backed by the Joint Chiefs of Staff, he said the plan called for "innocent people to be shot on American streets; for boats carrying refugees fleeing Cuba to be sunk on the high seas; for a wave of violent terrorism to be launched in Washington, D.C., Miami, and elsewhere.

"People would be framed for bombings they did not commit; planes would be hijacked," Bamford wrote. "Using phony evidence, all of it would be blamed on Castro, thus giving (the chairman of the Joint Chiefs) and his cabal the excuse, as well as the public and international backing, all they needed to launch their war," Bamford said. President Kennedy rejected the proposal.

According to Pentagon documents released in the late 1990s, a parallel early 1960s plan had the goal of creating "an incident which has the appearance of an attack on (U.S. facilities at Guantanamo), thus providing an excuse for use of U.S. military might to overthrow the current government of Cuba."

Under another plan, if a manned Mercury space flight failed, Cuba would be cast as the culprit. "This was to be accomplished by manufacturing various pieces of evidence which would prove electronic interference on the part of the Cubans," according to the plan. Whether the scheme would actually have been implemented if there had been a failed space flight is not known.

Castro has said the combined total of assassination attempts against him, irrespective of sponsorship, numbered well into the hundreds. He has said that more than three thousand people have been killed as a result of foreign-inspired, politically motivated plots against Cuba, most emanating from south Florida.

When Castro visited Chile in 1971 during the leftist government of President Salvador Allende, he told a gathering in Valparaiso that Chileans should be grateful that they don't that they don't live next door to the United States, as was Cuba's fate.

"Alégrense que estén por acá," he said. ("Be happy that you're down here.")

Guns and use of force were a critical component of Castro's Africa policy, especially in Angola and Ethiopia. He sent tens of thousands of troops to the two countries in the late 1970s and 1980s to assist the pro-Soviet governments, both of which were under assault from neighboring armies.

When Ronald Reagan took office in 1981, Washington was alive with rumors about a possible U.S. military attack against Cuba. Secretary of State Alexander Haig favored the idea but Reagan rejected it. But Castro was enhancing Cuba's readiness just in case. Castro began developing a sizable reserve force. Also, in Reagan's first year, the Soviets sent sixty-six-thousand tons of military aid to Cuba, according to State Department estimates. Between 1982 and 1986, these estimates show, the Soviets delivered six-billion-four-hundred-million dollars in military equipment to the island. Toward the end of the Reagan era, Cuba had more than two-hundred-sixty Soviet-made combat aircraft, including MiG jet fighters. Also, the island was ringed with surface-to-air missiles. At one point there were seventeen thousand Soviet troops on the island. Cuba reciprocated for Moscow's generosity by allowing the Soviets to have a bird's eye view of American military activities in South Florida from an intelligence monitoring facility outside Havana manned by a staff of twenty-one hundred.

During the 1980s, the Cuban military had one-hundred-seventy-five-thousand personnel under arms (thousands were in Angola and Ethiopia) and one-hundred-thirty thousand in reserve. As a percentage of total population, few countries, if any, had more troops. With his ambitious defense buildup in the Reagan era, Castro's message to Washington was clear: if you take us on militarily, we may not win but you will pay a heavy price and lose over time.

When impoverishment overtook Cuba in the early 1990s, Castro initiated a series of austerity measures. He brought home all of

Cuba's expeditionary forces and began a large-scale demobiliza-
tion. The military was asked to grow its own food so that more
provisions were available for the civilian population. Active military force levels eventually were reduced to forty-five thousand
from a high of three-hundred-thousand (other estimates put the
peak at closer to two-hundred-thousand). Survival of the revolution became Castro's top priority. He was too broke and his
people too hungry for him to continue his far-flung adventures.
He certainly did not leave Cuba defenseless. Perhaps taking a
cue from Vietnam, a close ally, he built a series of tunnels under
Havana and perhaps elsewhere to store weaponry and food and
to provide a haven for Cubans in the event of an American invasion. (I once was invited to take a peek at one tunnel; it wasn't
very revealing.)

Castro never doubted the American ability to invade and then
establish a government on the island. But he believed that the
tunnels would enable Cuba to mount a determined resistance
while offering safety to the population. As Castro saw it, the U.S.
occupation troops would eventually be forced to withdraw under
pressure from mounting casualties and international outrage.
There was no invasion; his thesis was never put to a test.

Castro knew the American side respected a driven, tena-
cious foe. Twice during the latter part of the twentieth century,
Caribbean regimes that were leftist but essentially defenseless
were brought down in short order by Republican presidents. The

first was in Guatemala in 1954 when the government of Jacobo Árbenz fell victim during the Eisenhower administration to shrewd maneuvering by the CIA in league with rightist military forces. The second was in Grenada in 1983 when U.S. troops under the direction of President Reagan invaded the leftist-led island at a time when the safety of seven hundred American medical students there was in question due to political turmoil. The invasion quickly ousted Grenada's pro-Castro leadership. An election was held soon thereafter, and a pro-American government was installed as a result.

Based on the events in Guatemala and Grenada, Castro calculated that Cuba might be America's next target. Gen. Rafael Del Pino, celebrated for his military exploits on behalf of Castro before defecting in 1987, said the Cuban leader, during a meeting three weeks after the 1983 Grenada invasion, raised the possibility of bombing the Turkey Point nuclear facility in South Florida in the event of American hostilities against Cuba itself. The resulting nuclear contamination would have claimed thousands of lives, probably including many sworn enemies of Castro in the Miami area. So far as I know, Del Pino's account has never been corroborated.

During the 1980s, the Soviets had sought as part of its aid program for Cuba to help the island overcome its grave energy shortages through the construction of a nuclear reactor in the southern city of Cienfuegos. The project proceeded for several years, and to the relief of Floridians, was halted in 1992 because Cuba could not meet the costlier financial terms imposed by the post-Soviet regime. The biggest U.S. concern was that the perceived lack of Cuban expertise could produce a horrific accident, comparable to the one in the Ukraine in 1986, leaving much of the Caribbean and the American southeast vulnerable to deadly nuclear contamination.

With the mothballing of the nuclear reactor project, Castro still had to rely throughout the 1990s on costly oil imports to meet energy needs. He finally got a break in 1999 with the accession of socialist Hugo Chávez as president of Venezuela, a major oil exporter. He soon began selling oil to his Cuban ally at cut-rate prices and provided him with other benefits. Castro finally had someone willing and able to replace the Soviet Union as a benefactor after by far the worst decade in the revolution's history.

CHAPTER 9

A SMALL NATION THINKS BIG

Imagine if the United States had a neighbor ninety miles away with a population of eight billion, a commanding nuclear arsenal and an unremitting hostility toward everything American. It shunned virtually all ties with America, including trade. Its huge military stockpile, coupled with its overall wealth and resources, dwarfed America's. A fanciful story line, of course, but put twenty-first-century America in Cuba's shoes, and Americans might have some idea of what it is like having a huge nuclear bomb-laden Goliath for an enemy. In Cuban' eyes, this basically was the fate of the island for much of the latter part of the 20th Century. In fairness, Fidel Castro, of course, provoked much of the hostility and seemed more comfortable with having America as an enemy than as a friend. In his forty-seven years at the helm Castro only on the rarest of occasions showed an interest in easing frictions with the United States.

Cuba knows what it is like to be the underdog, at least on paper. For every Cuban, there are twenty-seven Americans. In virtually every measure of overall strength, it was hard to exaggerate the American advantage. Cuba was a relative economic pygmy. In his competition with the United States from 1959 on, Castro made up for Cuba's lack of size and resources with extraordinary will and determination, including his creation of an ever-vigilant internal security apparatus. Anyone from within who dared to object to his rule was dealt with harshly. His prisons once bulged with political opponents. One, Ernesto Diaz, was confined for thirty years. Others who were disaffected either fled, usually to South Florida, or just kept quiet. To the extent that Cuba's economy was weak, he could always blame the enduring American embargo, whose first phase was imposed in 1960, before Barack Obama was born. It was strengthened in 1962 and tightened further afterward, although Congress eventually created loopholes for the sale of food and medical equipment.

American hostility, of course, has not been entirely gratuitous. As a daring provocateur, Castro may be unmatched. He seized more than fifty-nine hundred American properties without compensation in the early 1960s, while simultaneously fraternizing with the Soviet Union, a high-risk proposition given the Cold War tensions at the time. In 1962, he agreed to the installation in Cuba of Soviet offensive missiles, almost provoking nuclear war. Washington's missteps, most notably the failed U.S.-sponsored invasion at the Bay of Pigs, helped him consolidate his power. All revolutions need to be attacked by an external enemy in order to be true revolutions, Castro once said, and the United States accommodated him. All the while, Castro roiled the waters with Washington in other ways, backing armed rebel movements elsewhere in the Third World, at least for a time. He helped Moscow achieve some strategic objectives. Surely Castro knew that Washington, faced with such behavior, would not merely just look the other way.

He had long harbored ambitions much grander than merely running the largest island in the Caribbean. While he was still a guerrilla fighter in the summer of 1958, he penned the following note to Celia Sánchez, a friend and confidante: "When this war finishes, a war much longer and bigger will begin: the war that I'm going to launch against them (the Americans). I realize that is going to be my true destiny." A "war" on the United States? This was Castro at his most audacious. Once in power, he moved quickly to establish military and diplomatic ties throughout Africa, much of the Middle East, and with rebel groups in Latin America. All of this buttressed his credentials as a "*tercermundista*," literally "third-worldist" in much of the globe. Beyond Cuba, communism could claim a number of other post-World War II takeovers in large swaths of Europe and Asia. Castro perhaps saw the Cuban revolution as a continuum of a process already under way elsewhere.

In the end, it was an illusion. Over time, the communist regimes in Eastern Europe looked sickly next to their vibrant democratic neighbors to the west. They collapsed. In Asia, communists in

China and post-war Vietnam showed a lot more interest in economic development through capitalism than in spreading revolution. The Soviet Union disintegrated altogether.

For Castro, it was a case of reach exceeding grasp. He had envisioned many "Castroite" regimes but history was not on his side. By 1990, export of revolution was no longer his mission in life. After communism's collapse, he lowered his sights, devoting his final years power mostly to getting Cuba back on its feet economically and exporting medical care to needy countries. Socialism was still a goal but the path to achieving it, at least in Latin America, was left to Venezuela's Hugo Chávez, less radical than Castro but a leader who nonetheless offered an alternative to the political model favored by the United States—and had the money through oil exports to carry out his ideas. He sounded no less anti-American than Castro. He envisioned the day when the rest of Latin America would break free of America's "imperialist" grip and forge a new identity under the banner of socialism. But as of the summer of 2011, the issue for Chávez over the short term was not the hemisphere's future but rather the long-term implications of the discovery of a cancerous tumor, apparently in the pelvic region. It was removed by Cuban doctors. As of late 2011, his health prospects were uncertain.

The United States undoubtedly would have shown more tolerance for Castro in the early years of his revolution if he were a mere dictator. Many Americans were willing to give Castro a chance at the outset, but in just a few years he had alienated almost all segments of American society with his totalitarian ways, firing squads, pro-Soviet policies, property seizures, mass arrests of opponents and the stifling of a once vibrant press. If Washington, less than a decade earlier, had seen fit to sacrifice thirty-three thousand soldiers' lives in distant South Korea to preserve an anti-communist government under attack, it obviously would not take lightly the emergence of a Soviet ally at America's front door. Castro became an American nightmare—and vice-versa. He survived repeated U.S. efforts to bring him down, including assassination attempts and a trade embargo. He gave his collusion with Moscow a cast-in-concrete quality by enshrining the permanence of the Cuban-USSR friendship in Cuba's 1976 constitution.

He became known—and admired—in much of the Third World. He made a mockery of the original intent of the Third World's principal forum, the Non-Aligned Movement (NAM), by trying to push it in a leftward, pro-Soviet direction when he assumed the chairmanship in September 1979 and hosted a NAM conference in Havana that drew fifty-five heads of government. It was one of the largest summit gatherings in history until that point, no small achievement for a country which the United States had tried to isolate diplomatically for years. For me, covering the event was a memorable experience. Anti-American radicals seemed to be everywhere in the plush new *Palacio de Convenciones* in

Havana's eastern end. At a news conference, there was a pro-revolution flavor to all of the early questions asked of summit representatives at the podium. I raised my hand and was called on. Consistent with the rules, I gave my name and affiliation. The room erupted in laughter. Given the overall tenor of the proceedings, it was not a very hospitable environment for a reporter from AP, very much a part of the American news establishment. (It should be pointed out that there were a number of delegations at the summit who represented countries with good or at least "correct" relations with the U.S.) One foreign journalist who seemed particularly interested in befriending me at the summit was a woman correspondent from China. It was, after all, a time, 1979, of growing Chinese-American friendship and continuing frictions between Beijing and Moscow.

At a separate news conference convened by a high-ranking Cuban official at the start of the summit, a questioner asked him about the possible impact on the gathering of an oncoming tropical storm. The Cuban official looked directly at me and openly speculated about the possibility that the storm was the handiwork of forces interested in converting the conference into a flood-riven fiasco. The CIA clearly was the prime suspect but the official did not mention the agency directly. I'll never forget his steely look. The weather was indeed rainy but Havana was spared a direct hit.

The summit was perhaps the high point of Castro's long tenure. Then, things began to backfire. Three months after the conference, the Soviet Union embarrassed Castro by wantonly invading Afghanistan in support of an embattled communist government there. With this action, Moscow had flouted NAM's principles of non-intervention, a particularly egregious move in Cuban eyes because Afghanistan was a founding NAM member. Soviet troops were to remain in Afghanistan for eight years. (I was invited to the Soviet embassy in Washington in 1986 for lunch with several diplomats. They informed me that Moscow was planning to withdraw its troops from Afghanistan. In mock indignation, I shouted, "This is a sellout!" The Soviet hosts thought the comment was hilarious.)

Three months after the Soviet invasion, in April 1980, Castro faced the first domestic crisis of his rule when thousands of his countrymen began fleeing Cuba in boats from the port of Mariel. He dismissed the escapees as "scum." Before the exodus stopped five months later, one hundred and twenty-five thousand had left in search of a better life in America. It was a shattering blow to a country that had tried to portray itself as the wave of the future. (For an account of one family's experience during Mariel, see Addendum 2.)

Castro embarked on an entirely new adventure in early 1985 when he encouraged Latin American countries to renounce their burdensome three-hundred-and-fifty-billion-dollar debt to banks in the United States and Western Europe. At the time, democracy had spread throughout Latin America, but the region's economic fortunes looked bleak, mainly because of the debt. "There is no alternative," Castro told two American interviewers. "The cancellation of the debt or the political death of democratic processes in Latin America." Castro normally was dismissive about electoral practices in the region. *"Elecciones multipartidistas, multi-porquería"* ("Multiparty elections, multi-farce") was a typical barb. Critics said Castro's real purpose in pursuing debt cancellation was two-fold: to instigate bank failures that would cause an economic panic across America and Western Europe, and to liberate Latin Americans from their onerous debts, enabling them to fund badly needed social development programs. Signs sprouted around Cuba saying, *"La deuda latinoamericana es impagable. Hay que cancelarla."* ("Latin America's debt is unpayable. It must be canceled.") But the plan failed to win support in the region and quietly fizzled. Latin Americans apparently believed that debt renunciation would dry up their credit and come back to haunt them. Some elected leaders from the region, besides questioning Castro's motives, no doubt were reluctant to take economic advice from a Caribbean Marxist who was living off Soviet welfare. Castro figured it was worth a try. If the initiative had succeeded, it would have triggered a political and economic revolution in the hemisphere that would have reverberated for decades. Castro would have taken credit and emerged as perhaps the most con-sequential Latin American of the twentieth century. Instead, the proposal died a quiet death and was quickly forgotten.

(In a rare display of tolerance for alternative views, Castro included non-Marxists among speakers at a Latin American debt conference in Havana in July 1985. As a reporter there, I had one eye on Castro as he listened to one tedious speech after another. He was seated near the dais, his head turned sharply to the right, his eyes fixated on each speaker. So far as I could tell, he never averted his gaze during any of the numerous speeches. It was a remarkable display of self-discipline.)

Castro's audacity also was reflected in his Africa policies. A more prudent Latin American leader might have been content to zero in on domestic problems. But Castro had other ideas. He was determined to back anti-colonial struggles in Africa and to help governments in newly independent countries gain stability. In the mid-1970s, there were so many Cuban troops in Africa that Secretary of State Henry Kissinger facetiously wondered whether there were any left back home.

Countries where Cuban troops were sent did not have to pass human rights tests. In Ethiopia, during the seventeen-year reign of Mengistu Haile Mariam, tens of thousands of people were killed, tortured, or detained. Cuban troops were there virtually for the entirety of his rule. (After Mengistu was deposed, I saw him one year at holiday festivities in Cuba as an honored guest of Castro.) Castro also dispatched troops to the West African country of Equatorial Guinea, from which an estimated 25 percent of the population had fled because of the brutality of the regime of President Francisco Macias Nguema.

The heyday of Cuban engagement in Africa began in the mid-1970s. Tens of thousands of Cuban troops did wartime duty in Angola and later Ethiopia, protecting Marxist governments during years-long battles against enemy neighbors. Castro seemed undaunted by the complicated logistics of sending troops off to countries an ocean away, where there was little infrastructure, no support network, long supply lines, and formidable language barriers. As a committed revolutionary, Castro was not easily intimidated by such obstacles.

Cuban troops stayed in Ethiopia for fourteen years and in Angola for almost sixteen. Castro once said that a total of about four hundred thousand Cubans saw service in Angola, a mind-boggling figure considering Cuba's size, roughly ten million at the time. Cuban youths in their late teens were given a choice of either serving in Angola or helping to build tunnels under Havana and elsewhere to store food and hide weapons in the event of an American invasion. Castro's deployment of troops to Africa won him friends on the continent and served Soviet interests as well. It was a way of compensating Moscow for its generous subsidies to Cuba over the years. Angola was doubly important strategically because of its large oil reserves. (State Department officials said Angola used oil revenues to pay for the Cuban troops.) To the extent that Moscow had a foothold in Africa, it was largely because of Castro's actions.

Cuba reportedly had fifty-five thousand troops in Angola in 1988, forty thousand in the southern region where fierce fighting occurred. Another key foreign combatant was South Africa, then under apartheid, which was worried its security would be jeopardized if Marxism were left unchecked in nearby Angola. But when Cuban war planes seized control of the skies from the South Africans in 1987, the long Angola war soon ended with the pro-Soviet faction in Angola prevailing and firmly in control of the capital. Some analysts say the battle for Cuito Carnavale in southern Angola during this period may have been the bloodiest conflict in the written history of the African mainland.

No one could have predicted the positive turn the war-ravaged southern African region would take following the settlement in Angola. Perhaps tired of being cast as a pariah state and weakened by war and by U.S. economic sanctions, South Africa soon decided to release Nelson Mandela from prison, to grant independence to its colony to the northwest, Namibia, and to start dismantling not only apartheid but also its nuclear weapons program. Far-off Cuba had contributed indirectly to each of these developments, a remarkable feat—but at a high cost. The remains of more than two thousand dead (the unconfirmed official figure)

Cuban soldiers were repatriated and buried in Cuban soil. That death toll was roughly equivalent to fifty-four thousand dead U.S. soldiers, taking into account the difference in populations.

The time between Mandela's release from prison and his accession as the elected president of South Africa was a mere four years. He acknowledged the decisive Cuban role southern Africa a year after winning his freedom: "The Cuban international-ists have made a contribution to African independence, freedom and justice unparalleled for its principled and selfless character," he told a large gathering in Havana in July 1991.

But Castro's future hardly looked bright. The communist regimes in Eastern Europe had been falling, depriving Cuba of profitable political and commercial ties. The final blow came in late 1991, when Cuba's most important ally and aid donor, the Soviet Union, died at age seventy-four. The demise of Cuba's allies across the Atlantic ushered in the worst depression in Cuban history. Castro for the first time was forced to look inward lest his three-decade rule implode. There were to be no more mil-itary adventures abroad. Drastic cuts were made in the number of military personnel. Castro paid far less attention to foreign affairs so he could concentrate on saving his revolution. With communism on the ropes in 1991, Castro came under heavy pressure from sympathizers to undertake economic reform. Ini-tially, at least, he was unbending, telling his countrymen at one point, *"Viva la rigidez!"* ("Long live rigidity!") He equated reform with defeat, citing the example set by reformist President Mikhail Gorbachev of Russia, under whose watch the once-proud USSR disintegrated. Internationally, Castro had few close friends beyond the Third World. Many in Miami thought Castro's end was near. Eventually, he agreed to some capitalist reforms, and the economy began a recovery at mid-decade. But it took years—and the election of Hugo Chávez in Venezuela in 1998—for Castro to feel more secure economically. Finally, he had found somebody who could replace the long-gone Soviet subsidies. For Castro, Chávez was a godsend. The Venezuelan spent billions through subsidized oil sales to Cuba and providing help in other ways.

Castro always yearned to have allies in the hemisphere so that the United States would have more than one hostile country to contend with in the region. There were some breakthroughs for the left: Chile, (1970), Grenada (1979), and Nicaragua (1979). The regimes in each all were ousted eventually with varying degrees of American intervention. Venezuela was different. Chávez stood up to the Americans and didn't care what they thought.

Castro developed an appreciation for Chávez long before the Venezuelan was elected. A 1994 Chávez visit to Cuba after the Venezuelan's release from prison was a mutual admiration festival. Four years later, Chávez was elected president. Much like Castro himself, Chávez had demonstrated a penchant for risk-taking and radical politics. Castro had led an armed attack against the Batista government in 1953; Chávez launched his own insurrection in 1992 against an unpopular elected government. He was arrested and imprisoned. He was pardoned after two years, much like Castro was after his insurrection and imprisonment thirty-nine years earlier. Both became leaders of their respective countries four years after their release from prison. Castro shot his way into power in 1959, and Chávez emerged through a free election in 1998. The generation gap didn't seem to make much difference. (When Castro seized power in 1959 at age thirty-two, Chávez was a four-year-old tot.)

In return for Venezuela's assistance, Castro sent thousands of Cuban specialists to that country, notably doctors and health care workers. They collaborated in other areas as well. So tight was the relationship that Castro said the two countries had become one—"Venecuba," as he once called it. (A 2006 State Department cable, released by Wikileaks, said the two countries had forged an "axis of mischief," a reference to their efforts to promote leftist causes elsewhere in the region.)

With Venezuela's help, Cuba's economy did better for a time, but a drought from 2001 to 2003 proved costly. (At one point, Cuba even delivered water to the parched eastern region by train.) But the economy rebounded somewhat and by 2005, signs saying "*Vamos Bien*" ("We're doing well") appeared around Havana with Fidel's picture alongside.

The size of Venezuela's assistance to Cuba has been in dispute. The highly-respected *Economist* magazine estimated it at three and a half billion dollars annually as of 2011. Cuban-born economist Carmelo Mesa Lago of the University of Pittsburgh put the figure at eight billion dollars in 2010. If correct, this would easily top Cuba's combined revenues from tourism, nickel sales, exports of medical services, and remittances. (Sugar, once Cuba's chief export, represented only a small percentage of the total as of 2007.) It was difficult to exaggerate the importance to the Castros of Chávez's personal role in ensuring generous aid flows. In 2005, Fidel confidently predicted that a planned Venezuelan-funded electricity upgrade would end the Cuba's blackout curse — so long as Chávez was not assassinated. As Fidel implicitly saw it, he could not trust a successor leader to provide assistance to the degree that Chávez had. But in the summer of 2011, illness replaced assassination as Cuba's chief concern about Chávez's survivability. Cuban doctors removed a cancerous tumor, prompting questions about whether his life was in danger or, if it wasn't, whether he could handle a reelection campaign in 2012. .

Cuba had been dealt one near-lethal blow with the end of Soviet subsidies two decades earlier. The possible end of *Chavista* rule in Venezuela would be yet another because it is doubtful, as Fidel had indicated, that any successor would be as indulgent toward the island as Chávez. But Cuba was better positioned to absorb a cutback in Venezuelan aid than it had been to handle the sudden disappearance of European communism in the early 1990s. In contrast to that era, Cuba by 2010 had been receiving substantial income from tourism and remittances from overseas Cubans, not to mention dollar-earning Cuban medical missions which serve abroad. The country's less rigid economic policies also permitted self-employment and small business operations. Plans were even afoot to develop more than a dozen luxury golf resorts, including plush apartments, for use by foreign vacationers. Cuba also was attempting to tap into large oil deposits off its north coast but progress toward actual exports was expected to take years. Over the short term, though, the big variable in Cuban thinking as of late 2011 was Chávez's survivability.

Restless for new challenges abroad after focusing on domestic issues, Fidel turned in 2004—sometimes in collaboration with Venezuela—to the export of medical services, a path that would enable him to show off to the world Cuba's wealth of medical talent, help the infirm and earn money for Cuba at the same time.

Cuba won many friends in Latin America and Africa with an extraordinarily ambitious program called "*Operación Milagro*" (Operation Miracle). In these regions between 2004 and 2010, Cuba opened a number of eye care centers and Cuban doctors performed, according to official statistics, more than one and a half million sight-restoring cataract operations. A high percentage of these patients were poor and would have had no hope of paying for eye care at local rates. Francisca Antonia Guevara of El Salvador said the difference in her sight after her cataract operation in Havana was a night-versus-day transformation. (The Venezuelan government normally picks up some of the cost for procedures involving poor, non-Cuban patients.)

"As someone of few resources, I couldn't afford it (in El Salvador)," Mrs. Guevara said. "With the bad economic situation we have there, how are we going to afford this?" She spoke to a reporter after ending her brief stay at a Havana hospital. Cuba charges eye patients from middle-class countries; Portugal, for example, was paying a reported eighteen hundred dollars per patient. Panamá suspended Cuba's eye program without explanation, although it is believed that the government bowed to appeals from local eye doctors who may have complained that the presence of Cuban eye specialists meant fewer customers for them.

Under the program, Cuba generally supplies the technical expertise and Venezuela pays the overhead. In Cuba itself, the Pando Ferrer Hospital in Havana reportedly can perform three hundred eye procedures a day. Most involve cataracts but treatment for glaucoma also is available. Castro said in 2005 that fifteen hundred such operations were being performed daily in Cuba. (It is not clear how long those operations persisted at that rate. At some point, the supply of elderly patients in need of cataract operations had to run out.)

Other manifestations of Cuban outreach included an anticholera campaign in Haiti in 2010 and the care Cuba provided to many children from Ukraine who were victims of the nuclear disaster at Chernobyl in 1986. Also, Cuba sent more than two thousand health care specialists and tons of medical equipment to Pakistan in response to an earthquake in 2005. In addition, Cuba offered scholarships to one thousand poor Pakistanis to attend the ELAM medical school in Cuba. As of 2011, there were three hundred fifty-five Cuban health care workers in Guatemala and five hundred two Guatemalan graduates of ELAM in Havana.

There obviously are gaps in Cuba's universal health care system but there is no denying the extraordinary effort the country has made to deliver health services to the entire population, however shabby some facilities may be. The country's infant mortality and life expectancy rates rank with those of the most developed countries, according to Cuban statistics. Vaccinations and other forms of preventive medicine are universally available and Cubans with disabilities generally receive decent care, according to anecdotal evidence. (Some of the disabled do the family shopping because they have the right to maneuver their wheelchairs to the front of the line to pay for their selections. Other shoppers are stuck with a lengthy wait.)

As in every country, there have been grave instances of health care neglect in Cuba. One of the most notorious was the deaths of twenty-four patients at a psychiatric hospital outside Havana in January 2010 as a result of unseasonably cold temperatures and undernourishment.

After a year's investigation, the director of the hospital, Wilfredo Castillo Donate, was found guilty of abandonment of the disabled and diversions of funds. He was sentenced to fifteen years. Six others, all supervisors, received sentences ranging from seven to fourteen years. The *Granma* newspaper reported that the hospital staff failed to keep the patients warm and well-fed. A clinical assessment of the patients found "signs of malnutrition and a large number of cases of anemia and vitamin deficiency," despite the the hospital's receipt of enough food for two-thousand, four-hundred-fifty-eight patients, at a time when only one-thousand, four-hundred-eighty-four beds were occupied. The report substantiated complaints that hospital staff stole food and blankets that were sold later on the black market.

"The neglect and irregularities were already problems before, and you wonder how it is that no one saw them," Marta María Céspedes, a retired public affairs analyst, told the IPS news agency. "Weren't there inspections?"

Cuba, according to official statistics, has more doctors per capita than any country in the world. Many promising students choose medicine as a career because it satisfies a humanitarian instinct—or, perhaps more importantly, offers the opportunity to earn hard currency through service in one of Cuba's many foreign medical missions.

As of 2010, Cuba had thirty-eight thousand doctors and other health care workers serving in Third World countries, official figures show. Among foreign medical school graduates, thirty thousand were from Africa as of 2010. Much like Cuba's dogged military interventions in Africa a generation earlier, its ambitious medical outreach to some of the world's poorest areas was amazing in its scope, given Cuba's small size.

Katrin Hansing, an American who is writing a book about Cuba's medical diplomacy, told PBS, "If you have ever been to any developing countries where there are a lot of Cuban doctors or other professionals, Cuban doctors are loved, and, by extension, Cuba is loved in those countries.'

Sending Cuban doctors abroad—and training young foreigners to become doctors for service back home—helps the regime project an image of the island far different from the one that often portrays it as a serial human rights violator. It also provides a steady income, at least from countries with the ability to pay for Cuba's services. .

In a speech in 2005, less than a year before illness sidelined him, Castro talked about the priority given to health care by the revolution. Since 1959, his first year in office, he said Cuba had trained eighty-five-thousand-eight-hundred-eighty-seven medical doctors, adding that it was hosting more than twelve thousand medical students from foreign countries in that year.

Roughly half were from South America and the Caribbean. Of these, about ten thousand were enrolled at the Latin American Medical School (ELAM) in Havana, a huge number by the standards of typical medical schools. The number from the United States was one-hundred-twenty-nine. Room, board, and tuition were free (the biggest drawback was the cramped quarters in dormitories). At Cuba's request, the Congressional Black Caucus nominates students for possible admission to the school because of the low living standards in many CBC districts. According to Cuban officials, all receive full scholarships on the condition that they return to their home region once their studies are completed. The official figure for the number of foreign graduates was eight thousand five hundred eighty five from thirty countries as of March 2011.

The U.S. government, always trying to undermine Cuba, began in 2006 to encourage Cuban doctors serving abroad to defect. Show up at the nearest U.S. embassy and you get a visa, the doctors are told. A Wall Street Journal article said that as of mid-December 2010, one thousand five hundred seventy four Cuban doctors had abandoned their overseas posts and resettled in the United States. This was a relatively small percentage of the total. In Cuba, doctors earn only about twenty-five dollars a month but those in foreign missions get a fifty-dollar bonus, payable to their family in Cuba. In addition, they get direct payment in the host country of between one-hundred-fifty and one thousand dollars a month, depending on their mission, the Journal said. (In Cuba itself, it takes the average worker, doctors included, four or more years just to earn a thousand dollars.)

Dr. Darsey Ferrer, a dissident doctor in Cuba, said Cuban physicians "fight to get onto a mission because they can accumulate thousands of dollars." There were other incentives to sign up for the program. The Journal article said that about eight hundred doctors serving in Venezuela had defected to the United States by the end of 2010. Most of the rest came from Colombia and Curazao (these may have been escaped doctors from nearby Venezuela), as well as Guatemala and Perú. Others have come from Africa, the Middle East, and even distant Fiji. A *New York Times* account said that as a result of migration and desertion, there are six thousand Cubans in the South Florida health care industry. A Cuban-sponsored documentary on Cuba's foreign missions said "dropouts' from foreign missions average only 2 percent. It made no distinction between those who return home ahead of schedule and those who desert. Cuba goes to extraordinary lengths to prevent defections by doctors serving overseas. An earlier Journal article, in August 2010, reported that in some countries Cuban doctors work very long hours, are not permitted to drive a car, to leave their dwelling after a certain hour, to speak to the media, and must associate only with "revolutionaries."

Even before the U.S. visa program for Cuban doctors took effect, Castro castigated the U.S. for systematically "snatching" doctors from the countries where they are trained. He called the practice "scandalous" and said that a joint study by Harvard and the World Health Organization showed that fully 24 percent of doctors in the United States were immigrants. The figures for Canada, Great Britain, and New Zealand were higher.

Dr. James Thompson, a Houston psychologist, came away inspired by the Cuban health care system after a visit to the island with other Americans in 2010.

"Health care and education are provided to all citizens at no cost," he said on his return. "I was impressed by the loving, caring attitudes of the health care providers with whom we met. I didn't see long lines at clinics in spite of the fact that the doctors are pro-active and go out in the neighborhoods to assist needy patients." (Thompson's views cannot be accepted at face value because of Cuba's record of staging events for foreign visitors.) In all my visits to Cuba, I never heard a description of the health care system as glowing as Thompson's.

The guided tours of American academics and other experts are scripted and don't include the many health centers with long lines and shabby facilities. There are positive aspects to the system. Part of the job of one Cuban friend was to go door-to-door to encourage residents to visit a dentist if they had not had a recent checkup. The care is free but sometimes falls short, as was the case with a woman whose dentist insisied on extracting a bad tooth even though he had no novocaine available. She vowed never to see a dentist in Cuba again. (For more on dentistry in Cuba, see Addendum 2.)

It is uncertain how rare her experience was but overall it is doubtful that many Cubans would trade the care they receive—dental or medical—in Cuba for what is available elsewhere in much of the rest of Latin America, where treatment can range from mediocre to poor to non-existent for many. Rosa Martinez, a blogger, and frequent critic of the health care system, says: "Any Cuban who gets a sore throat, catches dengue fever, chicken pox, hepatitis or any illness can be treated at a first aid unit anywhere in our country." But another blogger, Alfredo Fernández, asked, "When did we stop caring that our hospitals had deteriorated to the point that they are today?" (See Addendum 2 for more from Martínez and Fernández.)

Because of Cuba's large investment in training doctors, none is allowed to emigrate. When the expertise of skilled doctors from developed countries is needed, Cuba invites them to the island to train local doctors in the latest techniques. Sending Cuban physicians abroad for such instruction is ruled out because of the possibility of defection.

With tens of thousands of doctors and medical professionals serving abroad, medical care in Cuba has declined, leaving some residents complaining about the government's priorities. Some clinics are short-staffed and others have closed. Complained one Havana resident after a long wait at a clinic, "Charity begins at home." Anecdotal evidence suggests months-long waits for special treatment are not uncommon. A former Cuba correspondent for Spanish Television, Vicente Botín, reports in a book on a Havana woman who was frustrated by the doctor shortage in Cuba. Police were summoned when she hung a sheet on her balcony with the words "Trade me to Venezuela." She told the officers, "Look, *compañeros*, I'm as revolutionary as the next guy, but if you want to see a Cuban doctor, you have to go to Venezuela."

There are continual reports that the best care and facilities in Cuba are reserved for hard-currency-paying foreigners, a situation that other countries practice as well. That issue gained international attention in 1991 when a prominent Cuban neurosurgeon, Dr. Hilda Molina, ran afoul of Cuban authorities after she objected to a government order to treat foreigners only at a neurosurgery center in Havana that she had founded a few years earlier. The government demand reflected its urgent need to obtain foreign exchange to confront a dire economic situation.   But Molina argued that Cubans should take precedence over foreigners. She resigned her post. Her outrage toward the government was evident during an interview I had with her at her modest home in Havana in the early 1990's. All told, the government denied her permission to leave the country for more than fifteen years to visit her expatriate son, his Argentine wife and their children. This stand was consistent with Cuba's policy of not allowing doctors (except those sent on missions) to leave the country. In 2009, the Cuban officials relented, and Dr. Molina, the once a committed revolutionary, was able to reunite with her family in Argentina.

CHAPTER 10

A DIPLOMATIC LINK IS ESTABLISHED

Jimmy Carter was far more tolerant of some dictatorships than he was of others. In his first few months in office he broke U.S. military ties with the several unelected governments with poor human rights records while reaching out to Cuba's communist government. In September 1977, after less than eight months in office, Carter's administration and the government of Fidel Castro opened diplomatic offices in each other's capitals. The two countries were actually on speaking terms for the first time in 16 years. But there was no exchange of ambassadors. They moved back into the same buildings that they had used previously. On the day when the Americans reclaimed their old seaside embassy, AP reporter Dick Pyle found a dusty Coke machine in the basement. The cost per bottle reflected the 1961 price: five cents. More than three decades later the two countries still don't have diplomatic relations but Carter apparently enjoys going to Cuba. And Fidel is always on his appointment list. During his last visit, in 2010, he called him an "old friend." Such displays of camaraderie irritate conservative Cuban-American groups which have been highly successful in pressuring successive administrations not only to preserve the embargo but also to support dissidents and to keep on the air U.S. government-sponsored radio and TV stations tailored for Cuban audiences.

Castro's stock in the United States, never high, plummeted during the Carter presidency when he consented to the 1980 Mariel boat lift, which brought one-hundred-twenty-five thousand disaffected Cubans to south Florida. During the exodus, it was disclosed that Castro, in an extraordinarily hostile act, had secretly placed thousands of common criminals and mentally ill Cubans aboard some departing boats.

Many Americans believed that U.S. authorities should never have admitted the refugees. They were ill-prepared for life in America. Newly arrived children caused overcrowding in Florida schools. Health clinics also were overburdened. Less than two months after the Mariel boat lift was called off, Carter's re-election bid ended in failure. Public dissatisfaction with Carter's handling of the exodus from Cuba no doubt cost him votes. Matched against Ronald Reagan, he carried only six states.

Life was often difficult for American diplomats assigned to the Havana office and for their Cuban counterparts in Washington. The latter had to receive State Department permission to go outside the Washington Beltway (except for a Beltway-hugging Virginia shopping center). American diplomats assigned to Cuba suffered harassment and the reverse was true as well. Intending to go to work in the morning diplomats assigned to each other's country sometimes found their tires had mysteriously flattened overnight. Outside the American office in Havana, diplomats could look out on a large nearby billboard that read: "*Señores imperialistas: no les tenemos absolutamente ningún miedo.*" ("Imperialists: We have absolutely no fear of you.")

Cuban diplomats in Washington were excluded from official invitation lists to attend, for example, inaugurations, State of the Union addresses or other official functions. It was much the same for the Americans in Havana. Until the Obama administration, the State Department had decreed that no U.S. official of a rank higher than mid-level could meet with Cuban officials in Washington. Cuba's posture toward American diplomats assigned to Cuba was frosty as well. One Reagan-era chief of mission, Curt Kammen, was so frozen out that he returned to Washington ahead of schedule to accept a different assignment. One of Kammen's successors informed the State Department in a cable that he was pleased with the access he was having to official circles. President Reagan's top aide for Latin America at the time, Elliott Abrams, brusquely served notice to the envoy that he was not sent to Havana to improve relations.

The U.S. diplomatic mission in Havana was quite large but over many years virtually its only function was to confer with would-be migrants and the Cuban government about migration issues. Political issues were off the table. (The Obama administration indicated an interest in opening discussions on improving relations. Raúl Castro responded positively only to be contradicted by Fidel, who reportedly said his brother had been misinterpreted.)

In the first fifty years after the revolution, more than one and a half million Cubans left the island for the United States; countless others yearned to leave but, absent other options, were stuck except those willing to pay a smuggler with a high-speed boat or to try a high-risk escape on a makeshift boat or raft.

Since 1995, the United States has been authorized to approve, partly through a visa lottery system, requests to migrate from twenty thousand lottery "winners" annually (although the actual number of departures was believed to be lower). Each departure meant one fewer disgruntled Cuban on the island, one fewer for the revolution to feed, house, and employ. It also usually meant more income for the government from taxes on phone calls from the migrants to the island and on remittances sent by the departed to friends and family in Cuba. In addition, the migrants had to leave behind all but small personal belongings. Days before the migrant's departure, an inspector took inventory of the family house to clarify what could stay and what couldn't.

In May of 1985, the Reagan administration began beaming anti-Castro programming across the island through a new station called Radio Martí, a mix of news, entertainment and anti-communist commentary. Judging by my travels around Havana at the time, the station had numerous listeners. Castro said the station would have no impact, a statement which precluded any effort to jam it. Radio Martí remained on the air for five years without interference. Jamming commenced in March 1990, coinciding with the concurrent jamming of a new U.S. anti-regime media instrument, TV Martí. Absent many listeners and viewers because of the interference, the two stations appeared to have minimal impact within Cuba. But, as of 2011, they remained on the air through continued congressional support.

The last high ranking U.S. official to go to Havana was roving U.S. ambassador Vernon Walters, who went there on a secret visit in 1982. (Word of the visit was leaked afterward by Cuban officials to reporters in Europe.) Walters, a former deputy CIA director, spent several hours with Castro. The meeting changed nothing. In a light moment, though, they talked about their respective educations in Jesuit schools as teens. In an interview with me, Walters said he told Castro that he remained a Jesuit: "*Yo me quedé fidel*,"— "I remained faithful." The implication was that Fidel didn't. Castro laughed. (In present day Spanish, faithful is *fiel*. In Spanish, it is *fidel,* or so Walters explained it to me. Walters' linguistic talents were legendary around Washington. He was fluent in seven languages.

Beyond Walters' jocular moment with Castro, there were other flashes of humor, albeit rare, between the two sides. In the early 1980s, Myles Frechette, head of the Cuban office at the State Department, read with interest a Cuban newspaper account of a speech in which Frechette was called a "troglodyte" (cave dweller), among other slurs. The mischievous Frechette phoned Cuba's top diplomat in Washington, Ramón Sánchez Parodi, and asked him if he could obtain a copy of the entire account because, he joked, it would give him a valuable career boost.

For many outsiders, the remittances that Cuban expatriates send back home are simply just a number. But these cash out-flows, estimated at between eight-hundred-million dollars and one-billion annually, have been a salvation for recipients on the island. Yoani Sánchez, the dissident Havana blogger, explains:" ... (T)housands of teenagers, the self-employed, seniors, students and babies depend on the uninterrupted growth in the flow between the families in exile and those on the island. In many Cuban homes the personal ability of thousands of individuals to overcome depends on maintaining this bridge, and their future as citizens rests in the arms of solidarity extended from outside."

Cubans on the island sometimes cope by relentlessly ingratiat-ing themselves with the regime while concealing their hostility. In her blog, Sánchez told of neighbors, a married couple named Bebe and Pablito, who would ritualistically go door-to-door exhorting neighbors not to miss an upcoming speech by Fidel at the plaza or a regime-sponsored parade or anniversary celebration. The couple reportedly served as trusted custodians for a petition that more than eight million Cubans signed (not voluntarily) in 2002 insisting that the country's socialist system be declared irreversible. It is now enshrined in the Constitution. One day Bebe and Pablito shocked the neighborhood by turning in their party documents at a meeting. They had secretly taken part in—and were winners in—the U.S. visa lottery. They soon settled in Miami suburb of Hialeah, their days as fake pro-Castro militants behind them.

Fidel often described the groups opposed to him as "*grupúsculos*," meaning they were tiny and inconsequential. That description was reinforced in a leaked Wikileaks cable, which alleged that a former chief of the U.S. diplomatic mission, Jonathan Farrar, said that dissidents "are more concerned with receiving money than spreading their proposals to wider sectors of Cuban society." Moreover, polling of Cubans seeking to emigrate to the U.S. disclosed "practically a total ignorance of the personalities in the dissident movement and their organizations," according to the leaked material. It was obvious, Farrar concluded, that the dissidents lacked "resonance among the Cuban people" and spend a lot of energy "obstructing each other." The leak delighted Cuban officials and reinforced what they had believed all along.

Taking aim at anti-Castro groups in Miami and Madrid, Farrar said dissidents complained that exiles were actually trying to discredit them "so that they (the exiles) can take power when the Castros are gone." He said that he doubted that exiles would play a significant role in a post-Castro government. Instead, the immediate successors probably would be mid-level officials who had served under the Castros, he said.

Some of Farrar's comments were echoed by Moisés Rodríguez Quesada, a secret Cuban agent who alleged that he duped the U.S. mission in Havana into believing that he was a human rights activist.

As such, Rodríguez enjoyed easy access to the mission, participated in meetings there, and once was even flown to Washington for consultations with State Department officials and meetings with U.S.-based anti-Castro human rights groups.

He discussed his activities in a March 2011 interview with the Communist Party newspaper *Granma* after retiring from his work as a spy. Rodríguez said that the U.S. diplomatic mission, formally known as the U.S. Interests Section, functioned as "the center of design and direction of the counter-revolution" in Cuba.

In the 1990s, he said, hopes rose among U.S. officials that with the defeat of communism in Eastern Europe and the Soviet Union, Castro, too, might be vulnerable.

In its reports to Washington, he said, the Interests Section exaggerated the number of human rights groups being formed in

Cuba. "The more reports we sent about (new) groups, the more money they sent us"—support that, he said, "was linked to Miami Mafia groups used by the U.S. government to channel large sums of money."

To the extent that dissident groups were active, the regime at times showed tolerance, then cracked down. Scores of arrests in February 1996 shut down an opposition umbrella group known as *Concilio Cubano* (Cuban Council) a week ahead of a planned all-party congress. Those arrested were released after a few nasty days in confinement but the group essentially was put out of business.

Rodríguez said he doubted the sincerity of Cubans who called themselves human rights activists. In majority of the cases, "the first chance they get they flee the country," he said. He added that he had permanent access to the Interests Section. "I could go as often as I wanted," he said. "I was well received, thanks to my long record as a 'counter- revolutionary': that was the guarantee."

Castro invariably referred to the embargo as a *"bloqueo"* (blockade), which is actually a misnomer because it erroneously suggests that no country could trade with Cuba. But there is some validity to Castro's claim that America's Cuba policy was purchased by his South Florida enemies through contributions to the most forceful anti-Castro candidates in U.S. elections. Take away just a fraction of the strong support of Cuban-Americans for George W. Bush in 2000, and Democrat Al Gore wins not only Florida but the presidency. On the other hand, the embargo is widely considered to be a failure because the Castros have survived it and given them an excuse for the country's poor economic performance. But the embargo is far less punishing than it once was. American food products flow freely into Cuba these days and non-food U.S. products, such as wearing apparel, often arrive in Cuba through third countries. The U.S. is the world's fifth largest exporter of goods to Cuba.

After taking power in 2001, President George W. Bush saw a policy of increased economic denial as the best way to weaken Castro. He appointed Cuban-American hardliners to senior positions. His government cracked down on illegal travel by Americans to Cuba, including an American grandmother, Joan Slote, seventy-five, who was fined more than nine-thousand-eight-hundred dollars by the government after her return from a cycling trip in Cuba. Technically, the travel was legal but not the eighteen dollars she spent there on souvenirs, under terms of the Trading with the Enemy Act.

Bush also took steps to curb travel by Cuban-Americans to Cuba and to cut down family-to-family cash flows to the island. (Obama subsequently eased some of these restrictions.) As of 2004, it was the official policy of the U.S. government to actively undermine any effort by Cuba to facilitate a transition of power in

Cuba from Fidel Castro to Raúl. Nonetheless, Washington was helpless to avoid that very outcome when Fidel fell ill in 2006; a seamless succession to Raúl quickly took place.

Espinosa Chepe, the economist/dissident, says the regime has been able to parlay the embargo to its advantage. "If anything has benefited the long nightmare of totalitarianism in Cuba, it has been the intolerance of extremist sectors in Florida," he says. A 2009 poll by Bendixen & Associates of Miami showed that Cuban-Americans were evenly split on whether the U.S. embargo should be lifted. In an earlier time, embargo supporters had a healthy advantage.

On the Cuban side, the most divisive issue apart from the embargo was the continuing detention in the U.S. of five Cuban intelligence officers convicted in Miami of espionage. They were sentenced to long prison terms. Cuba maintained that the men, imprisoned since 1999, were merely attempting to monitor potential anti-Cuba terrorist activities by Miami militants, of which there had been a long history. No foreign policy goal had been given higher priority by Cuba after 2000 than the release of the five. Their detention gave the regime another anti-American club to swing at the U.S. The national campaign on behalf of the five was relentless. A dozen years after their imprisonment, almost every Cuban knew who Antonio, René, Ramón, Gerardo, and Fernando, known collectively as as "*los cinco*" (the five), were.

This billboard sat for years in plain view of the American diplomatic mission in Havana. Translation: "Imperialists: We Have Absolutely No Fear of You!" After more than two decades, it was taken down without explanation.

CHAPTER 11

THE COMMITTEES FOR THE DEFENSE

Cuba's main weapon in detecting subversives has been the Committees for the Defense of the Revolution. The main task of these block-by-block groups is to be on the lookout for unauthorized gatherings or strange faces in their neighborhood. The committees were founded in September 1960. Castro was aware that the CIA had been able to topple Guatemala's leftist government, led by President Jacobo Árbenz, in a matter of days in 1954. Castro's CDRs, as they were known, were insurance against a similar outcome in Cuba.

Seven months after the committees were established, Castro suspected that an American-sponsored attack was imminent. During one feverish April weekend, some two hundred thousand suspects were rounded up, many pinpointed by local defense committees. Sure enough, a U.S.-armed and -financed Cuban rebel group soon attacked at the Bay of Pigs on the south coast. The Kennedy administration had hoped that the invasion would spark a national uprising that would oust Castro. But it took his forces only seventy-two hours to defeat the invaders. No one knows what would have happened without the mass CDR-led roundup beforehand.

Far from deposing Castro, the doomed counter-revolutionary invasion left him stronger than ever. He emerged as a giant killer, capable of overcoming almost any obstacle. Over time, of course, he made mistakes and suffered defeats, much like any other leader.

Besides their security role, the CDRs also perform social services. They ensure children are up to date with their vaccinations, dispense monthly ration books to neighbors, and organize cleanups and parties. They set up literacy drives and blood donations and convene "popular tribunals" to dispense justice to petty thieves or to people of questionable loyalty to the regime. (I assume the quality of the services performed by individual CDR units in carrying out these tasks varies greatly around the country. Stories are told about how some CDR captains bully neighbors or engage in illicit for-profit activities. Many others, of course, carry out their duties admirably.)

On the thirtieth anniversary of the CDRs, in 1990, Castro said the committees must remain vigilant. "We want to always have a proud and independent homeland instead of a Yankee colony," he said. "We must save the Revolution. We must save socialism. This is the task we urge the seven-and-a-half million CDR members to undertake."

One CDR role was to organize *"actos de repudio"* (acts of repudiation), which are street demonstrations in front of dissidents' homes. I can remember the day in March 1990 when I was alerted to one such gathering at the Havana home of Gustavo Arcos, once a close ally of Castro who later spent many years in prison for counter-revolutionary activities. The mob of several score hurled insults and rocks at the three-story house. (Arcos once told me seven other families lived there.) A government TV crew, alerted in advance, was taping the proceeding. One man in the crowd spotted me (I look like an American) and shouted: *"Ha llegado la CIA!"* ("The CIA has arrived!") We both laughed. Soon the gathering dispersed. It was a clear message to Arcos (and his friends) that he was being watched and should rein in his dissent. It is a tactic the regime has used many times over the years to scare opponents.

Days later, I went back to Arcos's home. Mrs. Arcos cautiously opened the door; the look on her face suggested that I, an American, was not welcome, certainly not so soon after the recent mob scene outside. Sensing her discomfort, I considered leaving but Gustavo spotted me at the door and invited me in. He seemed unperturbed by what had happened days earlier, looking on it as something dissidents must endure. We had a pleasant chat.

Increasingly, the regime prefers harassment to imprisonment. The last big roundup occurred in 2003 when seventy-five government opponents were arrested for anti-regime activities and sentenced after brief trials to long prison terms, most for more than twenty years. Internationally, the crackdown was a public relations disaster for the regime. The plight of the prisoners was highlighted by frequent demonstrations by the "Ladies in White," relatives of the detainees who were taunted by regime supporters during their periodic peaceful marches through Havana's streets. Persistent mediation efforts by Catholic church representatives helped to secure the release of many prisoners. All were freed within eight years. Some got early release for health reasons. The majority of the seventy-five were deported to Spain in exchange for their freedom.

The drawback to imprisonment of dissidents for the regime is that they can become a rallying point for its critics abroad. If they live at home, the regime is spared such criticism and can keep track of who the dissidents' friends are through surveillance of the home. It has become increasingly sensitive to international public opinion. It realizes that with modern communications, arrests of agitators quickly become fodder for international rights groups.

Arcos was four months younger than Castro. Virtually his entire life was spent dissenting against the status quo: first against Batista, then against Castro. It was Castro who recruited him to join the high-risk landing of eighty-two armed rebel soldiers by boat in eastern Cuba in 1956, the start of the rebel war against Batista. Arcos was shot in his right leg; he suffered pain for the rest of his life. Once in power, Castro named Arcos ambassador to Belgium, where he soon became concerned about Castro's dictatorial tendencies and his embrace of the Soviet Union. After returning to Cuba, he became a dissenter. He was soon imprisoned and spent much of the rest of his life behind bars. Arcos died in 2006 at age seventy-nine. His paid a great personal price for his ultimately unsuccessful pursuit of a democratic Cuba.

Elizardo Sánchez had been a dissident for forty-four years as of 2011. During eight of those years, he was a political prisoner. He is founder and president of the Cuban Commission for Human Rights and National Reconciliation. He works the rights issue in a way that doesn't provoke the authorities to take action against him. But thanks to Sánchez's many media and human rights contacts, he spreads word both within and beyond Cuba's borders of detentions (and releases) of rebels. Through his many contacts, Sánchez keeps track of such cases. His numbers show there were eight-hundred-two detentions, usually for brief periods, during the first five months of 2010.

At times, a security agent can be seen in a car outside the Sánchez home in the Playa section of Havana, watching comings and goings. (In the old days at least, they acknowledged each other with a wave.) He never underestimated the ability of the revolution to survive. "The government is in position to stay in power for years," he told me in 1992—a prediction that has certainly been borne out.

The CDRs are not the potent force they once were. Enthusiasm has dipped along with the faith of the people in the revolution. Attendance at committee meetings has declined. A museum in Havana honoring the committees gets few visitors. A reporter for *The Economist* magazine visited on a Saturday and found no one there except for a guard, who after greeting him, asked for an antihistamine. (Another tourist attraction is the "Dustbin of History Museum," with busts of former presidents. One item on display is a newspaper story announcing the death of Batista, Castro's rightist predecessor, in 1973.) A main purpose of many museums in Havana is to attract foreigners. For Cubans, a museum visit normally is not worth the inevitable transportation headaches.

Independent journalist Miriam Leiva said in a September 2010 blog that unlike an earlier period, the supposed CDR requirement for an overnight security guard on each block is widely ignored. Nonetheless, she said the CDRs still maintain "permanent scrutiny" over citizens and are in communication with state security officials. She pointed out that all children must register for CDR membership by age fourteen, lest they be labeled as politically suspect.

An October 2007 *Washington Post* account underscored signs of CDR-fatigue on the island:

"Once, in a bygone era when revolutionary fervor was at its apex, they were muscular entities, dominating street life and cementing Castro's hold on power. But over the years they have atrophied, becoming more creaking relic than shining showpiece, victim of the waning enthusiasms of a population weary of economic deprivation."

It also should be pointed that less vigilance is needed because some of the harsher restrictions of the earlier era have been relaxed. There are far fewer political prisoners than there were a generation ago, signaling a more tolerant attitude toward once-forbidden activities. Penalties for church attendance were eliminated decades ago. Religious Cubans no longer suffer discrimination. Intolerance toward gays is declining rapidly. In the mid-1960's, gays were sent to forced labor camps known for inhumane practices. Fidel has said he takes personal responsibility for the "injustices" of that period. A leading advocate of gay rights is a daughter of Raúl, Mariela, director of the National Center for Sex Education.

Despite the more permissive attitude of the CDRs, ordinary Cubans ignore the committees at their peril, as the *Post* story pointed out: "When a Cuban wants a job in the lucrative tourism industry—where a worker can earn three or four times the usual state salary—the CDR president's imprimatur is essential. Applicants labeled 'anti-social,' code for transgressions such as dissident activity or lack of interest in volunteer projects, are almost assured of being turned down."

Dariela Aquique, a *Havana Times* blogger, sees little merit in the CDR's. She wrote: "To be a part of this organization one must: pay monthly dues (which are next to nothing, by the way); attend countless numbers of meetings and ceremonies (complete wastes of time); participate in voluntary labor (which they never stop asking you to do); participate in late-night CDR block watches (to 'monitor' what the police should be on top of); maintain a positive attitude that translates into good human and social relationships with one's neighbors (which is nothing other than gossiping, back stabbing and other demonstrations of mudslinging). "

CHAPTER 12

AFRO-CUBANS

Pedro Pérez-Sarduy clearly remembers the day in January 1959 when Che Guevara appeared in the main square of the central Cuban town of Santa Clara hours after the surrender of President Fulgencio Batista.

It was there that, under Guevara's leadership, the final battle of Fidel Castro's war against Batista was fought. The city, one of Cuba's oldest, fell to rebel forces on December 31, 1958, and Batista fled that night. Support of the local population was decisive in that battle. In recognition of his exploits in Santa Clara, Guevara is buried there.

"The square was packed," Pérez-Sarduy said, recalling that long-ago New Year's day. "We were all excited and avid to see and hear this hero of the revolution. At the front of the crowd were the white Cubans, behind them were the mixed race people, and the blacks stood at the back. That's the way things were."

The revolution brought hope to millions of blacks in a country overwhelmingly dominated by the white elite of Havana, who, from appearances, paid little heed to the fate of the majority Afro-Cuban population.

Pérez-Sarduy says that it took the revolution too long to acknowledge the importance of Afro-Cuban history. "When I was studying in Cuba in the 1960s and 1970s, I learned all about Greece and Homer's *Iliad*, but nothing of my own culture," he said. "I learned of the massacre of black Cubans in 1912 from my grandmother." He noted that over time, black studies became part of the Cuban education curriculum. (In the 1912 tragedy, an estimated six thousand Cuban blacks were killed by forces loyal to white ranchers who feared growing black political power. The Cuban liberation army that ousted Spanish colonialists about a dozen years earlier was predominantly black. It was replaced by a largely white, American-trained national army.)

Castro has said that a half-century of revolution has improved health care, education, and employment for black Cubans but he also has acknowledged that these advances did not automatically bring an end to discrimination.

In a stopover in Harlem in 2002, part of an official visit to the United Nations, Castro said: "I am not claiming that our country is a perfect model of equality and justice. We believed at the beginning that when we established the fullest equality before the law and complete intolerance for any demonstration of sexual discrimination in the case of women, or racial discrimination in the case of ethnic minorities, these phenomena would vanish from our society.

"It was some time before we discovered that marginality and racial discrimination with it are not something that one gets rid of with a law or even with ten laws, and we have not managed to eliminate them completely, even in forty years."

Two years later, Castro inaugurated a new teacher-training school in Havana and described as "exemplary" the diverse nature of the student body.

"We are pleased to be advancing towards a society of full equality, equity, and justice, in which any remnants of the objective discrimination inherited from centuries of slavery and poverty, allowing only a part of the population to enjoy the fruits of education, are being definitely eradicated," Castro said.

But Pérez-Sarduy believes the overall situation of Afro-Cubans remains bleak. He said in 2009 that there had been a "severe weakening" of the moral fiber of Afro-Cubans and an increase in their rates of incarceration. Other problems included higher rates of prostitution and a loss of hope.

The Negritude Brotherhood of Cuba, which espouses racial equality, issued a forty-eight-point manifesto in June 2011 in which it insisted that "the racial question no longer be considered a taboo theme" on the island. Point 11 of the list called attention to poor housing conditions for Afro-Cubans. It said the annual plan for housing construction in Cuba should include "an appropriate proportion of housing destined to better the living conditions of families who reside in shelters, tenements, slums, etc."

The *Havana Times* in May 2011 had an interview with a Cuban, identified only as Omar, age forty-seven, who said he had worked as an athlete, trainer and book salesman. He described what life as an Afro-Cuban was like: "Everyone of color has suffered racism concretely, in the flesh and blood. You're out on the street you might see four white people pass by a police officer and nothing happens. But if you're black they'll ask for your ID card like it's nothing. For blacks everything is more difficult. They have to make twice the effort or be twice as good. If they're able to get an important position, everybody focuses in on them, watching for them to make a mistake and they'll screw them over as soon as they do… Look at the elite of this country, everybody's white. "

Pérez-Sarduy was fifteen on that day in January 1959 when Che Guevara spoke in Santa Clara. He was to become a multilingual poet, author, radio journalist, and columnist, and an expert on race in Cuba. He says that the race issue was rarely discussed openly in Cuba. He left the country in 1981 and now lives in London. He is a frequent visitor to the United States and, unlike many Cuban expatriates, is allowed to make return visits to Cuba. Some of his Spanish-language writings have been published in Cuba.

The Cuban government says that about 62 percent of the island's population has African blood, a figure that seems low to Pérez-Sarduy. As for the relatively small percentage of Afro-Cubans who have left the country, he says, "Black Cubans don't have anyplace to go into exile." Because of their color, he says, they would feel like strangers in Cuban areas of Miami or Madrid or any other place else they landed.

But there were many blacks among the one hundred and twenty-five thousand Cubans who fled the island for south Florida in the Mariel boat lift in 1980. Marvin Dunn, a historian and retired Florida International University professor, wrote about the newly arrived Cubans in his 1997 book, *Black Miami in the Twentieth Century*. He said these immigrants were given preferential treatment in hiring and in public funding for health and other social services. "That impact is still being felt today when you consider the number of African-Americans who did not get jobs back then and now have grown children who do not have jobs," Dunn wrote.

Visitors to Cuba, myself included, were struck in the earlier phases of the revolution by the absence of blacks in senior government and party positions. The seeming discrimination against blacks drew criticism from Wayne Smith, who once headed the U.S. diplomatic mission in Cuba. More senior level blacks can be seen in government nowadays but it was hard not to notice the continuing relative absence of black faces on television and on the staff at luxury hotels.

The government plan to promote self-employment and small business is expected to benefit whites more than blacks. The reason is that seed money available for startups is likely to flow to white entrepreneurs in Cuba from well-to-do—and mostly white—family and friends abroad. This point was acknowledged by two Afro-Cuban officials from Havana at a news conference in Washington in 2011.

American blacks and Cuban blacks have a common complaint: police harassment. "Driving while black" is the description used by Afro-Americans tired of being gratuitously pulled over by police cruisers. In Cuba, merely "walking while black" is enough for a young Afro-Cuban to attract unwanted police attention. (Credit Eugene Robinson, author of *Last Dance in Havana*, for noting the parallel phenomenon. "Young, tall and black Cubans tend to arouse suspicion much like they do in the U.S. Cops tend to stop them," he wrote.)

The leadership of the largest anti-Castro organization in Miami, the Cuban-American National Foundation, once viewed the dark-hued arrivals from Cuba with hostility.

Jorge Mas Canosa, the late CANF chairman, said in 1985, "When Americans see a black person attached to an issue or cause, all they see is welfare, poverty, hopelessness, illiteracy and crime; the cause becomes diminished. In order to make our (CANF's) program successful we must keep those black faces in the dark. If we have to bring them in, let's do so when there are no cameras."

The source for the statement is Alberto Jones, a Cuban refugee who lives in northern Florida and is a critic of the exile political establishment in Miami.

The perception that Cuba had a race problem was driven home in August 1994 when black youths rebelled near the *Malecón* seawall in Havana to protest the sinking of a vessel that had been hijacked off Havana's coast by Cubans attempting to flee to the U.S. Gunfire from military patrol boats foiled the attempt, and more than forty people were killed. The black-led protest that followed had few precedents in Cuba's revolutionary history. Castro, said to be unarmed, drove to the site in a jeep and was able to calm the situation, according to news accounts at the time. Far from directing anger at him, or perhaps fearful of retaliation, the demonstrators chanted "*Viva Fidel.*" He assured the crowd that those who wished to leave the country would not be stopped. Days later, tens of thousands of Cubans tried to flee on boats, only to be intercepted by U.S. Coast Guard cutters and taken to the *Guantánamo* base. All were eventually given visas and allowed to resettle in the United States.

Robinson, the American author, wrote that Castro, perhaps after noting the mostly black composition of the protest, ordered more race-sensitive hiring practices by the party and government.

There are no official statistics on the number of blacks in senior positions in Cuba; the government from time to time highlights race problems in the U.S. and has decried what it says is the disproportionate number of Afro-Americans in U.S. prisons.

Race issues at home aside, no non-African leader paid more attention to the problems of post-independence Africa than Castro.

He sent Cuban troops to a number of African countries starting in the early 1960s to assist in the transition to independence, to win goodwill for Cuba and socialist breakthroughs in the process. Cuban troops fought troops of South Africa's apartheid government in the 1980s. Castro won friendships on the continent and support in the United Nations on issues important to Cuba. These included the annual U.N. General Assembly resolutions denouncing the U.S. embargo against the island. Over American objections, Cuba was repeatedly elected with African support to a seat on the U.N. Human Rights Commission (later renamed the U.N. Human Rights Council.)

In the area of social development in Africa, Cuban contributions were undeniable. As of 2010, thirty thousand Africans had graduated from Cuban universities, according to Cuban officials. Countless others received care from Cuban doctors in Africa.

But while Cuba won acclaim and influence in Africa, many Afro-Cubans felt neglected. Referring to this community, Pérez Sarduy said, "An entire sector of the Cuban society" has been left "on the verge of collapse."

CHAPTER 13

ARTEMISA

On April 29, 1992, Fidel Castro went to a spacious field outside the town of Artemisa and, before a large gathering, exulted in a rare victory on the food front. At a time of mostly bad news for his revolution, Castro could at least trumpet a triumph in *"la batalla de las papas"* (the battle of the potatoes.) Soldiers, students, and farm workers had come together to harvest the crop, which had been threatened earlier by more than a week of rain.

Starting the previous fall, the weather had been the principal variable in determining whether potatoes would be added to the list of vegetables in short supply in Cuban markets. Overall, it was a time of testing for Cuba, coming not long after the costly, for Cuba, collapse of European communism and the dismemberment in late 1991 of the Soviet Union. Many around the world were wondering about Castro's ability to survive. Castro essentially had no reliable allies left outside the Third World, no help from any traditional partners. More difficulties were to come, including the tightening of the American economic embargo to a level never before seen. Cuba was faced with an economic free fall.

In the winter of 1991-92, Castro was worried about the prospective potato crop in fields to Havana's west, not far from the site where Soviet ballistic missiles had been installed thirty years earlier. Castro was dismayed that rains had largely prevented potato seed planting during November in Artemisa and other nearby farm communities.

The weather was far more agreeable in December. Seed plantings took place right up to New Year's Eve, as Castro recalled it. Thousands of workers were mobilized for the harvest starting around the first of April. But would the weather cooperate again? Would the workers give it their all?

The stakes were high. Food rationing had been in effect in Cuba for twenty-nine years, and seldom had the overall supply situation looked bleaker than it did that spring.

Alas, heavy rains came on April 2 and 3, and more fell between the seventh and the tenth, Castro said in his April 29 speech. He personally visited the area more than once to make assessments. "There was the danger of losing hundreds of thousands of quintals (hundredweights) of potatoes... No one knew how the potato harvest could be saved," said Castro.

Happily, the weather cooperated for the remainder of the month, and the harvest turned out to be bountiful. Castro shared the good news with workers, singling out for praise the groups that had labored the hardest. Some suffered cuts when forced to dig by hand; wet grounds had idled mechanized harvesters, and tillers proved to be only partially reliable. The regular labor force had been joined in the effort by military units, high school and university students, and foundry workers. The latter received Castro's most effusive accolade. "They were desperately harvesting potatoes so that not one would be lost," he told the hushed crowd (of which I was a part). Castro likes workers who go the extra mile and supervisors who push them to the limit. A "paternalistic attitude" can lead to unrealistically low standards, he said. The result, he added, is underperformance. At one point, Castro said he was outraged when told that the target for one work group was twenty thousand pounds. He said that was too low by thirty thousand pounds.

Speaking mostly without notes, Castro talked knowledgeably about planting deadlines, harvest times, pests, fumigation, irrigation, storage units, and weather patterns. Castro seemed to feel at home. After all, he was no stranger to rustic settings, having been raised in a large country house built on stilts in rural eastern Cuba, sharing it with farm laborers, and having cows, chickens, ducks, and turkeys as his outdoor companions.

In the Artemisa speech, he said that during an earlier visit, he had chastised workers who had put away their tools at five p.m. The sun still had not set, Castro said in his speech, mystified that anyone would call it a day two and a half hours before dark. (He was told later that the supply of corn seed had run out.) He also recalled that he reproached a university student brigade for listening to blaring music until 1:00 a.m., leaving them, he said, too tired for top efficiency the next day. He banned all music after 11:00 p.m., remembering how, as a guerrilla warrior thirty-five years earlier, marches that continued well after midnight would sap the energy of his troops, making them too weak to do much the next day.

Toward the end of his speech, Castro was clearly troubled by the prospect that the workers might be contemplating taking the day off two days later because it was May 1, an international holiday celebrated in honor of workers.

"There is work on 1 May," Castro said, a stern look on his face. Factory workers may be off that day but not those who work the field. "Agriculture does not wait," he said. "Agriculture does not know what workers' day is or 1 May is. It knows that corn must be planted. Not a single day can be lost. Not a single minute can be lost."

Later, however, he relented somewhat and ordered the workers to be on the job a half-day on May 1, noting that it was a Sunday. "I agree that Sunday is for rest. But I think that on May 1 we can honor the workers by working. Because we are not under capitalism; we are under socialism. We are not producing for the bourgeoisie; we are producing for the people."

He also pointed out that in Cuba, farm labor is provided by Cubans. It is unlike the United States, where Latin Americans dominate farm labor, or Europe, where Africans do the work, he said.

During his previous thirty-three years in power, Castro had acquired a reputation as a micromanager, an impression that certainly was reinforced that day in Artemisa.

Normally heads of state don't dictate work schedules of low-level employees, whether they are farm laborers or office workers. But there was Castro, announcing work shifts according to the whim of the moment. Pity the poor worker who thought he might get the day off on Sunday to spend with his family.

At Artemisa, it was impossible to know what the workers felt about the heavy demands placed on their shoulders. Their compensation certainly was small. Precise salary figures are difficult to access but Castro said in a separate speech not long thereafter that rice farmers in Cuba were making eighty pesos a month, roughly two dollars and fifty cents. That was too low, he said, criticizing the bureaucrats who had set the wage. Presumably farmers in other areas were being paid approximately the same. The Cuban Workers Central, better known by its Spanish initials CTC, is Cuba's main labor organization. It is under the control of the Communist Party and does not intercede on wage issues. Its mandate consists of raising the political consciousness of workers, and improving managerial performance and labor discipline. It is perhaps the only labor union in the world that plays no role in improving the wellbeing of the workers it presumably represents. Each May 1, there is a mass parade in Havana honoring workers. There are no banners calling for wage increases.

To the extent that many Cubans are dissatisfied with their lives, seldom do they blame Castro in conversations with American reporters. Even those who opposed the regime see Castro as a leader whose highest priority was the Cuban people, even though his economic schemes seldom produced positive results. When things went wrong in a particular neighborhood, it was not uncommon for people to say, "If Fidel only knew." Rightly or wrongly, he came across as the embodiment of Cuban patriotism.

When he stepped down in 2008, he was an international figure of some stature but certainly not for his management of the nation's economy.

CHAPTER 14

REGLA

The best way to get from Havana to the town of Regla is via ferry from Havana Harbor across the southern reaches of Havana Bay. On disembarking after a twenty-minute ride, I wondered whether the trip was worth it. The mood in Regla that Friday in 2007 was as bleak as the timeworn buildings. At times, architecture garbed in gray can look handsome, but that word hardly applied to the dirt-darkened eyesores in Regla, the legacy of a soot-spewing oil refinery. Many locals have fled Regla because of the contamination. The bright, sunny afternoon that Friday could not dent the griminess. My companion and I sat for a while in a park, occupied mostly by mothers awaiting the dismissal of their children from school. Most sat in silence on benches. Efforts to engage the women in conversation were brushed off.

We decided to move on. The faded sign on one building said "*Cafetería*" outside but that did not seem an apt description for what was inside. There was a counter with stools but no sign of food. The only visible item for sale was matches. The only sign of life was a dark-haired man dressed in white who was cleaning the counter as we sat down. My attempt at conversation was met with monosyllabic, one-word answers. He was about as communicative as the women on the park benches. I thought, *"Something terrible must have happened in this town."*

A middle-aged woman with a tired, unhappy face came in and sat on the last stool at the L-shaped counter. There, at least she could rest her back against the wall. She said to no one in particular, *"Quince años"* (fifteen years). She repeated it twice more. Wondering whether she was addressing us, we walked over to her. She told us it was the fifteenth anniversary of the death of her brother.

The counterman corrected her; *"Doce años"* (twelve years), he said. In any case, both knew what that anniversary, October 13, meant. It was a day that the people of Regla won't forget. Elena, not her real name, proceeded, cigarette in hand, to recount what happened on that day. Police, she said, shot her brother and two others to death while they were trying to escape to South Florida before dawn in a boat. At that time, Cuba was in the final phases of the worst economic crisis in the country's independent history.

One had to allow for overstatement when listening to Elena describe that life-transforming day twelve years earlier. Was there really a protest in which seven thousand people participated, infuriated by the fate unjustly meted out by police to the three would-be escapees? Perhaps the protest was smaller than she said it was. In any case, Elena became a marked woman, as she described it, labeled by police as a protest ringleader. She said she had no job, no money, no home—in effect, no life. Only through the generosity of friends did she have a place to lie down at night, she said. As we were leaving, I gave Elena some euros. So unaccustomed to good fortune was she that her only reaction was one of incredulity. Her jaw dropped. She was speechless. We wished her luck and left.

CHAPTER 15

CUBA'S IMMIGRANTS

William Brent was an American black power militant who high-jacked a TWA flight to Cuba in 1969 rather than risk getting caught for his role in a shootout in Oakland with police at a gas station.

He thought that the Cubans would welcome him as a daring fighter for racial justice. Instead, he was imprisoned on arrival and remained in custody for twenty-two months. His Cuban hosts thought he might have been a spy rather than a refugee from justice. It was a suspicion that the Cubans harbored for years although he was permitted to work as an English teacher, a farm hand, and as a radio disc jockey, among other jobs.

Twenty years of good behavior did not deter police from taking him into custody as part of a general roundup on the eve of a visit to Havana by Soviet President Mikhail Gorbachev in 1989. After Gorbachev left Cuba, Brent was allowed to go home. Given the long U.S. record during the 1960s of assassination attempts against Fidel Castro, perhaps Cuban officials can be forgiven for being extra cautious about Brent.

When I saw him in 2001, he was living in a comfortable river-side apartment in Havana with his American wife, Jane McManus. He made clear that he had never felt at ease in Cuba. He indicated that he might consider returning to the U.S. if he could be sure that he wouldn't be sentenced to death for his crimes. He certainly would have faced a lengthy imprisonment at a minimum.

He remained unrepentant about his life as a Black Panther but he acknowledged that he missed "my people, the struggle, the body language" of America. Brent died in Havana in 2006 at age seventy-five.

McManus, his wife, grew up in a Republican family in New England and became a far-left radical during the Vietnam war. Facing harassment in the U.S., she accepted a job offer to go to Havana with a Cuban magazine in 1969. Her initial enthusiasm for the revolution faded. She remained in Cuba but told an interviewer she considered Cuba to be a military dictatorship. Access to hard currency, a nice home, and freedom to travel to the U.S. made it worth her while to remain in Cuba. "Foreigners don't have to scramble to find where their next meal is coming from, or stand in line eternally, or go to hospitals that are filthy and don't have medicine," McManus said. She died in Havana at age eighty-five in 2005.

Soledad and Felipe Rodriguez, former rebels in El Salvador who emigrated to Cuba, are grateful to be there. They support the revolution and appreciate the eight-month free hospital stay given to Felipe after his kidney was removed in 1993. "What would we have done in El Salvador?" Soledad asked a reporter. "We wouldn't have been able to pay for his surgery."

She becomes impatient with Cubans who don't appreciate what they have. "In Cuba, everyone who wants a university degree can get one," she said.

CHAPTER 16

THE MILITANTS

In his early twenties, Orlando Bosch's goal was to become a pediatrician. Then along came Fidel Castro and his revolution, and Bosch embraced, with great fervor, a new mission: saving Cuba from communism.

In this pursuit, he was relentless, and often violent, for the next forty years, except for the eleven he spent in American and Venezuelan prisons. His main partner was compatriot Luis Posada Carriles. They hatched assassination schemes against Castro and sponsored politically motivated killings, bombings, and kidnappings in the U.S., mostly in Miami, Cuba, and elsewhere in Latin America.

Castro and Bosch were born five days apart in August 1926 and lived across the street from one another as university students in Havana in the mid-1940s. They knew each other well. When Castro took up arms against the Batista regime in the late 1950s, Bosch joined him.

When the revolution triumphed, Castro rewarded Bosch with the governorship of Las Villas province in central Cuba. In 1960, when Castro's intention to pursue one-man leftist rule by whatever means necessary, Bosch fled to Miami with his wife and family.

He and Posada became the best known of Castro's antagonists. They plotted for decades but always came up short. In July 2006, when a sudden intestinal illness left Castro near death, many of his enemies were jubilant but, curiously, not Bosch, then approaching his eightieth birthday. He was asked by a reporter from the Spanish newspaper *Vanguardia* whether he was relieved or frustrated by Castro's health crisis.

"I would have liked to kill that man to set an example for future generations," Bosch said. "The prospect that he will die in bed really upsets me."

Castro subsequently made a surprising recovery, but Raúl has been in charge almost since the day Fidel became ill in 2006. Bosch said Cuba's highly efficient internal security apparatus made it virtually impossible to eliminate him from within Cuba's borders. "It's quite clear that no organization (in Cuba) is doing anything," he told *Vanguardia*. Even if just three bombs were set off, he said, it would change the political climate because notions about Castro's invincibility would be shattered.

U.S.-based anti-Castro radio stations would be on top of the story, and create the impression that "things are topsy-turvy down there," said Bosch, believing that suppressed public hostility toward the regime would surface.

The closest an assassination plot came to success was in Santiago, Chile, in 1971, he said. Two hit men were there posing as reporters for a Venezuelan television station, one with a forty-five-calibre pistol hidden in a camera. "They were standing two meters away from Castro... The one who had to pull the trigger got cold feet and didn't shoot," Bosch said.

Posada paid little attention to politics as a young man but that changed with Castro's ascent. He was suave, handsome, calculating, and a womanizer. His darkest moment came not at the hands of his political enemies but reportedly when a Salvadoran general learned that Posada was romancing the general's wife. A gunshot wound left Posada's face permanently disfigured.

Days after the failed assassination attempt against Castro in Chile, another opportunity arose in Quito, Ecuador, part of the same Castro trip. Posada, a renowned sharpshooter, was waiting for him, rifle in hand, in an elevated area of the airport. Castro foiled the plan by ordering his pilot to land at a different runway.

(I was in Chile and Ecuador during Castro's visits and obviously was unaware of the assassination attempts at the time. I saw Castro in both countries but in other locations.)

The most spectacular joint venture undertaken by Bosch and Posada was the bombing of *Cubana* flight 455 shortly after takeoff from Barbados on October 6, 1976. The death toll was seventy-three. On board were fifty-seven Cubans, six teen-aged exchange students from Guyana, a young Guyanese family of five, and five North Koreans. Bosch and Posada, based in Venezuela, were accused of planning the attack. Venezuelan police took them into custody.

In her book *Without Fidel*, Ann Marie Bardach provides perhaps the most comprehensive account of the ten-year, tortuous legal process carried out by the Venezuelan judiciary against the two. "It was a case fraught with peril for its prosecutors, witnesses and judges, prompting unprecedented government interference and judicial dithering," Bardach wrote.

Two young Venezuelans, one employed by Bosch, the other by Posada, had planted the explosive devices and deplaned before the aircraft took off from Barbados.

Moments later, an explosion sent the plane tumbling into the sea. Two days after the bombing, CORU, a newly formed, Bosch-led anti-Castro organization, claimed responsibility, contending that the craft was a "military plane camouflaged as a DC-8 aircraft." Its passengers, the group said, "consisted of 57 Cuban Communists and five North Korean Communists." It was obviously a heinous crime—and a propaganda gift for Castro. His enemies had given him a perfect excuse to demonize them. He made the most of it. The investigative trail soon led to Bosch and Posada in Venezuela. Both were arrested. Venezuela had maintained close ties to Cuban anti-communists but, with the *Cubana* incident, everything changed. No longer would Caracas be a hub for Castro's opponents, a mini-Miami.

Venezuela's ties to the exiles worsened when, during the confinement of Bosch and Posada after their detention, angry supporters seeking their release set off bombs at five Venezuelan government facilities, including two in Puerto Rico.

Preparations for their trials were drawn out but, as Bardach described it, the trappings of their confinement were not unpleasant, more like a summer camp than hard time, with "common rooms to accommodate their steady stream of visitors—including a number of Miami's most influential politicians and power brokers."

As Venezuelan authorities wrestled with procedural issues, Bosch spent eleven years in prison—without even a conviction— and was released on grounds that the evidence against him was inadmissible because it was in English. He brazenly flew into Miami without proper documents—and with a parole violation hanging over his head. He may have thought that U.S. immigration officials would have waved him through because of his political clout in the city. Instead he was detained on his arrival.

Bosch certainly had no friends in the Justice or State Departments, as Bardach pointed out. He was regarded in these agencies as a terrorist. A call by Attorney General Richard Thornburg for his immediate deportation was ignored. Two years later, in 1990, President George H. W. Bush pardoned Bosch on the condition that he renounce violence. Bosch was free but had no intention of adhering to the condition. For him, it was terrorism as usual. He authorized bombings of buildings that in some way were identified with rapprochement with Castro. He occasionally was arrested but invariably was quickly released on orders from Washington, presumably from the White House. It was not America's finest hour.

In pardoning him in 1990, Bush took into account a number of political realities. Any attempt to deport or prosecute Bosch could have been politically costly for Bush and the GOP in South Florida. In November 1992, Bush, seeking re-election, edged out Democrat Bill Clinton in Florida but lost the overall election. It was the only presidential election of the nine held between 1976 and 2008 in which the winner failed to carry Florida. (Clinton fought hard for the Cuban-American vote, at one point declaring that it was time "to bring down the hammer" on Castro.)

Not surprisingly, the pardon for Bosch did not go unnoticed in Havana. Bush had given Castro a huge political opening, and the Cuban leader seized it; Castro often commemorated the October 6 anniversary of the bombing with a blistering speech. He claimed all along that the CIA was behind the bombing, although there was no proof. And the Bosch pardon was red meat for conspiracy theorists; Bush, after all, was CIA director at the time of the bombing. There was strong evidence that the CIA had prior information about the bombing but Cuba was never alerted, according to Peter Kornbluh, a senior analyst at the private National Security Archive in Washington. There were suspicions that Posada was playing a double role, informing the CIA about Bosch's plans to bomb an unspecified *Cubana* flight even as Posada himself was acting as Bosch's co-conspirator.

Nine years after his imprisonment in Venezuela, in 1985, Posada escaped and was immediately hired by the Reagan administration to assist Nicaragua's Contra rebels in their war against that country's leftist government. It was an amazing change of fortune for the accused mass murderer. He had eluded justice in Venezuela and moved quickly back to doing what he liked best: fighting communists. But he eventually resumed his struggle against Castro, hiring hit men to plant bombs in Cuba to disrupt the tourism industry in 1997. One bomb claimed the life of an Italian tourist, Fabio di Celmo. In 2000, an opportunity to assassinate Castro in Panama presented itself. The venue was an Ibero-American conference in November. But Posada and three companions were arrested before the conference began. They were convicted of illegal possession of weapons and sent to prison. (A charge of attempted murder was dropped.) Almost four years later, amid suspicions of a payoff, Posada was pardoned by Panamanian President Mireya Moscoso as she was about to finish her term in office.

As Bosch had done years earlier, Posada, a Cuban citizen, slipped into the United States in 2005 without proper documents. He was arrested and charged with lying to U.S. officials about his method of entry to the United States. During his trial in El Paso, Tex., the Justice Department surprisingly added three perjury charges against Posada concerning his alleged role in the 1997 Havana bombing that killed di Celmo. The U.S. action stunned Peter Kornbluh, the aforementioned Latin America research specialist. "The importance of this moment in U.S.-Cuban relations cannot be overstated," he said at the time, noting Posada's ties with the CIA in anti-Castro activities dating back to the 1960s, including planning for the Bay of Pigs invasion. In effect, the U.S. government had turned its back on a long-time collaborator. Cuba broke precedent as well by sharing with U.S. investigators information from its files about the alleged Posada-led bombing campaign in Havana. In the end, the El Paso jury acquitted Posada. His lawyer said the verdict was not an endorsement of terrorism but reflected what he said was the failure of the U.S. government to prove its case. None of the jurors who tried the case spoke publicly about their decision.

For a time in the 1960s, successive U.S. administrations were on the same wavelength as Bosch and Posada because of Castro's attempts to export his revolution, his disregard for basic human freedoms, and his enthusiastic embrace not only of communism but of the Soviet Union. The air in Washington during that period was thick with anti-Castro plots. Indeed, a Senate committee discovered in 1975 eight U.S.-sponsored assassination attempts during the 1960s against Castro. Eventually, though, the Americans' appetite for taking Castro out diminished, a reflection of Castro's less provocative behavior over the years. But Bosch and Posada never lost their fervor— until old-age caught up with them.

In their heyday, no act of violence seemed too extreme. The Bosch-led CORU, formed in the Dominican Republic in the summer of 1976, arranged within weeks of its founding for the assassination in Washington of leftist Chilean exile Orlando Letelier, an opponent of Chile's military dictatorship. He and a companion were killed in a Washington car-bombing, an event that shocked a city not accustomed to acts of international terrorism. Two weeks later, the *Cubana* plane was blown from the sky off the coast of Barbados. It was hard to see how either of these acts weakened Castro or radical leftist movements that were spreading elsewhere in the hemisphere that Bosch said he and his followers were fighting. Indeed, the *Cubana* bombing highlighted the brutality of Castro's more extreme opponents and, to some, enabled Castro to lay claim to the moral high ground in the continuing struggle over Cuba's fate. To others, of course, virtually any action against Castro could be justified because of his dictatorial ways, often cruel behavior and his role as a model for leftists elsewhere.

"In war, everything is valid," Bosch once said, explaining his penchant for violence. Said Posada: "It's a war." Their passions for bringing Castro down never wavered.

The Cuban media in 2011 took note of the saturation coverage given by the American press following the mass murder by a deranged Norwegian, and compared it with the seemingly indifferent American coverage of the *Cubana* bombing thirty-five years earlier. The Cuban reaction was understandable, given that the death toll in the two tragedies was roughly the same—seventy-three were on the *Cubana* flight and seventy-seven in the latter tragedy. But there were several reasons for the disparity in the coverage. One is that Europe is awash with international reporters who have responsibility for and easy access to virtually all capitals of the continent. For them, the events in Norway were an almost a once-in-a-lifetime opportunity to report on something truly shocking in a country known for its peace and harmony. Beyond that, as the day progressed, there was no ambiguity about the who the perpetrator was, the magnitude of his crime and his motives. A coherent whole quickly emerged within hours. There were few mysteries.

In Cuba, the events surrounding the 1976 *Cubana* calamity could hardly have been more different. There was no immediate information on whether the plane was the victim of pilot error, mechanical defects, or terrorism. Throughout he Caribbean, news staffs of international media outlets were thin, including Cuba. (The last evicted foreign correspondent stationed in Cuba was the American AP reporter in Havana, who left in 1969.) The first account of the *Cubana* story in the *New York Times* appeared on Oct. 19, almost two weeks after the bombing. There were brief references to the alleged perpetrators—Bosch and Posada, who were in the custody of authorities in Venezuela on suspicion of involvement in the bombing. So the coverage was understandably thin. It was hard for readers to be aware that the *Cubana* bombing was the worst terrorist attack in Western Hemisphere history until the attacks on the World Trade Center and the Pentagon on Sept. 11, 2001.

CHAPTER 17

THE U.S. AND BATISTA

How to deal with rightist military dictators in Latin America was a recurring problem for successive U.S. administrations during the Cold War. One example was President Fulgencio Batista of Cuba. The Eisenhower administration had the choice of distancing itself from Batista and his malodorous administration or to be a partner in curbing the pesky Cuban rebel movement led by Fidel Castro. The administration decided on a policy of support for Batista with an overlay of stealth. Batista was fine with the first part but not the second. One of the Eisenhower administration's contact men with Batista was Lyman Kirkpatrick, a CIA official whose recollections of his Cuba experiences were published in 1968 as a chapter in his book, *The Real CIA*.

Kirkpatrick landed in Cuba on a mission not long after Castro had begun his rebel campaign in the Sierra Maestra mountains in late 1956. Kirkpatrick said he had been instructed to urge Batista to energize a dormant agency designed to fight communism in Cuba. It was known as The Bureau to Repress Communist Activities, or BRAC, according to its Spanish initials. Less than two years earlier, CIA Director Allen Dulles had visited Cuba to help organize the BRAC. Batista agreed to a meeting with Kirkpatrick, and the wheelchair-bound CIA official weeks later was ushered into the presidential palace through a heavily guarded back door. During the meeting with Kirkpatrick, the white-suited Batista welcomed the idea of a more robust BRAC.

Communism seemed to be a remote threat in Cuba at the time. But with Marxism on the march in much of Europe, Asia and parts of the Third World, the Eisenhower administration was on the alert for potential security threats in all regions. During Dulles's visit, Castro was serving a prison sentence on the Isle of Pines for leading an attack on the Moncada military barracks in 1953. In a move Batista surely was to regret, he ordered the release of Castro in May 1955, a month after Dulles's visit.

The United States was fully supporting Batista at the time of Kirkpatrick's visit, providing military assistance. It also was forbidding U.S. diplomats from having contact with Castro's supporters because that would only give them encouragement.

Months after his initial visit in December 1956, Kirkpatrick returned to Cuba for a progress report on BRAC's status. After his discussions, he was told that Batista sent word on short notice that he wanted a briefing in his office on what the CIA official had learned. Joining him was U.S. Ambassador Arthur Gardner. After some discussion, cigars, and coffee, Batista startled the Americans by suggesting a group picture to commemorate the occasion.

For the CIA official, nothing could have been more unwelcome. He was assured that the picture was solely for private use but he was not convinced. What if the picture somehow were made public?

Efforts by the embassy to retrieve the picture from the palace that afternoon were unsuccessful. Kirkpatrick's worst fears were realized the next day when the supposedly private picture was published in no fewer than eleven Havana dailies the next day.

Accompanying news accounts described the call as official, he said, "and identified me by name, title, and organization. Thus I found myself being used to bolster a shaky and increasingly unpopular regime."

When Kirkpatrick returned to Cuba in September 1958, he found the Batista regime increasingly demoralized and resorting to ever-more brutal measures to counter Castro and his allies. Kirkpatrick predicted that Batista probably would not last until the end of the year. He fled the country on December 31. Castro was poised to take power.

The revolution was on. Cuba and the world would never be the same.

CHAPTER 18

CUBAN BASEBALL

Crewmen who traveled to Cuba aboard an American vessel introduced baseball to the country in the 1860s. Baseball was a perfect fit for a country that was mostly flat with only occasional frigid temperatures—and an endless supply of youngsters for whom throwing, hitting, and fielding seemed to come naturally. It was common during the early twentieth century for owners of the many sugar refineries scattered around Cuba to sponsor teams to represent their respective towns. Of the fifty-three Caribbean players who made it to the U.S. big leagues between 1900 and 1950, forty-three were Cuban; all were white. A professional Havana team competed in the 1950s-era International League, also comprised of teams from the United States and Canada.

No one had more of an impact on Cuban baseball than Fidel Castro, and it was not because of any on-field feats as a pitcher for the University of Havana team in the 1940s. Soon after taking power, Castro banned professional ball, substituting amateur ball in its place. He said in 1962, "Ballplayers are no longer bought and sold; there are no longer any enterprises which monopolize athletes and which can buy and sell an athlete as if he were a race horse. An athlete is no longer bet on as if he were a pedigreed rooster, a horse, or a dog." Castro forbade players from signing contracts with professional teams in the U.S. Those already play- ing in the U.S. could simply stay there or return to Cuba, never to leave. A Cuban wanting to play in the U.S. or simply migrate there would have to defect aboard a boat or raft or at an international tournament outside the Cuba. An estimated 60 revolution-era Cubans who deserted their homeland for the United States have played baseball in the U.S. Major Leagues. (Starting with the late 19th Century, about 155 Cubans have reached that level).

Perhaps the greatest Cuban player, Martín Dihigo, is a mem- ber of the halls of fame of Cuba, Mexico, the Dominican Republic, Venezuela and the United States, where he starred in the U.S. Negro League. He was a brilliant hitter and pitcher and played all nine positions during his career. In the Mexican League in 1938, his .387 average won the battling title and as a pitcher he won eighteen of twenty decisions with an 0.90 earned run average. About one-hundred-eighty Cubans are known to have played in the U.S. Negro League. Others are believed to be unaccounted for because of inadequate record keeping. Dihigo was appointed by Fidel Castro in 1959 as the revolution's first minister of sport.

In the pre-Castro era, dozens of well-known American ball- players competed in Cuba during the off-season, most notably Babe Ruth in the 1920's. It is reported (but not confirmed) that he received $2,000 a day for his participation. Cuban teams proved their worth by often outplaying visiting American teams. As an example, the Cincinnati Reds lost seven of eleven to the Havana and Almendares teams in the early 20th Century.

During the off-season, U.S. players flocked to Cuba in the 1950s when big league salaries were low and the extra pay, not to mention the balmy weather, were welcome. That all ended in the early 1960's when Castro abolished pro ball. Among the Dodgers who played for the team in the south coast city of Cienfuegos before the ban were Carl Erskine, Sal Maglie, Billy Herman, Don Zimmer and Joe Black.

The revolution keeps an eye out for young talent. The most promising teens are recruited for a countrywide development league. The best of these can wind up on one of the sixteen National Series teams, the country's premier baseball showcase. Players on teams representing Cuba in international play are drawn from these squads. Peter Bjarkman, an American expert on Cuban baseball, has written that Cuban teams "amassed the sport's most miraculous feat imaginable with either outright victory or at least trips to the finals of 50 straight major world-class venues" between 1961 and 2008.

National Series teams play a ninety-game schedule and are divided between eastern and western divisions. Each province has at least one team. It can   recruit only local players. This ensures an enthusiastic fan base but it also gives an advantage to the most populated provinces, Havana and Santiago, whose teams have won the most national championships. Salaries are reportedly about one hundred and twenty-five dollars a month, about six times the pay of average workers but still tiny by Major League standards. The price of admission to watch a game is a few pennies. (Movies in theaters are just as cheap.)

Sandy Amoros, a Cuban and a '50s-era Brooklyn Dodger, achieved instant fame by making an exceptional catch in the deciding game of the 1955 World Series against the New York Yankees. With two runners on, he caught the ball with his gloved right hand after a long run near the left field foul pole. It was the start of a double play that helped preserve a 2-0 Dodger victory, which brought the team its first World Series triumph in eight tries. Amoros was proclaimed "Hero of the Year" by *Carteles,* a Cuban publication. His career is remembered for little else. In seven Major League seasons he hit .255. He was washed up at age thirty and returned home during the second year of the Cuban revolution.

Castro offered him a job as manager for a local team. Amoros said no— and paid dearly. According to a 1989 account in Sports Illustrated magazine, Castro ordered the confiscation of Amoros' home, his car and his cash. He also refused him permission to join a team that had signed him in Mexico. He hated Castro for the rest of his life.

He managed to leave Cuba aboard a "freedom flight" to the United States in the late 1960's and settled in New York City where he was able to work only intermittently. Born into poverty in Cuba, he was to suffer poverty and ill health in America. He had to use a prosthetic device on one leg after a late-life amputation below the knee. He had few friends and died in Tampa in 1990. But he will always be remembered for those few seconds in left-field in Yankee Stadium in 1955 when he was the talk of the baseball world.

Bjarkman, the American expert on Cuban baseball, says Cuban-style baseball is superior to the American version. "The people of Cuba own a beautiful baseball, pure in its concept and artistic in its execution. Unlike its North American and Asian professional counterparts, the Cuban League version of the sport is played far more for pride and passion than for the tarnished purposes of supporting a highly profitable commercial enterprise. Cuban fans not only witness major league style talent in their own backyards but also enjoy a truly unique experience of rooting for hometown teams that actually consist of homegrown athletes— ballplayers born in the local village and not merely rented for a season or two before they peddle their talents on the open market to some other bitter league rival."

There are no distractions at games in Cuba—no advertising on walls, no exploding scoreboards, no din of rock music—just baseball. (In 2011, to entertain fans attending a minor league game in Ohio, a fan allowed himself to be shot from a cannon. He landed one-hundred-fifty-feet away, beyond the centerfield fence—a "human home run.")

At Latin American Stadium in Havana, built in 1946, the only hint of a commercial is the apartment building a few yards beyond the left field wall. It is painted blue and white, the same colors as the *Industriales*, as the oldest and most revered local team is known. The names of some stadiums which host National Series games have an anti-American flavor. One is *Victoria de Girón*, the beach where a Bay of Pigs battle was fought. It is home to the team from Matanzas, near Havana. Another, located in *Granma* province in the east, is named for a Viet Cong guerrilla, Nguyen Van Troi, who attempted to assassinate U.S. Defense Secretary Robert McNamara in the 1960s on a visit to Vietnam.

Many Cuban players find the salaries paid to big league U.S. players to be an irresistible lure. A steady rise in defections to the United States appears to have reduced the quality of play Cuba. The best known of the recent deserters are Aroldis Chapman of the Cincinnati Reds and Kendry Morales of the Los Angeles Angels. Chapman, a lefty pitcher, was in the Netherlands for a tournament in 2009 when he deserted. He received thirty million dollars for signing with the Cincinnati Reds. Morales was among a group of Cubans who fled in a boat in June 2004, his eighth attempt to leave. His best year was 2009, when he hit thirty-four home runs for the Los Angeles Angels.

The Cuban government sees defectors to the major leagues as traitors. Once they are gone, they become non-persons. More to the government's liking is former star player Antonio Pacheco who, when asked by *PBS* in 2000 why he didn't defect, said: "I think I represent to the fans the athlete formed by my country, the athlete that all Cubans want to see, the athlete who is a role model for all the Cubans who put their trust in me, the athlete who will never leave his people, the athlete who will never betray them, the athlete who will defend his flag with love and dignity... Cuba for me is like my mother, and I will never abandon my mother."

The Havana Industriales on March 8, 1990 as they prepared to board the team bus for a night game. They have won a number of national championships and are Cuba's best known team. The man without a uniform on the lower left is the author.

ADDENDUM 1

Following are excerpts from a speech by President Fidel Castro in Havana on May 1, 2003, International Workers' Day. In it, he describes what he considers to be the triumphs of the revolution.

"Cuba was the first territory free from imperialist domination in Latin America and the Caribbean, and the only country in the hemisphere, throughout post-colonial history, where the torturers, murderers and war criminals that took the lives of tens of thousands of people were exemplarily punished.

"All of the country's land was recovered and turned over to the peasants and agricultural workers. The natural resources, industries and basic services were placed in the hands of their only true owner: the Cuban nation.

"In less than 72 hours, fighting ceaselessly, day and night, Cuba crushed the Bay of Pigs mercenary invasion organized by a U.S. administration, thereby preventing a direct military intervention by this country and a war of incalculable consequences. The

Revolution already had the Rebel Army, over 400,000 weapons and hundreds of thousands of militia members.

"In 1962, Cuba confronted with honor, and without a single concession, the risk of being attacked with dozens of nuclear weapons.

"It defeated the dirty war that spread throughout the entire country, at a cost in human lives even greater than that of the war of liberation.

"It stoically endured thousands of acts of sabotage and terrorist attacks organized by the U.S. government.

"It thwarted hundreds of assassination plots against the leaders of the revolution. While under a rigorous blockade and economic warfare that have lasted for almost half a century, Cuba was able to eradicate in just one year the illiteracy that has still not been overcome in the course of more than four decades by the rest of the countries of Latin America, or the United States itself.

"It has brought free education to 100% of the country's children.

"It has the highest school retention rate—over 99% between kindergarten and ninth grade—of all of the nations in the hemisphere.

"Its elementary school students rank first worldwide in the knowledge of their mother language and mathematics.

"The country also ranks first worldwide with the highest number of teachers per capita and the lowest number of students per classroom.

"All children with physical or mental challenges are enrolled in special schools.

"Computer education and the use of audiovisual methods now extend to all of the country's children, adolescents and youth, in both the cities and the countryside.

"For the first time in the world, all young people between the ages of 17 and 30, who were previously neither in school nor employed, have been given the opportunity to resume their studies while receiving an allowance.

"All citizens have the possibility of undertaking studies that will take them from kindergarten to a doctoral degree without spending a penny.

"Today, the country has 30 university graduates, intellectuals and professional artists for every one there was before the revolution.

"The average Cuban citizen today has at the very least a ninth-grade level of education.

"Not even functional illiteracy exists in Cuba.

"There are schools for the training of artists and art instructors throughout all of the country's provinces, where over 20,000 young people are currently studying and developing their talent and vocation. Tens of thousands more are doing the same at vocational schools, and many of these then go on to undertake professional studies.

"University campuses are progressively spreading to all of the country's municipalities. Never in any other part of the world has such a colossal educational and cultural revolution taken place as this that will turn Cuba, by far, into the country with the highest degree of knowledge and culture in the world, faithful to Martí's profound conviction that 'no freedom is possible without culture.'

"Infant mortality has been reduced from 60 per 1000 live births to a rate that fluctuates between 6 and 6.5, which is the lowest in the hemisphere, from the United States to Patagonia.

"Life expectancy has increased by 15 years.

"Infectious and contagious diseases like polio, malaria, neo-natal tetanus, diphtheria, measles, rubella, mumps, whooping cough and dengue have been eradicated; others like tetanus, meningococcal meningitis, hepatitis B, leprosy, hemophilus meningitis and tuberculosis are fully controlled.

"Today, in our country, people die of the same causes as in the most highly developed countries: cardiovascular diseases, cancer, accidents, and others, but with a much lower incidence.

"A profound revolution is underway to bring medical services closer to the population, in order to facilitate access to health care centers, save lives and alleviate suffering.

"In-depth research is being carried out to break the chain, mitigate or reduce to a minimum the problems that result from genetic, prenatal or childbirth-related causes.

"Cuba is today the country with the highest number of doctors per capita in the world, with almost twice as many as those that follow closer.

"Our scientific centers are working relentlessly to find preventive or therapeutic solutions for the most serious diseases.

"Cubans will have the best healthcare system in the world, and will continue to receive all services absolutely free of charge.

"Social security covers 100% of the country's citizens.

"In Cuba, 85% of the people own their homes and they pay no property taxes on them whatsoever. The remaining 15% pay a wholly symbolic rent, which is only 10% of their salary.

"Illegal drug use involves a negligible percentage of the population, and is being resolutely combated.

"Lottery and other forms of gambling have been banned since the first years of the Revolution to ensure that no one pins their hopes of progress on luck.

"There is no commercial advertising on Cuban television and radio or in our printed publications. Instead, these feature public service announcements concerning health, education, culture, physical education, sports, recreation, environmental protection, and the fight against drugs, accidents and other social problems. Our media educate, they do not poison or alienate. They do not worship or exalt the values of decadent consumer societies.

"Discrimination against women was eradicated, and today women make up 64% of the country's technical and scientific workforce.

"From the earliest months of the revolution, not a single one of the forms of racial discrimination copied from the south of the

United States was left intact. In recent years, the revolution has been particularly striving to eliminate any lingering traces of the poverty and lack of access to education that afflicted the descendants of those who were enslaved for centuries, creating objective differences that tended to be perpetuated. Soon, not even a shadow of the consequences of that terrible injustice will remain.

"There is no cult of personality around any living revolutionary, in the form of statues, official photographs, or the names of streets or institutions. The leaders of this country are human beings, not gods.

"In our country there are no paramilitary forces or death squads, nor has violence ever been used against the people. There are no executions without due process and no torture. The people have always massively supported the activities of the revolution. This rally today is proof of that."

QUOTES FROM FIDEL

As leader of Cuba, Fidel Castro was known for his long speeches. It is doubtful that any leader spoke more words in public than Castro. It was not unusual for Castro to speak more than four hours at a time. No researcher could complain of a lack of material when searching for an illuminating Castro quote. Here are some:

"I am one who believes sincerely in freedom. I am among those who believe that everyone has the right to say what he thinks... The system will never deprive anybody of his rights, of imprisoning intelligence, of muzzling thought, for any reason in the world." Speech in Montevideo, Uruguay, 1959. (Note: He did not announce his intention to create a Marxist-Leninist state until December 1961.)

"We believe that there must not be bread without liberty but that there must not be liberty without bread. This is what we call humanism. We want Cuba to be an example of representative democracy with true social justice." April 28, 1959, four months after taking power

"The duty of all journalists is to report what happens, and only with freedom of the press can there be political liberty." February 14, 1959

"I am a Marxist-Leninist and I will be a Marxist-Leninist until the last day of my life."
December 2, 1961

"The journalist is a militant of the revolution, the press is an instrument of the revolution and the first duty of the journalist is to support and defend the revolution." September 1997

"The great battle of the eggs has been won. From now on, the people can count on 70 million eggs every month." Interview, March 2, 1964 (Note: As of 2010, Cubans were entitled to ten eggs a month under the rationing system.)

"By 1970, there will be 5,000 experts in the cattle industry and about 8 million cows and calves which will be good producers of milk. There will be enough milk to fill Havana Bay with milk." (Note: The milk bonanza never materialized. Reliable supplies are assured only for children under eight years of age.) Speech to the Federation of Cuban Women, December 1966

"At this moment (during the Cuban missile crisis), I want to share with you (Nikita Khrushchev) my personal opinion. If the imperialists invade Cuba with the objective of occupying it, the danger of this aggressive act for humanity would be so great that, in the aftermath, the Soviet Union should not allow under any circumstance that the imperialists be the first to launch a nuclear attack against it. I make this point because I believe that imperialist aggressiveness is extremely dangerous and if they in fact carry out the brutal act of invading Cuba in violation of moral and international law, that would be the moment to eliminate the danger once and for all through a legitimate act of defense and although it would be a hard and terrible solution, there is no alternative." Excerpt from a letter from Castro to Soviet leader Nikita Khrushchev, October 25, 1962

"If Cuba decided to carry out terrorist acts to respond with terrorism to the terrorists, we are sure that we would be very efficient terrorists. Let nobody think otherwise. If we decide to be terrorists there is no doubt that we would be very efficient. But the fact that the revolution has never resorted to terrorism does not mean that we have renounced it... Let this be a warning!" From a speech on June 6, 1976

"No (Cuban) woman is obligated to sell herself to a man... those who do it do it for themselves, voluntarily... We can say they are very educated and healthy prostitutes." Speech to the Congress of Young Communists, April 4, 1992 (Note: The revolution had virtually abolished prostitution during the early years. It made a comeback when the economy collapsed in the early 1990s.)

"Cuba has benefited enormously from the departure of all those people (from Mariel). We authorized everyone who wanted to leave. I believe it was the greatest cleanup in history." International Workers' Day speech, May 1, 1980 (More than one hundred and twenty-five thousand Cubans fled the island in boats between April and September 1980.)

"You cannot judge a country, nor a country's ideas, nor a country's system, when (the United States) is endeavoring to prevent its development at all costs. It is not fair to judge Cuba on the one hand and, on the other, attempt to drown and stifle it, to bring it down by famine and disease. It is not a question of judging Cuba, but rather of judging those who have tried at all costs to prevent the development of our country." In response to France-2 TV network question on whether a flawed economic system caused the depression of the early 1990s, shown on October 20, 1994

"The mass political knowledge of the Cuban people is unrivaled in any other country." International Workers' Day speech, May 1, 2002

"(What will happen in Cuba after my death) is not my problem; it's the problem of others. I think a man should not live beyond the age when he begins to deteriorate, when the flame that illuminated the most brilliant moment of his life begins to deteriorate." Interview with CNN, October 23, 1995

ESSAY ON CHE

The following essay was written by Ariel Dorfman, a Chilean writer and intellectual, on the occasion of Time magazine's selection of Ernesto (Che) Guevara as one of the hundred most important figures of the twentieth century:

Though communism may have lost its fire, he remains the potent symbol of rebellion and the alluring zeal of revolution.

By the time Ernesto Guevara, known to us as Che, was murdered in the jungles of Bolivia in October 1967, he was already a legend to my generation, not only in Latin America but also around the world.

Like so many epics, the story of the obscure Argentine doctor who abandoned his profession and his native land to pursue the emancipation of the poor of the earth began with a voyage. In 1956, along with Fidel Castro and a handful of others, he had crossed the Caribbean in the rickety yacht *Granma* on the mad mission of invading Cuba and overthrowing the dictator Fulgencio Batista.

Landing in a hostile swamp, losing most of their contingent, the survivors fought their way to the *Sierra Maestra*. A bit over two years later, after a guerrilla campaign in which Guevara displayed such outrageous bravery and skill that he was named *comandante,* the insurgents entered Havana and launched what was to become the first and only victorious socialist revolution in the Americas. The images were thereafter invariably gigantic. Che the titan standing up to the Yanquis, the world's dominant power. Che the moral guru proclaiming that a New Man, no ego and all ferocious love for the other, had to be forcibly created out of the ruins of the old one. Che the romantic mysteriously leaving the revolution to continue, sick though he might be with asthma, the struggle against oppression and tyranny.

His execution in Vallegrande at the age of 39 only enhanced Guevara's mythical stature. That Christ-like figure laid out on a bed of death with his uncanny eyes almost about to open; those fearless last words ("Shoot, coward, you're only going to kill a man") that somebody invented or reported; the anonymous burial and the hacked-off hands, as if his killers feared him more after he was dead than when he had been alive: all of it is scalded into the mind and memory of those defiant times. He would resurrect, young people shouted in the late '60s; I can remember fervently proclaiming it in the streets of Santiago, Chile, while similar vows exploded across Latin America. *!No lo vamos a olvidar!* (We won't forget him!).

More than 30 years have passed, and the dead hero has indeed persisted in collective memory, but not exactly in the way the majority of us would have anticipated.

Che has become ubiquitous: his figure stares out at us from coffee mugs and posters, jingles at the end of key rings and jewelry, pops up in rock songs and operas and art shows. This apotheosis of his image has been accompanied by a parallel disappearance of the real man, swallowed by the myth. Most of those who idolize the incendiary guerrilla with the star on his beret were born long after his demise and have only the sketchiest knowledge of his goals or his life. Gone is the generous Che who tended wounded enemy soldiers, gone is the vulnerable warrior who wanted to curtail his love of life lest it make him less effective in combat and gone also is the darker, more turbulent Che who signed orders to execute prisoners in Cuban jails without a fair trial.

This erasure of complexity is the normal fate of any icon. More paradoxical is that the humanity that worships Che has by and large turned away from just about everything he believed in. The future he predicted has not been kind to his ideals or his ideas. Back in the '60s, we presumed that his self-immolation would be commemorated by social action, the downtrodden rising against the system and creating—to use Che's own words—two, three, many Vietnams. Thousands of luminous young men, particularly in Latin America, followed his example into the hills and were slaughtered there or tortured to death in sad city cellars, never knowing that their dreams of total liberation, like those of Che, would not come true. If Vietnam is being imitated today, it is primarily as a model for how a society forged in insurrection now seeks to be actively integrated into the global market. Nor has Guevara's uncompromising, unrealistic style of struggle, or his ethical absolutism, prevailed. The major revolutions of the past quarter-century (South Africa, Iran, the Philippines, Nicaragua), not to mention the peaceful transitions to democracy in Latin America, East Asia and the communist world, have all entailed negotiations with former adversaries, a give and take that could not be farther from Che's unyielding demand for confrontation to the death. Even someone like *Subcomandante* Marcos, the spokesman for the Chiapas Maya revolt, whose charisma and moral stance remind us of Che's, does not espouse his hero's economic or military theories.

How to understand, then, Che Guevara's pervasive popularity, especially among the affluent young?

Perhaps in these orphaned times of incessantly shifting identities and alliances, the fantasy of an adventurer who changed countries and crossed borders and broke down limits without once betraying his basic loyalties provides the restless youth of our era with an optimal combination, grounding them in a fierce center of moral gravity while simultaneously appealing to their contemporary nomadic impulse. To those who will never follow in his footsteps, submerged as they are in a world of cynicism, self-interest and frantic consumption, nothing could be more vicariously gratifying than Che's disdain for material comfort and everyday desires. One might suggest that it is Che's distance, the apparent impossibility of duplicating his life anymore, that makes him so attractive.

And is not Che, with his hippie hair and wispy revolutionary beard, the perfect postmodern conduit to the nonconformist, seditious '60s, that disruptive past confined to gesture and fashion? Is it conceivable that one of the only two Latin Americans to make it onto Time's 100 most important figures of the century can be comfortably transmogrified into a symbol of rebellion precisely because he is no longer dangerous?

I wouldn't be too sure. I suspect that the young of the world grasp that the man whose poster beckons from their walls cannot be that irrelevant, this secular saint ready to die because he could not tolerate a world where *los pobres de la tierra (the poor of the earth),* the displaced and dislocated of history, would be eternally relegated to its vast margins.

Even though I have come to be wary of dead heroes and the overwhelming burden their martyrdom imposes on the living, I will allow myself a prophecy. Or maybe it is a warning. More than 3 billion human beings on this planet right now live on less than $2 a day. And every day that breaks, 40,000 children—more than one every second!—succumb to diseases linked to chronic hunger. They are there, always there, the terrifying conditions of injustice and inequality that led Che many decades ago to start his journey toward that bullet and that photo awaiting him in Bolivia.

The powerful of the earth should take heed: deep inside that T-shirt where we have tried to trap him, the eyes of Che Guevara are still burning with impatience.

ADDENDUM 2

This section includes essays that illuminate the varied frustrations of ordinary Cubans.

One deals with the country's shortage of milk. Another describes the challenge a mother faces in finding shoes for her daughter. Male chauvinism on Havana's streets is discussed, as are the shortcomings of the health care system. A Cuban-American woman recalls her traumatic departure from Mariel in 1980 as a teen. A committed revolutionary writes about Cuba's need for reform. A security guard talks about his humdrum existence. The first and longest piece is about a man who has made leaving Cuba his life's ambition.

THE WOULD-BE ÉMIGRÉ

The following is a transcript of an interview in Entrevista *(Interview) magazine (Spanish) with a Cuban man who had failed three times in efforts to flee Cuba aboard a homemade boat for the United States. The question-and-answer portion begins after the interviewer, Yoani Sánchez, a Cuban dissident who writes mostly for foreign publications, provides background* :

The relativity of distances obsesses the Cuban *balseros* (rafters, i.e., those who try to escape to the U.S. by sea). "So close yet so far," the strip of sea that lies between Cuba and the United States seems to say.

When the Institute of Meteorology announces several days with good weather, then the remote Cuban coast sees the rafters arrive, the men and women whom the nation is losing, who no longer stay to employ their talents, their time, their lives, in Cuba. Some will blame this illegal emigration on the "economy," as if economics and politics could, in Cuba, each go their own way.

Carlos Manuel (not his real name) has made three attempts to leave the country illegally. On the first attempt, he was betrayed by one of the group and didn't even get away from the coast. The second took him outside the territorial waters until he and his fellow rafters were intercepted by the U.S. Coast Guard. Now, he has just returned from third trip where the propeller broke and the engine seized up for lack of oil.

While he shows me the drawings of a "boat" manufactured with irrigation pipes, he says that this summer he will succeed. He agrees to share his story in an interview, but not before enlightening me that I should not give his real name, nor say from which part of the north coast he plans to exit. The interview begins:

You have already tried three times to reach the coast of the United States. Why this obsession with reaching it or, if you prefer, leaving?

I have been thinking of leaving this country for over ten years. At first I wanted to do it through a letter of invitation to Italy, but it didn't work because between the exit permit, passport and ticket, what I had to pay totaled more than a thousand dollars and I just could not bear these costs and neither side knew anybody there to help me. So I reflected a bit and I told myself: "I know the sea very well, from when I was very small, I have been in the water." So I decided to use the sea to fulfill my dream of leaving Cuba.

At first it was the same to me, where I would go, I just wanted to close my eyes and be away from all the things that annoy me every day. Being a thousand kilometers from the end of the line for bread... and also my family, since we don't all fit in the house and coexistence becomes very difficult.

Some of my friends went to Spain, others are married to foreigners and now I get postcards from incredible places. Others preferred to stay and really don't do well.

When I meet them they tell me that they still live with their parents and now receive from their workplace an extra bag, once a month, with soap and detergent. I do not want that for my life, I do not want to be in my sixties and have a pension that won't support me and have to sell cigarettes to survive, and all of these things in my own country. I do not want my life to depend on the whims of a few top people who will decide this month whether I will eat peas or lentils. I want to experiment, I want to try other things, and I don't think that in the next ten years I can do that here.

The second time you were caught by the U.S. Coast Guard and the Americans returned you to the island. Can you tell us the details of this process from the time the raft was illuminated by spotlights until the Cuban police left you at your house?

It was very hard for everyone in the raft when we realized we had been intercepted. We had invested money from the sale of all of our personal belongings to make the raft, so in a few minutes all those resources, plus the time and energy for many months that we had used to construct the boat, went down the tubes. The first reaction we had was not to let them catch us, but we were far from the coast and there was no escape, so we had to surrender.

The American Coast Guard neutralized us quickly, without violence, but with a professionalism and authority that left us no other choice but to cooperate. They took us in a small boat to a ship that serves as a shelter for all those they stop on the high seas. They bring together all the people who have been intercepted so they have a lot of people to return to Cuba.

I found the people on that ship fantastic. Although most were very young, we also saw some elderly people and even women with very young children. Each of us was interviewed by an immigration officer and they confiscated all we were carrying. Luckily

I was able to hide the GPS, which was the most valuable thing I had; it was the same one I used the third time.

Three days after being in that "floating hostel" they brought us back and handed us over to the Cuban authorities. They made a record with our personal information and led us to a bus that took each of us to his own home. On my block they contacted the president of the CDR (Committee for the Defense of Revolution) and explained that I had made an attempt to leave the country illegally. I felt like a child that a teacher was scolding front of its mother.

Hasn't it occurred to you to free your mind of this obsession and to use your talents and energies in this country?

I've passed through many stages. At one point I was seriously looking for a job and I decided to make my life here. But after six months I stopped. On the one hand was the administrator who was sticking it to me because he knew I was the one who had returned after trying to leave on a raft; on the other hand I couldn't find a space where I could say what I felt about everything around me, until it got to the point where I came to believe I was sick because everything bothered me. But talking to people my age I realized that a wish to leave the country is widespread, perhaps more than people think. I realized I was not a rare bird but that if there are those who are fighting for the dream of studying in college, or to be a famous artist. I was going to use my energies to fulfill my dream of traveling. With that I don't think you do any harm to anyone, it's a personal decision and ought to be respected as one.

I also tried to make some handicrafts to earn a little extra money and to gain some independence from my parents but it all ended when they confiscated some wild cane I took from Lenin Park to make some ornaments. I stopped everything with tremendous apathy. You are just thirty years old, so you were a Pioneer, you repeated the slogan of "Pioneers for communism, we will be like Che."

You belong to the generation that had to be "a new man" and shouted anti-imperialist slogans in front of the American diplomatic mission; how is it that the raft ended up being the path you chose?

I ask myself that. Because when I was a kid leaving the country was very frowned upon. I remember that my mom had some aunts who left in the eighties from Mariel and their names could not be mentioned at home. One day they sent some jeans to my dad and we had to hide them because if we didn't everyone would say that we were related to the worms. (Worm means "gusano," a pejorative term for counter-revolutionary.) But what is bad always becomes very attractive, and I started to be very interested in what was happening outside of Cuba. For a long time I thought that anyone who left was a traitor to the country. When I got the itch to leave Cuba, I reasoned that the others who had left were traitors but I was not. It's only now that I realize neither they, nor I, are betraying anybody.

What I see on television makes me more curious, because it can't be that everyone else out there is so bad, so I thought I should go see for myself. What attracts me to the United States is the same as for Mexico, or Finland or Australia. I want to leave here.

Normally they paint people like us, the balseros, as the lowest of the low, crazy to take the risk without knowing what they want. But I'm no fool. I was about to graduate in engineering only I got discouraged and left. All the people that are planning this with me now, we are all educated, we even have a cybernetics specialist who is going to handle the rudder.

Tell us a bit about preparation for the exit.

Normally you must first decide what kind of boat you are going to make. There are many variants, for example the one we are building now is irrigation pipe cut in half and then converted into plates that come together with rivets. As I know a little naval engineering, I'm very demanding with the details and I don't want to set sail on anything improvised. I am a bit of a perfectionist and do the math so that later, at sea, there won't be any unpleasant surprises. So each part for me takes at least about six months to collect materials and begin construction. Once the materials are stored somewhere near the coast, then comes the building, which normally can not be inland because then it would be very heavy to carry to the sea. In water up to your chest, you work somewhere where there's enough vegetation to hide the work, for example in a small river. Sometimes it moves a little and then the police discover the boat before it's ready and you lose everything. That happened to me once.

Buying the engine is the most difficult because of the fuel and it must be in good condition so it can operate for long hours. We need to begin to find out who has an engine to sell and do so with discretion so as not to be detected. After that there is caulking the structure, as was done with irrigation pipes, and having a good location for the engine and rudder. The quality of propeller is very important; it was because of a defect in the propeller that I was frustrated in my last attempt.

I know that your great-grandparents chose this country to escape the rigors of Spain in the '20s. Why now do you want to do it in the other direction? Why do you think Cuba is no longer a country of immigrants and has become one of migrants?

Well, I don't know much about that. What I know is that my maternal great-grandparents came here from Asturia in Spain looking for better opportunities. But my family here depends on economic help sent by their parents, who left, to be able to live.

Sometimes, when I go to a coffee shop or I walk through Old Havana, people think that I am a foreigner because I have light eyes and very white skin. At first I am treated very kindly but immediately when they hear me speak like a Cuban they totally change their attitude. That hurts me, because I feel that as a Cuban I am on the lowest rung of the ladder and it can't continue to be this way. However, I see my friends, also Cuban, who left a couple of years ago and now they return and they can stay in a hotel, rent a car, speak more freely about what they think and they're allowed to have a cell phone, and the truth is, I feel humiliated.

You're young and you've already spent more than ten years of your life in a dream that you haven't attained. You don't think this means you should modify your plans and abandon the idea of emigrating?

I don't think about dropping this idea. I've spent a lot of time on the plan and I am completely "burned out," I mean everybody knows that. It's like when you spend half an hour waiting at a bus stop and know that you could walk but you're going to regret it if the bus passes you. Anyway, how can I "modify my plans"? By trying to climb the ladder of the system, or sign up with the opposition?

What do you think awaits you on the other side?

I am not one of those who paint castles in the air and think of nothing else but having a car and a home. What I want is to work, and I want to be able to use what I earn with my job to have a normal life without having to steal or pretend. The truth is that I do not think so much about material things that can be found there, but about everything that I can do there. For example, I dream about being able to navigate the Internet, because I believe in all these years I haven't been connected for even one hour reading all the information that interests me.

I want to travel and I want to do what I want, whether it's paint my hair green or join the Green Party. Anything, as long as I can decide. That is what most attracts me to living outside Cuba, the possibility of leaving behind all these restrictions that we Cubans face, all the discrimination in our own country, all the absurd bureaucracy that turns any small thing you do every day into an ordeal of paperwork and limitations.

I have a friend who married a German and now lives in Berlin, and tells me that if a hotel in that city didn't let someone stay because of their nationality, either German, Turkish or Iranian, that would be a scandal that would generate press coverage and popular protests. Yet here, every day, we Cubans cannot access places in our own country and services that tourists can use. (Note: All Cubans can now access hotels.) For that reason, I want to try in another country, to see what I can achieve, what I can do for myself that I can't here.

Here I will not be able to change things as I want, because citizens do not have it in our own hands, we don't have the time or resources to accomplish it. It pains me to leave my country, but unfortunately my life is going on and I can't wait any longer for the "bright future" I was promised as a child. This is the best time of my life when I have the energy to work and accomplish projects and I don't want all those hopes of doing something to be lost in waiting.

If you want to stay I respect your decision, but I do not see it, because they throw insults at me, "stateless," "worm" or "traitor," just because I have decided to make my life elsewhere. I do not understand all the limitations for entering and leaving the country, these concepts of "final exit" or the confiscation of property from those who go.

I remember having heard as a young boy that the construction of this system is a voluntary thing, so I have every right to not want to participate. At least I'm honest with what I want and I have not pretended for years and then defected during an official visit, as do many artists, athletes and officials, who until yesterday were swearing allegiance to the Revolution on television. I only count on my raft, with my energies to take to the sea, with my ability to orient myself, with my youth, I do not want anything more than what I can earn with my effort.

LEAVING

Mirta Ojito left Cuba as a teen with her family during the 1980 Mariel boat lift. This excerpt is taken from a collection of essays published in By Heart/De Memoria—Cuban Women's Journeys In and Out of Exile, *edited by María de los Angeles Torres. It describes Mirta's final hours on Cuban soil, starting with a knock at the door of their home.*

My mother opened the door. A burly officer, unshaven and dressed in olive green pants and a white tee shirt, walked in. Without introducing himself, he read our names aloud... He said we were leaving. He also said he wanted to do an inventory of the house. He (poked) his nose in every drawer, cabinet and shelf in the house. As I gathered what I wanted to take with me—a tear-smeared handkerchief, a wilting rose, a picture of Varadero Beach, a chocolate-covered lipstick and two pens—I heard the conversation between the officer and my neighbor.

"Why don't you call the other neighbors and arrange something for these people?" he asked her. He was talking about an *acto de repudio* (act of repudiation), the kind of mini-riot—and sometimes large riot—organized and carried out by neighborhood committees for practically every person who was leaving through the Mariel boat lift. In 1980, the country turned against itself for the first time since the beginning of Fidel Castro's regime

in 1959. Neighbors turned against neighbors to harass and tor-
ment them for their decision to leave the country. It went something like this: When word got out that someone was leaving,
block leaders called on the rest of the residents to stand in front
of the house of the person who wanted to leave. They stood there
for hours, sometimes days, yelling epithets and throwing rocks
and tomatoes at the house. Sometimes windows were shattered;
sometimes doors were pushed down; sometimes people were
killed; sometimes people killed themselves, trapped inside their
homes. That is what the officer wanted for us.

Our neighbor, a woman who had fought with Castro's guerrillas
in the Sierra Maestra mountains, who held the rank of lieutenant
and was married to an army colonel, looked the officer up and
down and told him, "Nobody touches this family. I've seen these
kids grow up."

(Later, Ojito brooded about possessions she had to leave
behind.) Are the orange curtains my mother made by the light
of a *quinqué* (oil lamp) a thing, part of a house, or are they part
of my heritage, part of my mother's? Are the dolls collected over
the years just toys or testaments of an imaginative childhood, a
remembrance of countless hours spent pretending to be a mom?
Are my much marked and read books just paper and scrawls or
are they my memory, my intellect? Are pictures just that or are
they proof of my life, my past? Can a yellow crystal necklace
really be replaced?...

(Ojito and her family left their home in a police car and went to Mariel, the beachside town from which most Cubans were departing for south Florida after pickup by boats of friends or relatives.)

Thousands of people gathered together on the sand, waiting, for what we did not know. Where was our boat? Where was my uncle? Sometime during the evening, they called our names though loudspeakers, and that was how we learned the name of the boat that would takes us to the United States: The Valley Chief... As night fell, my mother and sister found a thin mattress and went to sleep. My father and I sat in plastic beach chairs in front of them... We did not speak much that night but we observed and what we saw was pitiful. A grown man, a chemistry professor from Santiago de Cuba, was on his knees begging an officer to let him join his wife and children who were already in the bus (for the short trip to their boat). Her name had been called but his, inexplicably, had been omitted. When the officer refused to let him go, the wife said she wanted to stay with him to avoid dividing the family. The officer said no to that, too. She must go. He had to stay. And stay he did, crying on his knees, two centimeters from the officer's boots.

At about noontime (the next day), our boat was called... Soon we were sitting in a windowless bus. The windows were there, actually, but the glass was gone, leaving us exposed to the fury of the mob outside. As we left, we ducked, not certain of what to expect. Those who did not were pelted with tomatoes and eggs thrown by the furious mob that waited outside.

(At the next stop), we formed a long line in the midst of a rocky wooded area. Surrounded by tall trees that offered a respite from the unrelenting sun, we waited our turn. What we were waiting for we did not know, but because Cubans were trained to wait in line everywhere, often without knowledge of what was available, we obeyed. Soon it became apparent that what awaited us was not pleasant.

People were taken one by one inside a little house with a green roof. There they were interviewed, their papers were reviewed and they were strip-searched. We had already turned in our identification papers... El Mosquito was the final stop to strip us of our identity and remaining possessions. If something questionable was found during the search, the person was taken away through a side door that we could clearly see from where we were standing in line. At one point we heard the agonizing screams of one young man who minutes before had been standing before us. We did not see him go out through any door. I assumed there were holding cells inside the house. While we waited, we wondered what could have triggered the ire of the searchers...

Our turn came. Someone asked my name and what I was carrying. I showed him my possessions. He took the two pens, which my uncle had brought from the United States the year before. (I was sent) to a little booth with a curtain. A woman asked me to take off my pants and panties. Midway through the process she must have realized that I was not hiding anything, and, mercifully, let me go.

Unknown to us, my little sister, who went through the same process, had a plastic bag hidden in her underwear. It contained a picture of our grandfather and a letter that our downstairs neighbor, who loved her like a granddaughter, had sent her from the Soviet Union, where he had been sent before to train for six months. The officer let my sister keep her things...

We emerged from the house without money or identity, not quite sure of what to expect next. What came next was an olive green tent with no walls. Inside there were two rows of olive green bunk beds... Picture this: We had no towels, no sheets, no clean underwear, or extra clothes. We had not taken a shower or brushed our teeth since we left our house the day before. We had not slept on bed or taken off our shoes or had one minute alone. We also had not gone to the bathroom...

We assembled around one bunk bed and decided to break the night into seven shifts, one hour each. The head of each family would stay awake to listen for the name of our boat... In the morning, unexpectedly, our boat was called... We rode a bus to our final stop in Cuba... I caught a glimpse of my uncle in the distance—dirty with a beard from 17 days at sea... Behind him, white and motionless, waited the boat that would take us to the United States.

A SECURITY GUARD'S STORY

The following interview appeared in the Havana Times in December 2010. It was written by Omel Almaguer.

Mauricio Ortega, 57, is a native of *Guanabacoa,* a municipality of the city of Havana. With a ninth grade education, among the jobs he's held are street sweeper, security guard and ambulance driver. Currently he works for AGESP (the Security and Protection Agency), one of the most important security companies in the country. He lives alone in a one-room apartment with a bathroom. Mauricio (not his real name) doesn't have any known family members living in Cuba.

Mauricio, what does your job consist of as a security and protection agent?

I stand guard twelve hours a day. Every three days, I'm on duty for two days and I have the third one off. The first shift is during the daytime and the second one at night. You have to remain standing all that time. You can only sit down when the shift boss puts another agent in your place. Then you take advantage of that time and eat the lunch (sandwich and soda) they provide, or—if you want to, sell it—and bring a lunch container with your own food.

Who buys the lunches you sell?

They're almost always the bus drivers; I work in a depot. The drivers make good money, so they can pay us 20 pesos ($1) for a lunch. To me its good business to sell it, because with 20 pesos I can go to the cafeteria in front of my house and I buy several biscuits for one peso each, along with a croquette or something fried. It's lousy but I have money left for the days when I don't work. I can use it to buy cigarettes and to get a buche (a shot of cheap rum).

If you figure it out, during the 15 shifts I do each month, I sell 22 snacks for 20 pesos each; that adds up to 440 pesos ($22), which is a lot more than my pay.

And when you're not on guard duty, how do you deal with the issue of lunches and dinner?

I have lunch in the old people's dining rooms, and I can also buy rice and cooked beans there for dinner. At night I eat that with some of the mincemeat that comes in the cafeteria biscuits.

Do you keep it in the refrigerator and then eat it cold?

No, since I don't have a "frigidaire."

So don't the beans go bad?

They sometimes get a little smelly, but if you're good and hungry you can get by that.

Have you thought about improving your situation?

A heap of times. Since I separated from my wife, we swapped our old house for this room for me and for an apartment for her and the little girl. I've thought about improving things little by little, but there's not enough on a guard's income.

I understand that at AGESP they pay $25 CUC a month [about $30 USD] and a wage that's about 250 pesos in domestic currency [about $10 USD]. Couldn't you save a little of that?

That's difficult. In fact, I hardly ever get paid my full amount of hard currency CUCs. The agency's incentive system is a little screwed up. If you miss one day of work—even if you're dying—they'll dock you to the very last cent. I remember when I missed work because I had an abscess in my molar; no only was I docked, but they went so far as to send me to the disciplinary council.

Sometimes the team boss, who's above the shift boss, pressures me to buy him a beer. And it's better to just buy it, because it's much worse if he has a problem with you.

I like to drink shots of rum from time to time. So sometimes I show up on my shift with alcohol on my breath. According to the agency's regulations I should be sent straight home, but since he knows I need it, he lets me go on into the job in exchange for the favors I just mentioned.

In fact, they'll deduct your hard currency pay for any silly little thing. A demerit in the incident report book means a loss of 5 percent of your hard currency. This is how they blackmail us all the time.

It's very difficult to be perfect for 12 hours straight. They know it and they're always keeping their eyes out for a chance to "give you the knife." Sometimes they make you believe they are your friends. Then, when you find out that they've reported you, you're forced to admit, for example, that one day you climbed up in a bus to sleep because the cold and the mosquitoes had made the night impossible.

Then you have co-workers who aren't comrades or anything else. They too keep an eye on you to knock you out of position and win brownie points with the bosses. Well, the truth is that I stay on here because I don't have any alternative left. If I did, I swear I'd get myself as far away as I could from the agency, with its damned CUCs, its discipline and its extremism.

I think about how I'm stuck here as a guard while there are other people living the sweet life…with air conditioning in their rooms, eating good and with beautiful women. But what woman is going to look at me if all I have for a home is some little rat trap, or if I don't have any decent clothes or money to invite her out to a nice place?

The worst thing is that those people haven't done anything to earn what they have; it dropped down from out of the sky, just like this misfortune dropped on me.

But don't you think that there are people who right now are in worse situations?

That's true. But if I think like that then I'm screwed. It's always better to look up. If you accept what you have, you'll never escape misery. I know that in Africa there are people living under subhuman conditions, with undernourished children whose noses are full of snot, like they show on television. I know that in many countries of the Americas it's the same thing. And that in China, whose economy is booming, there are millions of Chinese going hungry—at least that's what they say on the news. But yet and still, no one who's screwed wants to live like us Cubans. Everybody wants to be live like the Americans, or like the French... But what do I know?

My very own daughter left with her mother for Venezuela. She left on an aid mission and she got married there to some guy with money. She did the right thing. If I could have, I would have done the very same thing. Right now I'm trying to get in contact with her to see if they can help me a little from there.

And what do you like to do when you're not working?

I go to the stadium. Or I play dice with my partners and we have a few shots. There ain't nothing else. Now I'm just hoping the years will pass and I'll hit my retirement age. I'll see if I can stay home. I figure I can live off the 200 pesos a month (less than $10) that are due me.

LOOKING FOR FOOD

Daisy Valera is a nuclear chemist in Havana. The following essay appeared in the Havana Times in November 2010.

Anyone would think that with the weekend should come the chance to relax after a demanding work week. But that's not the situation for me. Saturday and Sunday are days for going out scouting for food.

I'm not the only person who finds herself in this situation of continuing to work during the time supposedly reserved for leisure.

The fact that many families are in this situation is a topic among the crowds of people who turn out every weekend at the Carlos III Agricultural Fair.

Carlos III proper is a central thoroughfare whose name they decided to change to Salvador Allende Avenue at some point in time, though no one paid attention to that re- christening.

On Saturday mornings I throw on a daypack, with who knows how many plastic bags stuffed inside, and I head out for the popular street market.

What can I find there?—almost everything, from recycled clothes, soap, air fresheners, children's bikes, earrings and plants, to food stands from Havana restaurants selling products like shrimp or beer.

But the thing is that I'm not searching for any of those products; I go to look for something very basic: food, the kind that's supposed to exist at an agricultural fair.

But at Carlos III, what's scarcest is food and what are in excess are people looking for the same thing as me.

So, it's not unusual for the lines that form even in front of lemon stands to stretch for miles, or for the would-be buyers—drained by the heat—to end up doing everything from screaming at each other to fighting.

If you happen to be interested in buying fruit, in the best case scenario you'll have to choose between only two alternatives. I've been making guava juice for the past three months because I don't like papaya.

And if you have a taste for salad, you may well end up leaving with empty hands, which is what happens when the only things they have to offer are avocados and you don't like them.

The fair is a battle between all those who want to buy produce without first getting in line, and with the sellers who strive—I don't know how—to make the scales always mark in their favor.

You leave exhausted, wishing to never again return to a place like this, but knowing full well you have no choice.

In addition to being tired, I end the day upset, because I know that there are people who don't have to invest their Saturdays and Sundays in this struggle. Those are the ones who I can't figure out where they get the money to buy shopping carts full at supermarkets that sell in hard currency CUCs, those same stores where it's hard for me to buy a bar of soap.

SHOES

Countless millions of poor families around the world lack shoes or affordable day care for their children. In Cuba, shoes are available at highly subsidized prices and day care is free. Still problems arise, as Cuban blogger Rosa Martínez points out in an essay published in the Havana Times *in February 2011.*

For the last three months I've had several experiences related to footwear. I went to stores almost every day for about a month but didn't find anything appropriate for my youngest daughter. I finally gave up and decided to take the advice of a friend and just wait, assuming I didn't spend the money before then.

Yet, the inevitable occurred. The only pair that she had for day-care fell apart. As one of my uncles said, "The car broke down for a lack of wheels." Her poor tennis shoes couldn't take any more so she had to use her dress shoes. But these—though they were new and had hardly been ever worn—only lasted her eight hours. The same day I had put them on her, all their leather fell off. Little black strips were lying all over the nursery.

"What could she wear tomorrow?" I wondered. I didn't have a dime to buy her anything at the store; plus, what would I have been able to find if there's hardly any footwear for girls, at least in Guantánamo. The following day the good news came.

My only alternative was to go to a friend who also has a girl, but a year older. I was hoping she had some used pair that she could sell me to get me out of this situation.

"God might push us under, but he doesn't let us drown," I said when she pulled out a couple pink sandals that she gave to Claudia and that fit her perfectly. She also had some white tennis shoes in good condition, but these I had to buy, though she sold them to me at a good price.

In any case I was very grateful. My little girl could go to daycare and I could go to work the next day. All I needed to do was continue saving money to be able to buy her some new ones. What more could I ask for?

For several weeks she wore the nice white tennis shoes. But there was no way to get her to put the sandals on.

"Mom, these are ugly," she told me.

"No, Mimi. They're not ugly; they're used but they're not ugly," I told her.

"Look how cute they look with your polka-dot dress," her father told her, trying to convince her.

"Oh, Dad, I don't like them; they're ugly," she said again, this time crying.

I didn't insist. When I looked at them more closely, I could see they were pretty beat up (maybe that's why my friend hadn't charged me anything for them). I decided that my daughter could continue wearing the white tennis shoes. The only bad thing was that she couldn't wear them with her dresses. It didn't matter, it was starting to get cool outside, so wearing pants would be better—I thought, to cheer myself up—though I really felt like screaming.

At the beginning of December came some unexpected humanitarian assistance from an old classmate from the university. She gave me 100 CUCs (about $120), which didn't even have a chance to warm my hands: I immediately went to another province and bought three pairs of sandals for my daughter (one pair of dress shoes, and two practical and strong pairs for daily use). I also took advantage of the opportunity and bought her some brown boots that she could wear with shorts or pants.

You can imagine the happiness I felt when I had them in my hands. I couldn't believe that this anguish had ended, at least for the time being.

That day I slept like I hadn't in weeks, and I imagine that even after I fell asleep the smile stayed on my face.

Although I was exploding with happiness, it wasn't until the following day that we showed the shoes to our daughter. We know her well and we know that when she has something new she wants to put it on immediately, whatever it is.

"Claudia, look at the shoes we bought you," I said.

"These are for getting dressed up, and these two are for the daycare center, and this pair is also for the daycare but for when you wear shorts or pants. Let's see. Which ones do you want to wear today?" her dad asked.

"Mommy, I want to take all of them to daycare with me," she exclaimed.

I was astonished. This was too much. She wants to wear all of them at the same time? It's true that these kids aren't easy, I said to myself.

"Why do you want to take all of them?" I asked her, trying to be calm. "Do you want to give a pair to a friend?" I smiled.

"No, Mom. It's so Jennifer can see them. She says I don't have any shoes."

I just stood there...speechless. I couldn't believe it. My daughter is only three years old.

With much effort we were finally able to convince her that she shouldn't take all the shoes, but who was there to convince me not to cry?

MISBEHAVING MALES

This essay by Daisy Valera, an independent blogger, appeared in the Havana Times *in 2010.*

Last month I had a little more free time than usual. It wasn't that I wanted it, but it was do to the impossibility of speeding up the paperwork that would allow me to begin working.

And in my case, having a lot of free time has been synonymous with having a lot of time alone—walking along the many streets of my city, catching buses and going into various establishments, alone.

Perhaps because I used to always spend my free time going out with my partner or my friends, I never felt like I do now: Harassed!

Thus going out on the street has turned into a challenge for me, one that I have to tolerate. Apparently, fifty years since the 1959 socialist revolution and the (work) foundation of the Federation of Cuban Women (FMC) have not been enough.

The attitude of many men on the island is far from being respectful; they definitively don't look at us as their equals. I feel that somehow, instead of shining as a woman, I more closely appear as a piece of meat. I have to put up countless obscene allusions regarding the most varied parts of my body. They walk beside me bothering me for more than a block and even try me to buy me with a can of beer.

On occasion the anger makes me respond by calling them har-assing cavemen, others I totally ignore.

If we agree that I don't have the body or face that these types are accustomed to seeing in magazines or on TV, and that I gen-erally don't wear clothes that are very colorful, nor do I ever put on makeup, then one could deduce that this experience doesn't happen exclusively to me.

I've noticed that many women are also under this same type of pressure. We are still relegated to the old role of sexual object, one which is possible to buy, and that the man can treat any way he so desires.

While I battle with the lustful eyes, the saliva-dripping tongues hanging out of their mouths, and the gross language from all those I consider more animals than men, I'm at a loss as to how to respond.

I understand that these harassers are victims of their histori-cal past, that because of their ignorance they don't know how to please a woman, but this doesn't allow me to accept being dealt with so abusively.

I end up wanting all men who commit such acts of disrespect to be fined or tried like in some other countries. But this isn't going to happen. Nor do I see any type of campaign aimed at raising aware-ness around this issue. In Cuba, women have not attained the same status as men, and I haven't seen any serious work on this problem.

But after 50 years…isn't it about time!

AN INSIDER'S CRITIQUE

Cubans who are members of the communist establishment usually keep criticism of the regime to themselves. One who didn't was Soledad Cruz, a veteran journalist and former ambassador of Cuba at the U.N. Economic and Social Council in Paris. She is hostile to the United States and remains committed to the socialist ideal. But she has become disillusioned with many aspects of the Revolution, as she made clear in a long essay she wrote in 2007. Following are translated excerpts:

Hiding the truth does not serve the revolution. This is one of the maxims of José Martí that I embrace even though this has cost me dearly during my long years of service. I don't say that I have the absolute truth, which doesn't exist... I'm referring to the habit of telling what I see, the facts... One of the Stalinist defects from which Cuban socialism has not been able to free itself is the existence of a journalistic ethic heedless of the Cuban reality, of the often conflictive nature of society and of the complexities of creating a more just society in a country that is poor and blockaded (a reference to the U.S. embargo).

In Cuba, the majority of the population wants to save the revolution at all cost. The intelligent majority knows they can't expect anything better from capitalism, even less from the United States and the tramps from Miami.

...With the problems that affect socialist society, there have to be free, and not obligatory, elections because when elections are compulsory, you get an outcome like that which occurred in Eastern Europe.

Nobody can deny that (Cuba) has to produce, to do it efficiently and to have earnings that only under socialism can be distributed in a just way to achieve equality among the people (in the context of) wellbeing and not poverty.

Regrettably, the ones (Cubans) with the best economic possibilities are not the scientists who make vaccines, or the Olympic champions, or labor heroes but those who, in spite of all the decrees and regulations, have enriched themselves illegally or they receive large remittances from abroad.

MILK

By Verónica Fernández, a blogger for the Havana Times

I was born in the town of Regla, on the other side of Havana Bay. Over the years, many people from Regla have gone to live in Cojímar, fleeing the contamination from the petroleum refinery in Regla. That's what my family did when I was just four years old. Since I was a little girl I have been drawn to the arts and letters. Poetry and narrative writing are my favorites. I had the good fortune to study philology, a branch of the human sciences dealing with language and literature, at the University of Havana with top notch professors. As a Capricorn, I adore organization, people who are mature, the romantic things in life and the lack of self-interest that is the backbone of these times. I enjoy our typical Cuban food, (white rice, black beans, pork and yucca with garlic sauce) and also Italian food. I also like chocolate and drinking a *mojito* (rum cocktail) in the historic center of my city.

Aida, my friend's grandson, is now eight years old and he loves milk. When he was born his mother was unable to breast feed him so they began giving him powdered milk bought at the corner bodega store with the ration book until he was seven. Now, having turned eight, he's no longer entitled to receive milk as a part of the basic staples available through the rationing system.

My friend is now going crazy because for the last few days she hasn't been able to find anyone selling milk on the black market. As for the dollar store, a bag of only two pounds of powdered milk cost more than 5 CUCs ($6.25); therefore it's impossible to quench the boy's thirst for milk for a whole month on the wage of a single parent who's paid in domestic currency the equivalent of only 10 CUCs every thirty days in regular pesos.

The grandmother commented to me that she had to change her whole wage to CUCs last month to buy her grandson two bags of milk. Even combined with the wages of her daughter (the boy's mother) they had to perform magic to make it through the month, though they had to forego a number of needs.

Her daughter also earns the equivalent of 10 CUCs a month, but of course they have to buy cooking oil, tomato puree and bath soap. In short, they not only need to purchase food, but other things like toiletries in order to have the very minimum in a home in order to subsist. She told me that her sole longing in life was to be able to raise her grandson so that he's a strong and healthy man, nothing more.

Today I ran into her very worried while walking down the street in *Cojímar*. As she stopped to assess her situation, she told me that at that moment not even the dollar store had milk for her grandson, and that she didn't know what to do, where to go, and that she could no longer deal with the situation. It's incredible but true;

there are periods when such necessary products can't be found in any of the stores in the neighborhood or even in other adjacent neighborhoods.

Again, what first comes to mind is the US economic blockade against Cuba and the major limitations that we face as a result. But what I can't figure out is why they haven't prioritized this essential and basic product for sale in places aimed at the general public, though it is sold in CUCs at astronomical prices. People who are responsible for a child or an elderly person should at least have this option for guaranteeing a glass of milk in the morning or at night to those who need it most.

In fact, I'd never seen the dollar store in my neighborhood without this product. However, life is ungracious, because right now in these stores that are lacking any powdered milk, they have these big beautiful toys on display that dazzle everyone who goes into these establishments. Of course these are prohibitively expensive, but they are available for children.

Is this normal? Is this in line with our situation and our needs? On the contrary, most of the parents and grandparents of these children couldn't afford those toys no matter how much their children and grandchildren begged for them.

They, just like me, suffer from the contradictions in our world. Imagine the ungraciousness and unpleasantness that we are made to feel because there are people who make things so difficult and make our situations so desperate.

How can we afford the luxury of displaying amazing toys in our stores for sale in CUCs if we can't offer what is most necessary and sought out by the public? Are we trying to bury our heads in the sand? Why is it necessary to support this incongruity in the market? Why don't we plan better so that basic products are always available in this Cuban dollar store?

It's completely laughable and in turn ironic to run into these situations, which almost seem like they're created on purpose and with all the ill intentions in the world.

Like always, many people (among them me) say that the severest blockade is the one enforced by us on ourselves by making people feel discouraged and demoralized each and every day.

I think there's no reason or motive to show off things like those expensive toys, which are unattainable for most people, and not have basic products available. At least the Cuban public could have a minimum of respite knowing these are there and—with extraordinary effort—are potentially attainable.

THE DENTIST

Another essay by Havana Times blogger Verónica Fernández

At the end of last year, two of my molars began to hurt. I immediately went to my dentist since we had already become friends over the time that she's been treating me. I've found that in addition to her being very professionally competent, she's also an excellent person.

As soon as I got to the dental clinical in *Cojímar,* I began to look for her. They told me that she hadn't worked there for more than a month because her father was ill. Since she's the only daughter, she had to request an unpaid leave to be able to attend to him.

This news was terrible for me because now I had to face a problem more difficult than my intense molar pain. I went to her house, where I found her in a state of such desperation that I felt bad for having come at such an inopportune moment. Her father was in an advanced stage of dementia.

Nevertheless, after I explained the nature of my ailment to her, she recommended that I see a certain other dentist. Like her, this was someone who had a lot of experience and who she was certain would take good care of me because this dentist too was very professional. I left her house feeling bad about her situation but also about mine, because I then knew that I wasn't going to be able to have her as my dentist for a long time. In fact, I had no other alternative but to turn to this new dentist.

I got home stunned by my pain but also fearful about having another doctor put their hands in my mouth, despite the strong recommendation. I don't consider myself a cowardly person, but in these types of cases everyone is fearful of the unknown.

After going through a hellish night, because nothing relieved my pain, I left early in the morning in search of the new dentist. She told me that I had to wait a little while but that she would attend to me. After waiting more than two hours, I was still there waiting for them to call me. Suddenly the door to the dentist's office swung open and she appeared. It seemed she had come out to get something to eat and when she saw me; she only said that she had forgotten I was there. My face was the reflection of my soul as I requested loudly that she see to me because I couldn't take any more.

I finally sat down in the daunting dentist's chair, and I can only say that no one could imagine what happened there. The anesthesia I was given did absolutely nothing. After going through that entire odyssey, the dentist explained to me that for more than a year they hadn't been given the types of supplies with which to work and all that they have is the result of negotiations with friends and other institutions. She told me more. She said that if she were to wait for them to give her the supplies she needed to care for the public, she'd never work. Therefore, what she does is buy the materials herself, but she has to charge. What she refuses to do is stand around doing nothing while seeing people coming to the clinic in need of care.

She told me that dentists in general have to do their work wherever they are needed; therefore it's unethical to sit around in their offices doing nothing because they haven't been given the needed supplies. The whole group that works with her thinks the same, and it's for that reason they're able to treat patients.

While I was listening to what this dentist was telling me, several questions came to my mind: Is it possible for us to continue saying we're a medical power? Are the senior officials within the Ministry of Public Health unaware of what is happening? How is it possible that the Cuban people cannot enjoy such a basic human health service? If we don't have the resources necessary in the country to give the appropriate attention to our people, why do we prioritize other countries? If we don't have indispensable dental materials for caring for the public, why do we continue graduating so many dentists every year?

In fact, this situation is shameful and terribly unfortunate because it discredits us in all aspects. We cannot suggest that our basic health care system is the best if it's not undergirded by a solid material foundation.

In our system, no medical doctor in Cuba should have to occupy himself with having to search for supplies to treat their patients.

What is the value of so many (international) campaigns against dengue fever, cholera, or drug addiction if the first things that we have to get working as they should be are our own health facilities?

QUESTIONS

Written by Alfredo Fernández for the Cuban diaries section of the Havana Times

When did Perú get so screwed up? So begins the great novel *Conversación en la Catedral* (Conversation in the Cathedral), by Mario Vargas Llosa.

It turns out that this question posed by Zavalita to a friend in a mid-1950s Lima café can be extended in time to present-day Cuba.

When will those born on this island stop seeing subsistence as an ephemeral period and (an anomaly) and begin conceiving of it as life itself?

When did we begin to accept as normal that our wages always have to be excessively low, requiring us to constantly concern ourselves with our immediate survival?

When did we decide to accept the decisions of politicians as being indisputable, despite their ineptitude?

When did we decide not to protest what is wrongfully done, since things couldn't turn out worse than already are—and nothing will change otherwise?

When did we decide to pay to continue to be Cuban when we're abroad?

When did we stop caring that our hospitals had deteriorated to the point that they are today?

When did we accept that the fact that wages of a police officers are higher than those of a doctor or a teacher?

When did it become normal for us to spend three days in a bus terminal waiting to travel?

When did we begin to conceive of emigrating as the sole way to solve our problems?

When did love and friendship become transformed into means of obtaining material goods that are impossible to obtain through work and honesty?

When did we learn to "live" with family, friends and lovers who, in the best of cases, we only contact by e-mail or see them a single week each year?

When did we decide to leave all the solutions to the country's problems up to biology?

When did Cuba get so screwed up?

ADDENDUM 3

THE PHOTOGRAPHER

Author's Tribute to Charles Tasnadi

During the 1980s and early '90s, I averaged about two trips to Cuba per year. On each, I was accompanied by Charles Tasnadi, an amiable Hungarian who migrated to the United States in the 1960s by way of Venezuela. He was perfect for Cuba assignments. He spoke Spanish and was tireless, sometimes working around the clock. He and I would rent a Cessna in Miami and fly to Havana, me with one suitcase and Charlie with seventeen, almost all filled with photographic equipment. For years, Charlie would pack scuba diving equipment on the chance Castro could be lured to the beach for snorkeling; Charlie supposedly would take underwater pictures of him. But the Cuban leader never showed interest.

Charlie always rented two rooms at our hotel—one for sleep and one to develop pictures and transmit them on phone lines. The Cubans liked to see Charlie come down because he spent so much money sending pictures. He would make a phone connection and then start to send a picture to Washington. With a good line, the picture would arrive in twenty minutes. But Charlie was almost never that lucky. I remember one trip when he started sending a picture of Castro at 8:00 p.m. Every time he tried, the line would disconnect. At 2:00 a.m., he finally succeeded. At three dollars per minute, the phone charges that night were huge, as they were other nights as well. On the last day of each visit, Charlie would sit down with a Foreign Ministry official to tabulate the phone bill. Invariably, it was well into the thousands of dollars.

He and I never traveled to Cuba without sixty-watt bulbs because the low-wattage hotel bulbs were almost useless. Charlie, of course, needed a dark room in those days to develop his pictures and would ask the Cubans for help in screening out all light with black tape and other material. One of the few times I ever saw Charlie get mad was when workers informed him that his room was ready, that it was as dark as a moonless night. On entering the room, he exclaimed, "This is not a dark room! It's more like the Sahara Desert!" It took time, but the workers finally got the room dark enough to satisfy Charlie.

Much more common was the gregarious Charlie, who greeted hotel maids like long-lost friends and even waiters he had never met before. We were having a bite one day at the Hanoi restaurant in Santiago on Cuba's eastern tip. The waiter came with the menus. Charlie smiled and shook his hand. The waiter came back for our order. Charlie smiled and shook his hand. The waiter brought the meal. Charlie smiled and shook his hand. The scene repeated itself several more times. I'm sure the waiter had never met anybody like Charlie Tasnadi.

END

INDEX

Made in the USA
Charleston, SC
24 May 2012